An Original & Complete Curriculum of Druidical Study

The CELTIC GOLDEN DAWN

About the Author

JOHN MICHAEL GREER (western Maryland) has been a student of occult traditions and the unexplained for more than thirty years. A Freemason, a student of geomancy and sacred geometry, and a widely read blogger, he is also the author of numerous books—including *Monsters*, *The New Encyclopedia of the Occult*, and *Secrets of the Lost Symbol*—and currently serves as the Grand Archdruid of the Ancient Order of Druids in America (AODA), a contemporary school of Druid nature spirituality. Greer has contributed articles to *Renaissance Magazine*, *Golden Dawn Journal*, *Mezlim*, *New Moon Rising*, *Gnosis*, and *Alexandria*.

The CELTIC GOLDEN DAWN

— △ —

An Original & Complete Curriculum of Druidical Study

— ▽ —

JOHN MICHAEL GREER

Llewellyn Publications
WOODBURY, MINNESOTA

First Edition
First Printing, 2013

Book design and edit by Rebecca Zins
Celtic knot: iStockphoto.com/Trudy Karl
Cover design by Kevin R. Brown
Interior illustrations by John Michael Greer

Llewellyn Publications is a registered trademark of Llewellyn Worldwide Ltd.

Library of Congress Cataloging-in-Publication Data
Greer, John Michael.
  The Celtic Golden Dawn : an original & complete curriculum of Druidical study / John Michael Greer.—First edition.
       pages   cm
  Includes bibliographical references (pages   ) and index.
  ISBN 978-0-7387-3155-1
1. Druids and druidism. 2. Hermetic Order of the Golden Dawn. 3. Magic, Celtic. 4. Cabala.
I. Title.
  BL910.G7455 2013
  299'.16—dc23

2012041078

Llewellyn Worldwide Ltd. does not participate in, endorse, or have any authority or responsibility concerning private business transactions between our authors and the public.

All mail addressed to the author is forwarded, but the publisher cannot, unless specifically instructed by the author, give out an address or phone number.

Any Internet references contained in this work are current at publication time, but the publisher cannot guarantee that a specific location will continue to be maintained. Please refer to the publisher's website for links to authors' websites and other sources.

Llewellyn Publications
A Division of Llewellyn Worldwide Ltd.
2143 Wooddale Drive
Woodbury, MN 55125-2989
www.llewellyn.com

Printed in the United States of America

Table of Contents.

Contents

Contents

The Bardic Grade

The Druid Grade

Introduction.

The Golden Dawn and the Celtic Twilight

THE FOUNDATION OF THE Hermetic Order of the Golden Dawn in 1888 marked the zenith of one of the most creative periods in the long history of occultism and the convergence of trends that had been building in British and European occult circles for many decades. Too many students of occultism these days, whether they believe that the Golden Dawn system was handed down from the immemorial past or think that it was patched together more or less at random out of scraps of forgotten lore from the collections of the British Library, see it as a unique phenomenon. The truth of the matter is far more interesting.

The beginning of the flood tide of magical innovation that brought the Golden Dawn into being can be dated to 1854, when the French occultist Alphonse Constant—writing under his pen name Éliphas Lévi—published the first volume of *Dogme et Rituel de la Haute Magie* (*Doctrine and Ritual of High Magic*).[1] Lévi, as he may as well be called here, was an extraordinary and too-often underrated thinker who studied for the priesthood in a series of Catholic seminaries, left before ordination, and was active in radical politics for several years before finding his life's work as the first great modern writer on magic. At a time when popular opinion dismissed occultism as superstitious nonsense, Lévi was able to restate the basic principles of magic in a form that the reading public of the nineteenth century found understandable and appealing. In the process, he kickstarted a revival of magic that is still ongoing.

Lévi's genius was that his theory of magic combined a first-rate knowledge of traditional occultism with an equally keen understanding of those intellectual currents of his time so that a contemporary audience could make sense of magic. He reworked the old philosophy of magic, which was heavily tinged with the scholasticism of the Middle Ages and opaque to most people by his time, in terms drawn from the cutting edge of

---

1 The English translation by A. E. Waite is titled *Transcendental Magic*.

nineteenth-century philosophy and science. The German philosopher Arthur Schopen-hauer, then hugely popular, wrote about the world as the product of will and representa-tion; Lévi borrowed this by positing that magic is the product of will and imagination. Nineteenth-century physics accepted the idea of a subtle substance pervading the uni-verse, providing the basis for light, heat, electricity, and magnetism; Lévi borrowed the idea, renamed it "the Astral Light," and postulated that it was the medium that transmits magical influences from mind to mind—or from mind to matter.

Another key to Lévi's success was the way he redefined the image of the practitio-ner of magic. During the Renaissance, when magic had last been popular and respected in Western culture, magicians had envisioned their art as a way to the fulfillment of the highest reaches of human possibility. Since that time, reduced to a hole-and-corner existence as members of a despised subculture, magicians had done as socially marginal groups so often do, accepted the wider culture's negative opinion of them without ever quite noticing that this was what they were doing. Lévi restored magic to its old dig-nity, but in updated terms: in an age that was intoxicated with the dream of conquering nature, he offered the promise of nearly limitless power and wisdom to those who were willing to rise to the greater challenge of conquering themselves.

This act of redefinition relaunched occultism back into the popular culture of Lévi's time, giving it a foothold in the collective imagination for the first time since the onset of the Scientific Revolution two centuries earlier. In the wake of *Dogme et Rituel de la Haute Magie* and a string of sequels from Lévi's busy pen, an occult subculture emerged, first in France, then in other European countries and overseas as well. As the new subcul-ture expanded, it found an unexpected audience among Freemasons.

Freemasonry itself was finishing up a century of extraordinary innovations when the nineteenth-century revival of magic began. When it originally went public in 1717 with the founding of the first Grand Lodge of England, Freemasonry had only two degrees of initiation, Entered Apprentice and Fellow Craft. A third, Master Mason, was added around 1720; the Royal Arch, the first of what came to be known as the higher degrees, appeared at some point before 1743, the date when it was first mentioned in Masonic records. Thereafter the floodgates opened, and literally thousands of new degrees came into being. Most of these lasted only a little while, but some of the best found their way into an assortment of rites, or systems of degrees, that took shape around the beginning of the nineteenth century. The York Rite of ten degrees and the Scottish Rite of thirty-three were the most successful of these rites, and both of them are still active today.

By the second half of the nineteenth century, partly as a result of this wave of creative innovation, Freemasonry was far and away the most influential voluntary organization in the Western world. The Craft,[2] as its members still call it, served many purposes—social networking and charitable work, among others—but it also very often provided an outlet for the interests of men who were intrigued by ritual, symbolism, and mystical philosophy. Lévi's updated occultism made a good fit with these interests. One of the consequences was an explosion of new organizations, some connected to Freemasonry and others simply inspired by it, that combined initiation rituals modeled on those of the Craft with instruction in magic modeled on the writings of Lévi and the many authors who followed him into the realm of the occult.

*   *   *

AS THE ORIGINAL HOME of Freemasonry, Britain saw a particularly large number of these new occult lodges. One of the earliest and most influential was the Societas Rosicruciana in Anglia (Rosicrucian Society in England), or SRIA, which was founded in 1867 by English Freemason Robert Wentworth Little. Open only to Master Masons, the SRIA based its degrees on the traditions of the Rosicrucians, a mystical and alchemical society of early seventeenth-century Germany, and attracted a great many British Freemasons with occult interests. Several other orders of a similar kind came into being within Freemasonry, while outside the Craft, occult societies such as the Hermetic Brotherhood of Luxor, the August Order of Light, and the Royal Oriental Order of the Sat B'hai competed for members.

The spread of occultism in nineteenth-century culture went into overdrive in 1875, the year of Éliphas Lévi's death, when the Russian expatriate Helena Petrovna Blavatsky and a group of American occultists founded the Theosophical Society in New York. The first public organization for occult education in modern times, the TS, as it was usually called, grew explosively over the decades that followed, helped substantially by Blavatsky's talents as a writer and publicist. Unlike Masonry and many of the other initiatory orders, the TS was open to women as well as men, and it attracted a great many

---

2 This same term, along with various other bits of Masonic terminology and practice, was borrowed from Freemasonry by the founders of modern Wicca.

women who were interested in occultism but too often found themselves on the wrong side of lodge doors.

By the late 1880s, the popularity of Lévi's new vision of magic, the proliferation of occult lodges and secret societies, and the rapid spread of Theosophy created a substantial market for a magical lodge that would admit women as well as men and teach not simply occult philosophy but also practical magic. That niche was filled in 1888 when William Wynn Westcott and Samuel Mathers—both of them Freemasons, Theosophists, members of the SRIA, and more than usually competent occultists—launched the Hermetic Order of the Golden Dawn. Westcott, the driving force behind the order in its early years, had been active in British occult lodges, Masonic and otherwise, for years; Mathers was a gifted writer of rituals. Their raw materials included the famous "cipher manuscripts," which outlined the rituals and teachings of what became the Golden Dawn's Outer Order, but the two of them also drew on the accumulated experience of decades of magical societies and more than a century of Masonic innovations.

The story of the Golden Dawn's rise and fall has been told many times and need not be retold here in detail. Like too many other occult organizations before and since, the Golden Dawn ended up with an inner circle composed of people who were better mages than managers and who discovered the hard way that esoteric wisdom is no substitute for the forbearance, cooperation, and common sense that any group project needs to succeed or even to survive. The first major blowup came in 1900, splitting the order into two factions; a more serious explosion followed in 1903. One round of troubles followed another until the last Golden Dawn temple with a charter from the original order finally went out of existence in the 1970s.

The years before the troubles began, though, were spent in a continuing creative ferment. Not only Westcott and Mathers but many of their inner circle of students and initiates kept busy bringing new material into the Golden Dawn synthesis; some of this new material was drawn from older occult literature, but a significant portion of it was entirely new. In the process, a number of Golden Dawn initiates ventured into other parts of the busy alternative spirituality movement of the time—and one of the things they encountered there was the revival, a century and a half old by then, of the spirituality of the ancient Druids.

*   *   *

THE DRUID REVIVAL, as it is usually called these days, first took shape around the time that Freemasonry was establishing its first public presence. A tradition in modern Druid circles, in fact, dates the organization of the first Druid order of modern times to 1717, though documentary evidence is lacking. There was certainly a documented Druid Revival group meeting in suburban London in the early 1740s, however, under the chiefship of the genial Rev. William Stukeley, a noted scholar of British antiquities, and the movement expanded rapidly from there. By the 1790s, according to contemporary records, there were Druid societies in Dublin and in the Hudson River Valley of the newly independent United States, and Druid ceremonies were being openly celebrated at Primrose Hill in London.

Behind this phenomenon lay a complex history. The ancient Druids were the priests, wizards, and philosophers of the Celtic peoples of Ireland, Britain, and Gaul (modern France). There are a handful of scrappy references concerning them in Greek and Roman records, and accounts in Irish legends written down centuries after the last Druids went extinct, but none of these sources provide a clear view of what the Druids were and what they taught. Some accounts portrayed them as savage priests spattered with the blood of human sacrifices, while others extolled them as wise sages in forest sanctuaries contemplating the secrets of nature and passing on exalted moral teachings to their students. Whatever they might have been, the Romans suppressed them in Gaul and Britain, and Christian missionaries finished the job in Scotland and Ireland; they last appear in history in the ninth century, when they tried and failed to prevent the Picts of eastern Scotland from converting to Christianity.

There the story might have ended, except for two factors. The first was the mystery that surrounded the standing stones and earthen mounds scattered across the countryside in Ireland, Britain, and France. Today's scholars argue on the basis of radiocarbon dating, as well as currently accepted estimates of when the Celts arrived in the far west of Europe, that those monuments could not have been built by the Druids. In the seventeenth century, however, when the cultural ferment of the Renaissance sparked the first serious historical research in France and England, nobody had access to radiocarbon dating or historical linguistics. As scholarly curiosity turned toward the tall stones and low mounds that dotted the landscape, the idea that they had been built by the ancient Druids was hard to dismiss. That possibility inspired researchers to comb old documents for references to the ancient Druids, and accounts of the little that the Greeks and Romans had said about the Druids found their way into circulation.

The second factor, which arrived with shattering force in the early eighteenth century, was the first wave of the Industrial Revolution. Modern historians like to paint this as a great leap forward, but many people who witnessed it at the time were appalled by the human and environmental cost of a transformation that forced several million rural people off lands their ancestors had farmed for centuries, offered them the hard choice between emigration and work in the vast smoky factories of the new industrial order at starvation wages, and blighted the land itself with coal smoke and sprawling industrial earthworks. The two respectable ideologies of the time—dogmatic Protestant Christianity on the one hand and an equally dogmatic scientific materialism on the other—insisted that all this was for the best. Those who disagreed ended up seeking a third option; some of them found it in what little was known about the ancient Druids.

The newly created Druid groups that emerged from the collision between these factors pursued various paths. Some took an active role in the struggle of the Welsh people for cultural survival and self-determination, an allegiance that ended up transmitting Druid Revival ideas and organizations to the Celtic peoples of Cornwall and Brittany a little later on. Some modeled themselves on Freemasonry and concentrated on social networking and charitable works. Some followed up on the original religious and environmental agenda that seems to have launched the movement, laying the foundations for a movement of nature spirituality that would blossom in a later century. By the second half of the nineteenth century, as a result, there were plenty of Druid orders of various kinds scattered around Britain.

Some of these orders had substantial overlaps with the subculture of magical lodges and Masons with occult interests mentioned earlier. The same Robert Wentworth Little who founded the SRIA in 1867, for example, went on to found a Druid Revival organization, the Ancient and Archeological Order of Druids (AAOD), in 1874. The connections that gave birth to the subject of this book, however, had a different origin: they took shape in the wake of a remarkable cultural shift that still influences the English-speaking world today.

*   *   *

THE CULTURES OF THE Celtic nations that were part of the United Kingdom in 1800 were by and large despised not only by their English conquerors but by many of the Celts themselves. In Ireland, Scotland, Wales, and Cornwall, those who wanted to rise in the world copied the culture and language of England and did their best to rid themselves of what a great many people at that time considered the outworn relics of a barbarous past.

During the century that followed, though, an astonishing transformation occurred: the Celtic nations rediscovered themselves. Languages, music, traditions, and lore that had been on the verge of dying out found new defenders as people in the Celtic lands redefined themselves as members of distinct cultures and nations with their own values and histories. That in itself was remarkable; what was still more remarkable was that the English themselves began to fall under the spell of the peoples they had conquered. By the late nineteenth century, Celtic arts, literature, and music had become wildly popular in England as well as other European nations.

The fascination with all things Celtic that pervaded English culture during the heyday of the Golden Dawn might have left the order untouched, except for three factors—or, more exactly, three people. The first was Samuel Mathers, one of the order's founders, an enthusiast for all things Celtic who claimed to be descended from the MacGregors, one of the most famous and romantic of the Highland clans of Scotland. The second was Mathers's wife Moina, a gifted clairvoyant and occultist who played a leading role in the order straight through its history and who was as much of a Celtophile as her husband.

The third was a figure of much greater importance: the Irish poet and playwright William Butler Yeats. Winner of the 1923 Nobel Prize in Literature and one of the twentieth century's most influential poets, Yeats was also a capable and passionate occultist. He founded the Dublin Hermetic Society in 1885, then was initiated into the Hermetic Order of the Golden Dawn in 1890 and quickly rose through the order's grades of initiation, becoming one of its leading members. At this same time, Yeats was one of the major forces in the Irish cultural renaissance, both through his own work and through his encouragement of two generations of Irish creative talents. Yeats's collection of stories and essays entitled *The Celtic Twilight*, published in 1893, was so influential in its day that the entire Celtic literary and artistic revival of the period is commonly called "the Celtic Twilight" after it.

It was probably inevitable that Yeats's occult interests and his labors on behalf of Ireland would fuse at some point, and in 1895 that fusion began as Yeats drew up the first plans for a Celtic magical order on Golden Dawn lines: the Castle of Heroes. Samuel and Moina Mathers were among a good dozen Golden Dawn initiates who assisted in the project, which was to be headquartered in a castle on an island in Lough Key, County Roscommon. Five grades of initiation were drawn up, along with outlines of the training required of initiates. It was a workable project, and it might have gone forward if the Golden Dawn itself had survived.

Instead, the first round of political crisis in 1900 put the Matherses and Yeats on opposite sides of a bitter divide, and the struggles that followed scattered the members of the working group that Yeats had gathered around his project into a number of mutually hostile factions. The devastating impact of the First World War, Ireland's successful war of liberation against England immediately afterward, and the Irish Civil War that followed finished off any further hope of accomplishing the project in Yeats's lifetime. The extensive papers from the Castle of Heroes project are now in the National Library of Ireland, silent witnesses to one of the many might-have-beens in the history of Western magic.

*   *   *

IN THE AFTERMATH OF the Golden Dawn's self-immolation, various groups of former members regrouped and organized lodges and orders of their own. Very little is known about most of them, but a curious factor appears in the few records that survive: a noticeable number of these successor groups apparently drew a great deal of their inspiration from Celtic sources, while bits of unmistakably Golden Dawn material also began to surface in Druid Revival groups in England at this same time. Robert MacGregor-Reid, an influential Druid leader of the following generation, was exaggerating considerably when he said to surrealist painter and author Ithell Colquhoun, "Doesn't it occur to you that the Druid Order is the survivor of the Golden Dawn?"[3] Still, there were certainly a number of Druid organizations in the early years of the twentieth century that had close formal or informal connections with the Golden Dawn tradition.

---

3 Ithell Colquhoun, *Sword of Wisdom*, 117.

One of these was the Ancient Order of Druid Hermetists (AODH), which appeared on the London occult scene in 1926. Its head, Mrs. E. A. Ansell, was a student of Irish occultist P. G. Bowen, head of the Dublin Hermetic Society founded by Yeats. The documents that survive—notably, copies of the AODH periodical *The Pendragon*—suggest that a fair amount of Golden Dawn teaching filtered into the AODH system by one means or another.

The Cabbalistic Order of Druids, a group of which little but the name seems to be known, also came into being sometime in the 1920s. If its name is anything to go by, it combined Druidry with the Cabalistic magic that had been central to the Golden Dawn system. There were several others, at least one of which is still quietly active in England today.

There were also a certain number of temples—that is, local working groups—of the Golden Dawn's immediate successor orders that went in a Celtic direction. The most famous of these was the much-rumored Nuada Temple, which was apparently founded in 1916 and, according to Ithell Colquhoun, met for many years in the London suburb of Clapham[4]; it was affiliated to some extent with the AODH, though the exact degree of connection is anyone's guess at present. Standard practice in the original Golden Dawn was to name each temple after a deity—for example, the main London temple was the Isis-Urania Temple, the temple in Bristol was the Hermes Temple, and so on—but Nuada Temple seems to have been the only one named after a Celtic deity, the Irish god Nuada of the Silver Hand. Another London temple, headed by William Carnegie Dickson, apparently practiced the standard Golden Dawn rituals but combined them with a series of workings drawing extensively from the legends of King Arthur and Merlin.[5]

The remarkable magical career of Dion Fortune also intersected with the current of the Celtic–Golden Dawn fusion in significant ways. Fortune—her real name was Violet Firth, but few people nowadays remember her by anything but her magical nom de plume—came to occultism years after the original Golden Dawn had blown itself apart. She had some of her training in two of the successor orders that emerged from the fragments of the explosion and a great deal more in the wider world of British occult societies and magical lodges; her principal teacher, Dr. Theodore Moriarty, was a Freemason and a Theosophist with connections in several corners of the occult scene.

4   Ibid., 129.
5   These are discussed in Alan Richardson and Geoff Hughes's *Ancient Magics for a New Age*, 5–102.

The magical order Fortune founded, the Fraternity of the Inner Light, had three degrees of initiation and a distinctive system of teaching that included borrowings from the Golden Dawn, Theosophy, and Christian mysticism, among other sources, as well as a great deal of material that was entirely original to Fortune herself. Celtic traditions played a significant role in Fortune's synthesis, and the teachings of the Inner Light came to include a substantial body of material on the occult dimensions of the legends surrounding King Arthur; much of this has been published by Fortune's student Gareth Knight as *The Secret Tradition in Arthurian Legend*, a book that has gone on to inspire a significant amount of Arthurian occultism.

The Society of the Inner Light, as it is now called, is still very much a going concern, as are several daughter orders founded by Inner Light alumni in the years since Fortune's death in 1946. The vast majority of the groups that embodied the fusion between Celtic traditions and the Golden Dawn, however, went out of existence in the Second World War and the years that followed it. Between the disruptions caused by the war years and the postwar rise of Wicca and other freshly minted Neopagan traditions that embodied a vision of magic and spirituality radically different from the one that had been central to the Golden Dawn and the Druid Revival alike, few people had any interest in the old, no-longer-fashionable magical lodges—too few, ultimately, to enable them to keep their doors open. It is an old story and an uncomfortably familiar one to those of us who have an interest in the magical traditions of the Western world.

*   *   *

IT IS AT THIS point that the story this introduction tells takes an unavoidably personal turn. In 2003 I was elected to the position of Grand Archdruid in the Ancient Order of Druids in America (AODA), a Druid Revival order founded in 1912 as the American branch of the Ancient and Archaeological Order of Druids, founded by Robert Wentworth Little back in 1874. I came to the job after most of a decade with the Order of Bards, Ovates and Druids (OBOD), a large and lively contemporary Druid order with its roots in the Druid Revival traditions; I came to OBOD, in turn, after nearly two decades of intensive personal work with the traditions of the Hermetic Order of the Golden Dawn.

When I joined it, AODA had fewer than a dozen members, and I was the youngest by some thirty years. The same shifts in fashion that doomed the British occult orders of the early twentieth century had an even more devastating effect on the once thriving American occult scene. In the wake of the sixties, an astonishing number of young Americans attracted to occultism seem to have convinced themselves that magic consisted solely of what had been invented in England between the founding of the Golden Dawn and the emergence of modern Wicca. To many of these newcomers, if it didn't come from the Golden Dawn, Aleister Crowley, Dion Fortune, or one of the first generation of British Wiccan personalities, it simply wasn't of interest. In the face of such attitudes, AODA was fortunate to survive even in its shrunken form; hundreds of American occult societies and magical lodges went out of existence in the second half of the twentieth century, in most cases taking all their accumulated knowledge and rituals with them.

The rituals and teachings of AODA (which I have discussed at some length in other books[6]) have very little direct connection with the Golden Dawn tradition, though they share a great deal of material with the British Druid Revival scene. Beginning in 2003 and continuing for several years thereafter, however, as word of my election to AODA's "hot seat" got into circulation, I began to be contacted by people who had had some previous connection with AODA or one of the other esoteric orders associated with it in the past. The common thread in these communications was some variation on the theme of "Since you're the Grand Archdruid now, you ought to have this." What "this" was varied from person to person, and by no means did all of it have anything to do with AODA or even with Druidry; still, among the things that came my way during those years were fragmentary documents concerning two different Golden Dawn–Druid hybrid orders, one of them probably the Ancient Order of Druid Hermetists, the other less identifiable.

As a Druid with a Golden Dawn background, I was fascinated by this material, and not just for the obvious reasons. Like most students of the Golden Dawn, I had thought that its methods and teachings were unique, since I had found nothing else comparable to them; it had never occurred to me that they might have been simply the only surviving examples of a much broader current of related magical traditions. Just as it only became possible to conceive of the theory of evolution once scholars considered the evidence

---

6   *The Druidry Handbook* (Weiser Books, 2006), *The Druid Magic Handbook* (Weiser Books, 2008), and *The Druid Grove Handbook* (Starseed Press, 2011).

from fossils and saw how they bridged the gaps between living forms, the excavation of these "fossil" rituals and teachings allowed me to fit the Golden Dawn into a context that had not previously been visible.

What I came to see, if I may sum up the results of a great deal of research in very few words, is that the Hermetic Order of the Golden Dawn was simply one of the more elaborate flowerings of an occult movement that had its roots in the impact of Éliphas Lévi's redefinition of magic on the Masonic and quasi-Masonic occult scene of the nineteenth century. Though they drew a great deal of raw material from ancient sources, neither the Golden Dawn nor the broader movement were ancient in any real sense; they were, rather, a creative response to the opening up of new possibilities in the field of magic, and both the Golden Dawn and the broader movement kept on displaying an impressive capacity to innovate throughout their history. In the process, they also created highly effective ways of practicing magic and of carrying out the work of personal transformation that Lévi, as well as the Golden Dawn and its successors, called initiation.

*   *   *

TO SPEAK OF THE Golden Dawn as the creative and innovative product of a tradition is to risk falling afoul of some remarkably deep-seated prejudices in the contemporary occult and Pagan communities. Both these communities, in America and elsewhere, are very largely split down the middle between partisans of tradition who bristle at the thought of innovation and partisans of innovation who see no value whatsoever in tradition. The reality is that any spiritual or magical practice worth the name necessarily includes both tradition and innovation, but this simply adds spice to the bubbling cauldron of acrimony that too often results from this split.

Thus there are plenty of people on the occult scene these days who insist that the rituals and teachings of the Hermetic Order of the Golden Dawn must be studied and practiced exactly as written, or that some other body of written magical teaching taken in the most pigheadedly literal manner is the only valid basis for magical training. On the other side of the scene are at least as many people who insist that all of the traditional lore of magic is stuff and nonsense that should be tipped into the dumpster in favor of notions derived from current intellectual vogues and imagery copied from today's pop culture.

This same divide runs through the midst of the contemporary Druid scene as well. There is a small but vocal faction of Druids and Celtic Pagans that devotes its time to denouncing anyone whose Druidry fails to copy whatever reconstructions of ancient Celtic spirituality might happen to be in fashion in the academic world. The fact, and of course it is a fact, that the Druid Revival has been a vibrant, creative, and meaningful movement for close to three hundred years, evolving traditions and creating lineages that can have value in their own right irrespective of any relationship to the ancient Celts, never finds a place in the resulting diatribes. On the other side of the balance are those who simply make things up out of whole cloth as they go along and call it Druidry.

It needs to be said that there is nothing wrong with following the Golden Dawn tradition exactly by the book or with choosing to practice a personal spirituality that copies every detail of currently fashionable academic interpretations of archaic Celtic spirituality. Equally, there is nothing wrong with making things up as you go along and seeing how they work. The problem emerges when these two options are treated as the only possibilities that exist, when one of them is treated as the only valid one, and when the huge middle ground—which is where magic and spirituality, by and large, have their home—is dismissed from consideration.

This sort of thinking is, among other things, a complete misunderstanding of the nature of tradition itself. A tradition—the word comes from a Latin root that means "that which is given across" or, as we would now say, handed down—is simply a collection, accumulated over time, of things that work. In magic, as in anything else, having a good idea of what has been tried in the past is an enormous asset, but it has to be combined with a willingness to adapt the lessons of the past to the needs of the ever-changing present. A body of knowledge that remains absolutely fixed over time, incapable of absorbing new lessons and insights, is not a tradition but a corpse.

In the same way, the refusal to learn from the lessons of the past, far from being a sign of originality or what have you, simply guarantees that a great many mistakes made long ago will have to be made again. Those who refuse to learn from the past, as the saying goes, are condemned to repeat it—and as Karl Marx pointed out a long time ago, while the first time around may be tragedy, the second is generally farce.[7]

---

7 In the opening sentences of *The Eighteenth Brumaire of Louis Bonaparte* (1852).

Nor is it ever possible either to follow or to reject tradition totally. No matter how rigidly traditionalist a magician thinks he is, he inevitably reinterprets the teachings and rituals he receives in the light of his own experience of life and responds to the blanks that are always left by a system of teaching by filling them in with material that, consciously or otherwise, is invented for the purpose. The older the tradition, the more comprehensive the innovations will be, since (for example) no American in the twenty-first century is even remotely capable of experiencing the world in the same way as a Celt in the fifth century BCE. No matter how cutting-edge and avant-garde a magician thinks she is, in the same way, the very concept of magic itself in contemporary society—to say nothing of the fashionable philosophies and pop culture that provide today's avant-garde magic with so much of its raw material—are freighted with so much existing magical material that it's no wonder cutting-edge magic generally ends up looking very much like the old-fashioned magic it claims to be rejecting.

The most successful magical traditions, in turn, are generally those that combine a solid awareness of tradition with a willingness to innovate freely, using tradition as a base. The Hermetic Order of the Golden Dawn was among the best examples of this. Westcott, Mathers, and the other adepts of the order came to their work with a wealth of tradition inherited from the movement set in motion by Lévi, by the documents remaining from older systems of magic, and from the occult end of Masonry and quasi-Masonic magical orders. That gave them their basis in tradition. On that foundation they built a structure of astonishing creativity—and that structure became part of the body of tradition that later orders had available for their own work.

The Celtic–Golden Dawn hybrid orders of the early twentieth century drew, in turn, on the traditions that the Hermetic Order of the Golden Dawn enriched. It is an accident of history—or perhaps the working of those subtle factors that occultists have so often sensed moving through history—that the teachings and practices of the Hermetic Order of the Golden Dawn have become famous while those of the Castle of Heroes, the Ancient Order of Druid Hermetists, and their peers have been ignored or lost. It could easily have gone the other way; there are many people in today's Druid and Celtic Pagan communities who find the Judeo-Christian symbolism of the Golden Dawn teachings less than congenial and likely would have welcomed similar traditions built up on a Celtic polytheistic basis. It simply happened that while the hybrid orders were still a going concern, modern Pagans were generally practicing Wicca if they were doing anything at all, and once the Neopagan movement expanded to the point where people were interested in a wider range of alternatives, nearly all the hybrid orders had died from lack of new members.

*   *   *

THE KNOWLEDGE LECTURES, PAPERS, and rituals that follow this introduction may thus be seen as an imaginative effort to stand history on its head. It probably needs to be said that they are not the materials from a Druid–Golden Dawn hybrid order that actually existed. As mentioned earlier in this essay, the materials I received were fragmentary, so much so that creating a working system out of them would have required at least as much work as creating an entire system from scratch.

I have also been told, though I have no way to verify this claim, that there is at least one Druid order in Britain still working the system sketched out in one of the sets of fragments I inherited. Publishing rituals and teachings that belong to a order that still exists is a very serious matter, magically speaking, as well as a breach of the common courtesy one Druid tradition owes to another. Nor, for that matter, would such a disclosure help communicate the point I hope to get across here, which is that the Golden Dawn system—like any magical or spiritual system—is the product of a lively dance in which tradition and innovation take the lead by turns.

For these reasons, among others, I have done the logical thing and created an original system of Druid magic—or, to introduce the old-fashioned form consistently used in the papers that follow, Druidical magic—which is based on the same template of Golden Dawn tradition used by the Celtic–Golden Dawn hybrid orders but fills in that template, as they did, with material from a variety of sources. The most important of these sources is the body of Druid Revival teaching and tradition common to most of contemporary Druidry, which derives largely from the brilliant Welsh innovator Iolo Morganwg (Edward Williams)[8] and was developed further by generations of Druids in the various Revival orders.

---

8   Like a great many innovators in the fields of magic and alternative spirituality—including the founders of the Golden Dawn—Williams found it useful to conceal his originality behind dubious claims of an ancient lineage. It bears remembering that the value of his innovations does not depend on the accuracy of their myth of origin.

There is also a great deal of straightforward Golden Dawn material, though this has been altered in a number of ways—for example, in the pentagram rituals of the system that follows, the pentagrams of the five elements are drawn in a different way, and the assignment of the elements to the Tree of Life is also different. These distinctions follow from the basic structure of the system, which works with elemental influences exclusively, rather than combining them with planetary influences. This strictly elemental focus follows the lead of most Druid Revival orders, which put a great deal of emphasis on the elements but do not include astrology in their systems of symbolism and practice.

To the sources just named are added a number of other branches of occult lore that either play a role in the Druid Revival traditions or fill a necessary niche in the system. These include sacred geometry, spagyrics (herbal alchemy), and divinatory geomancy, among others. The more traditionalist end of the Druid scene will no doubt be incensed at these additions, but it has to be remembered that the Golden Dawn tradition is by definition eclectic and syncretistic. To draw up a system of Golden Dawn magic that was anything other than a wildly diverse combination of materials from different sources would thus be hopelessly inauthentic.

The structure of the teachings and rituals of the Druidical Order of the Golden Dawn, the invented order presented here, is drawn partly from that of the original Golden Dawn and partly from the exigencies of the tradition's later years. In place of formal initiation rituals conferred by a team of experienced members, which are not currently available, the material that follows uses the slower but equally effective method of the repeated practice of self-initiation rituals backed up by regular meditation and inner work with the important symbols of the system. The three degrees of initiation offered in most of the older Druid Revival orders—Ovate, Bard, and Druid, in that order[9]—provide the framework. The Ovate, like the member of the Outer Order in the original Golden Dawn, is given a sequence of knowledge lectures and basic practices; the Bard, like the member of the Portal Grade, receives more complex teachings and practices to prepare him for the demanding work of ceremonial magic; the Druid, like the Adeptus Minor, is handed the keys to the tradition and then expected to get to work with them.

---

9 This was the standard order of grades in nineteenth- and early twentieth-century Druid organizations. Ross Nichols, the founder of OBOD, deliberately altered this in his order, putting the Bardic Grade first to emphasize the poetic and artistic side of the tradition.

Introduction

The material that follows can be approached in at least two ways. First, for those who find a Druid Revival–oriented system of Golden Dawn magic appealing, it can be studied and practiced exactly as it exists. I have myself practiced the material that follows, and it works: that is, anyone who learns and practices it systematically will, on completing the course of study that follows, have mastered an effective system of magic and spiritual development that can be used with good results for the rest of a lifetime.

To reach this goal, however, the student will need to work through the lessons and practices that follow in their proper order. This is as true for those who already have extensive experience in other magical traditions as it is of complete beginners. It is too rarely noticed that the initial stages of training, which focus on the symbolism and philosophy of a system, have to be absorbed through study and meditation for the later stages to have their effect. Furthermore, it is my experience that even the most learned of occultists has a great deal to learn by revisiting the basics now and then.

On the other hand, a great many readers may find one or another part of the Druidical Order of the Golden Dawn system unwelcome. They may, for example, prefer Irish gods, symbolism, and terminology to the Welsh material I have used; they may wish that I had used some other form of divination or included planetary influences or put in or left out something else; they may, for that matter, have no interest whatsoever in a Celtic Golden Dawn but may be eager to see whether something of the same sort can be done to make the Golden Dawn approach fit whatever spiritual tradition they themselves find appealing. They and their interests are at least half of the reason why the book has been written.

Creating a system of ceremonial magic and occult initiation along the lines of the Golden Dawn tradition is not an easy thing, but it is within the reach of anyone who is willing to study both the original Golden Dawn material and the papers that follow, and triangulate from these in the direction of whatever set of symbols or purposes it is that calls to them. Inevitably some of the systems produced in this way will flop; others will turn out to be workable; and it is always possible that one or two will surpass anything that has yet been done in the Golden Dawn tradition and go on to become major influences on the magical lodges and teachings of the future. If that happens, I cannot help but think that Lévi, Westcott, and a great many of their peers would be pleased.

A Note to the Reader.

THE MATERIAL THAT FOLLOWS has been written and presented in such a way as to resemble as closely as possible the papers that would have been given to the student of an early twentieth-century Druid–Golden Dawn hybrid order. From one perspective, this is simply a lengthy literary joke; from another, it is what the old alchemists used to call a *lusus serius*, a "serious game," in which a certain degree of deliberate absurdity becomes a framework for communication on more than one level. Still, the process has involved certain departures from standard practice.

One of these that may be controversial has to do with gendered pronouns. The use of the masculine pronouns "he," "him," and "his" to refer to human beings in general was so universal in English prose in the early twentieth century that even the most radical feminists of the time used it, and I have done the same here in order to catch the flavor of the language of the time.[10]

Another issue that may be challenging to current readers is that all the books I have listed as recommended reading were published before 1930. Excellent books on all these subjects have been published more recently, of course, and I have included recommendations in an appendix, along with notes on the sources I have used for the material in these papers.

Like the teaching documents of other occult societies and magical lodges at that time, the papers that follow are designed to be studied carefully and explored in daily meditations, not simply read through once in a casual manner. They do not cover every topic in detail; in many places, a great deal of room is left for the student's own thoughts, contemplations, and insights, and not all questions implied by the text are answered. The initiate of a magical tradition cannot expect to be spoonfed.

---

10 Just at the moment, the English language has no gender-neutral singular pronoun suitable for human beings, and "his or her" or the reverse very often makes for awkward prose. In some of my other books, I have ducked this difficulty in other ways—for example, in *A World Full of Gods* (ADF Press, 2005), I use the feminine pronouns "she," "her," and "hers" to refer to human beings in general.

Those readers who intend to learn and practice the teachings of the Druidical Order of the Golden Dawn may find it entertaining, if nothing else, to imagine that the following pages are, in fact, the legacy of some long-defunct Druid order in the Golden Dawn tradition, hidden away for decades in some unlikely place. The twine around the bulky envelope yields reluctantly to your shaking hands, but the glue on the envelope's seal has long since turned to dust, and it opens readily. You pull out the papers inside, and read...

DRUIDICAL ORDER OF THE GOLDEN DAWN

△

The Ovate Grade

▽

Thrice welcome, Aspirant!

We are pleased to welcome you to the first stage of your studies on the Druidical path, and we trust that you will there find light, wisdom, power, and peace, as many others have done before you.

The work immediately before you is divided into seven knowledge lectures, each of which presents certain elements of Druidical teaching for you to learn and certain magical and spiritual practices for you to perform. The knowledge lectures should be studied in order, and you will find it the most productive approach to be sure that you have thoroughly grasped the material presented in each lecture before going on to the next. You should expect to spend at least four months at this work, and it is never a mistake to take longer if this assists you to learn the teachings more thoroughly.

The practices that are assigned to this grade include, among other things, a ritual, a form of meditation, and a form of divination. These three in particular form the foundation for your future progress as an initiate of our path, and they should be practiced as regularly as possible. Should you complete the training of the first, or Ovate, grade and proceed to the second, or Bardic, grade of our Druidical Mysteries, you will be expected at that time to set aside time each day for these three practices, and the sooner you are able to make room in your day for this, the more rapidly you will progress and the more benefits you will gain.

With these words of encouragement, we welcome you again to the Druidical path!

The Guardians of the Order

First Knowledge Lecture.

I. THE FOUR ELEMENTS of the ancients are general conditions of:

    Heat and Moisture: Air

    Heat and Dryness: Fire

    Cold and Moisture: Water

    Cold and Dryness: Earth

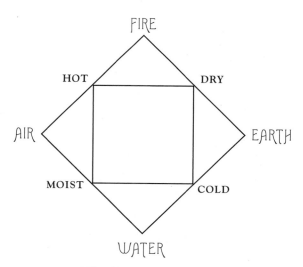

The Four Elements

The elements are present in all phenomena and are not limited to the material forms that bear the same names. The student will benefit from learning to recognize them in all things: for example, when contemplating a leaf, note the presence of earth in terms of the solid material substance of the leaf, water in terms of the sap, air in terms of the

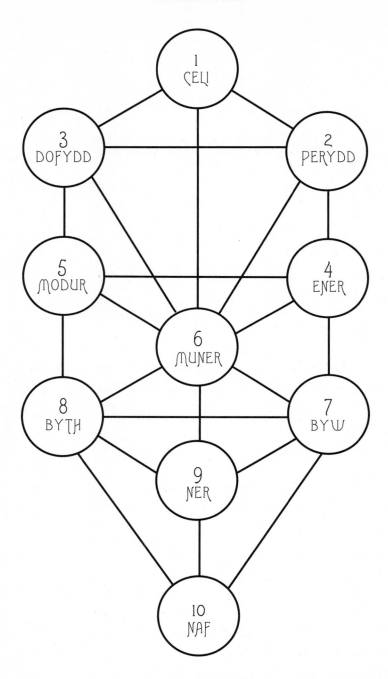

The Tree of Life

elements of the atmosphere entering into and exiting from the pores, and fire in terms of the energy of life therein.

2. TO THESE ELEMENTS correspond directions, times, seasons of the year, and colors:

To air:	East	Dawn	Spring	Yellow
To fire:	South	Noon	Summer	Red
To water:	West	Dusk	Autumn	Blue
To earth:	North	Midnight	Winter	Green

The element of spirit is added to the four material elements in the Druid teaching. It occupies the center of the symbolic circle, and its correspondences are as follows:

To spirit:	Center	The Now	Eternity	White

3. IN THEIR MYSTERY Teachings, the ancients made use of a variety of symbolic patterns upon which the symbolism of the Mysteries could be usefully arranged. With the creation of a universal symbolism of the Mysteries, these were resumed in the pattern of the Tree of Life. In Druidical teachings, the ten stations, or spheres, of the Tree of Life have the following names, which are traditional titles of deity. Each name is followed by its meaning and pronunciation; it should be noted that "dd" is pronounced "th" as in "these," not as in "thin."

1. **CELI**, the Hidden ("KAY-lee")
2. **PERYDD**, the Cause ("PER-uth")
3. **DOFYDD**, the Tamer ("DOV-uth")
4. **ENER**, the Namer ("ENN-er")
5. **MODUR**, the Mover ("MO-dir")
6. **MUNER**, the Lord ("MINN-er")
7. **BYW**, the Living ("BE-oo")
8. **BYTH**, the Eternal ("BITH")
9. **NER**, the Mighty ("NER")
10. **NAF**, the Shaper ("NAHV")

The Tree of Life is shown on page 26. To it, in the Druid teachings, are assigned the three circles of existence:

THE CIRCLE OF ABRED—that is, "Release," pronounced "AB-red"—corresponds to the stations of the Tree from Naf up to Byw. This is the circle of incarnate life in the realm of the four elements.

THE CIRCLE OF GWYNFYDD—that is, "Luminous Life," pronounced "GWUN-vuth"—corresponds to the stations from Muner up to Ener. This is the circle of discarnate life in the realm of the three modes of spirit.

THE CIRCLE OF CEUGANT—that is, "Empty Circle," pronounced "KYE-gant"—corresponds to the stations from Dofydd up to Celi. This is the circle of the divine presence that can be traversed by no created being.

First Meditation

LET THE OVATE TAKE a seed of some kind—a pea or bean will be suitable—and soak it for twenty-four hours in clean, fresh water. Let him then place it upon moistened cloth or blotting paper and keep that moist. After several days, the seed will be found to have sprouted. Let it be kept moistened until the first root and seed leaves have appeared. It may then be placed in the ground, if a suitable spot exists and the season is favorable, or returned to the earth in some other manner.

When this has been done, let the Ovate take the sprouting of the seed as a theme for meditation. Let him note the ideas to which this gives rise. Concentrating his faculties on this, let him endeavor to realize the presence and power of life within matter.

Begin by finding a suitable physical position, balanced but comfortable. The one commonly used is sitting upright in a chair, sufficiently far forward that the spine does not rest against the chair back; the feet are flat upon the floor, the hands resting upon the thighs, the head balanced, the gaze slightly lowered. Breathe rhythmically for several minutes until the body is still and the mind quiet. Remain in this state for a few minutes at first, and for longer as you get more used to preventing the mind from wandering. Afterwards, think of the theme of meditation in a general way, considering such of its aspects as come to mind; choose one train of thought that unfolds from the theme, and follow it to its conclusion. A few cycles of rhythmic breathing then complete the meditation.

The best method for rhythmic breathing for this stage of the training is the Natural Breath:

1. Breathe in slowly, drawing the air down to the bottom of the lungs. Allow the muscles of the abdomen to relax so that the abdomen moves slightly forward with the in-breath, then relax the midriff so that it expands, and then relax the chest, with the same result.

2. Allow the breath to remain in the lungs for an interval, no longer than feels comfortable to you. This should be done without closing the throat.

3. Breathe out slowly, first by gently contracting the muscles of the abdomen, then those of the midriff, then those of the chest. Finish with the lungs empty but without strain.

4. Pause briefly before beginning with the in-breath again.

The three phases of each in-breath and out-breath should take approximately equal times. With practice the rhythm becomes automatic, and a few minutes of breathing in this rhythm will quiet your body and mind for meditation.

WHEN YOU HAVE MEDITATED upon the seed and its sprouting often enough that no new ideas or insights occur to you, proceed to the teachings included with this knowledge lecture, particularly the lecture on the Three Rays of Light. All these must be studied closely and contemplated in meditation so that they may sink deep roots in your mind; only thus will they flower and bear fruit.

The Lesser Ritual of the Pentagram

THIS RITUAL IS AMONG the foundations for all the ceremonial work of the Druidical Mysteries. It should be performed daily. Alternate the summoning and banishing forms of the ritual so that you summon in one day's practice and banish in the next. Pay close attention to the differences you perceive in the effects of the two forms of the ritual.

1. *The Rite of the Rays*

This is performed as follows:

FIRST, stand facing east. Imagine yourself expanding to a vast height until your head is among the stars, the sun is at your solar plexus, and you stand upon the round earth. Then raise your hands up from your sides in an arc above your head and join them palm to palm, fingers and thumbs together, and then draw them down until your thumbs touch the center of your forehead. As you do this, visualize a ray of light descending from infinite space above you to formulate a star of brilliant white light above the top of your head. Vibrate the word *Mae* (pronounced "my"). (The meaning of "vibration" in this context is explained on page 34.)

SECOND, bow your head slightly, and visualize a ray of light shining from the star in your head down the midline of your body and descending into infinite space directly below you. Vibrate the word *Alawn* (pronounced "ALL-own," the last syllable rhyming with "crown").

THIRD, leaving your left hand at forehead level, move your right hand down and to your right in an arc until it forms a single diagonal line from shoulder to fingertips. The palm should finish facing forward. As you do this, visualize a ray of light shining from the star in your head along the line of your right arm and descending into infinite space below and to your right. Vibrate the word *Plennydd* (pronounced "PLEN-nuth," with the "th" voiced as in "these," rather than unvoiced as in "thin").

FOURTH, make an identical motion with your left hand, extending it down and to your left until it, too, forms a single diagonal line from shoulder to fingertips. As you do this, visualize a ray of light shining from the star in your head along the line of your left arm and descending into infinite space below and to your left. Vibrate the words *A gwron* (pronounced "ah GOO-ron").

FIFTH, cross your arms across your chest, right arm over left, with your hands resting on the front of your shoulders. Visualize all three rays of light and vibrate the words *Y teyr pelydryn goleuni* (pronounced "ee TEIR pell-UD-run go-LEY-nee"). Then, in a single smooth motion, sweep both arms up, out, and down to your sides, then bring them palm to palm and raise them to the center of your chest, fingers pointing upwards and thumbs touching your chest. Vibrate the word *Awen* (pronounced "AH-OO-EN," with the three syllables held for an equal length of time). This completes the first phase.

The words spoken in this rite are in the Welsh language and mean "Alawn, Plennydd, and Gwron, the three rays of light." The three names mean "harmony," "light," and "virtue," and according to tradition they were the names of the three original Bards of Britain; they have another meaning as well, which will be considered in due time.

2. The Summoning Ritual of the Pentagram

This is performed as follows:

FIRST, face east and perform the complete Rite of the Rays.

SECOND, go to the eastern quarter of the circle. Using the first two fingers of your right hand, with the others folded under your thumb in the palm of your hand, trace a summoning pentagram in the fashion shown below, starting down and to the right from the topmost point and then continuing clockwise around to the same point. The pentagram should be two or three feet across. As you do this, visualize it taking shape before you, as though your fingers were drawing it in a line of golden light. When you have finished, point to the center and vibrate the divine name *Heu'c* (pronounced "HEY'k").

The Summoning Pentagram

THIRD, with your extended fingers, trace a line around the circumference of the circle a quarter circle to your right, ending at the southern quarter of the circle; visualize it in golden light as you trace it. Trace a pentagram in the south in the same way as in the east, point to the center, and vibrate the divine name *Sulw* (pronounced "SILL-w").

FOURTH, repeat the process, tracing a line another quarter of the way around the circle to the west, visualizing it in golden light, and tracing and visualizing the pentagram as you did in the east and south. Point to the center of the pentagram and vibrate the divine name *Esus* (pronounced "ESS-iss").

FIFTH, repeat the process once more, tracing a line around to the north, tracing and visualizing a pentagram there, and vibrating the divine name *Elen* (pronounced "ELL-enn").

SIXTH, trace a line as before back around to the east, completing the circle, and then return to the center and face east. Extend your arms down and out to your sides, once again taking on the posture of the Three Rays of Light. Say:

Before me, the Hawk of May and the powers of air. Behind me, the Salmon of Wisdom and the powers of water. To my right hand, the White Stag and the powers of fire. To my left hand, the Great Bear and the powers of earth. For about me flame the pentagrams, and upon me shine the Three Rays of Light.

As you name each of these things, visualize it as solidly and intensely as you can. You are surrounded by the elements—a cloudscape to the east, a desert scene of blazing heat and flame to the south, a seascape to the west, and a forest to the north—with the animal guardians visible against these backgrounds. The pentagrams and circle form a pattern like a crown surrounding you, and the Three Rays of Light shine down from the starry center of light in your head as in the Rite of the Rays.

SEVENTH, perform the complete Rite of the Rays as before. This completes the ritual.

3. The Banishing Ritual of the Pentagram

This ritual is performed in the same way as the Summoning Ritual except that the pentagrams are drawn in a different way—from the topmost point down and to the left, and then around counterclockwise to the same point, as shown below. All other words, actions, and visualizations remain the same.

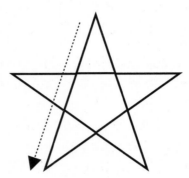

The Banishing Pentagram

A Note on Vibration

Among the most important skills you will learn as you proceed in the work of the Druidical Mysteries is vibration, which is a particular mode of speaking or chanting names, words, and phrases of power. To vibrate a word is to utter it in such a way that it produces a buzzing or tingling sensation in your body. To learn how to do this, take a vowel sound such as "ah" and draw it out, changing the way your mouth and throat shape the sound until you feel the sensation just described.

In the early stages of your training, simply getting this effect whenever you vibrate a word or phrase is enough. With practice, however, you will find that the sensation can be localized in any desired part of your body; for example, when you point to the center of a pentagram and vibrate a divine name, the vibration can be localized in the fingertips, and this will grant increased force to the working.

Concerning the Three Rays of Light

IN THE FIRST PART of *Barddas*, the great collection of Welsh Bardic lore, we read the following about the creation of the world:

God, when there was in life and existence only Himself, proclaimed His Name, and co-instantaneously with the word all living and existing things burst wholly into a shout of joy; and that voice was the most melodious that ever was heard in music. Co-instantaneously with the voice there was light, and in the light, form; and the voice was in three tones, three vocalizations, pronounced together at the same moment. And in the vision were three forms and three colors, which were the form of light; and one with the voice, and the color and the form of that voice, were the first letters. It was from a combination of their vocalization that every other vocalization was formed in letters. He who heard the voice was Menw the Aged, son of the Three Shouts, but others say that it was Einigan the Giant, that first made a letter, the same being the form of the Name of God, when he found himself alive and existing co-momentaneously and co-instantaneously with the voice.

Elsewhere in the same section it says the following:

Einigan the Giant beheld three pillars of light, having in them all demonstrable sciences that ever were, or ever will be. And he took three rods of the quicken tree, and placed on them the forms and signs of all the sciences, so as to be remembered; and exhibited them. But those who saw them misunderstood, and falsely apprehended them, and taught illusive sciences, regarding the rods as a God, whereas they only bore His Name. When Einigan saw this, he was greatly annoyed, and in the intensity of his grief he broke the three rods, nor were others found that contained accurate sciences. He was so distressed on that account that from the intensity he burst asunder, and with his parting breath he prayed God that there should be accurate sciences among men in the flesh, and there should be a correct understanding for the proper discernment thereof. And at the end of a year and a day, after the decease of Einigan, Menw, son of the Three Shouts,

35

beheld three rods growing out of the mouth of Einigan, which exhibited the sciences of the Ten Letters, and the mode in which all the sciences of language and speech were arranged by them, and in language and speech all distinguishable sciences. He then took the rods, and taught from them the sciences—all, except the Name of God, which he made a secret, lest the Name should be falsely discerned; and hence arose the Secret of the Bardism of the Bards of the Isle of Britain.

And likewise in the same section is the following:

Pray, my beloved and discreet teacher, show me the signs that stand for the Name of God, and the manner in which they are made.

Thus are they made—the first of the signs is a small cutting or line inclining with the sun at eventide, thus, / ; the second is another cutting, in the form of a perpendicular upright post, thus, | ; and the third is a cutting of the same amount of inclination as the first, but in an opposite direction, that is, against the sun, thus \ ; and the three placed together, thus, / | \ . But instead of, and as substitutes for these, are placed the three letters O I W.

THE SIGN MADE BY these three lines or cuttings, / | \ , is the emblem of the Three Rays of Light that brought the world into being, and they form the holy sign of the Druids. Each ray, as has already been suggested to you, has a name: the left-hand ray is Gwron, "virtue," and to it is assigned the quality of knowledge; the right-hand ray is Plennydd, "light," and to it is assigned the quality of power; and the central ray is Alawn, "harmony," and to it is assigned the quality of peace. Knowledge, power, and peace are therefore manifest in and called forth by this sign.

The threefold pattern of the Three Rays of Light is among the most important keys to the Druid Mysteries, for it is a first step in the understanding of those Mysteries to recognize that all things are threefold. The same insight may be found in other Mystery Teachings. "The Mind of the Father said that all things should be cut into three, whose Will assented, and immediately all things were so divided," says the Chaldean Oracles.

The following themes should be considered in this light:

1. A standing stone on an open plain will produce a shadow at dawn as the sun rises, reaching westward across the plain. At the summer solstice, when the

sun rises farthest north of east, the shadow extends south of west; at the winter solstice, when the sun rises farthest south of east, the shadow extends north of west; at the equinoxes, when the sun rises due east, the shadow extends due west.

2. The ancients taught that a virtue is not the opposite of one vice but the midpoint between two, which are opposed to each other as well as to the virtue between them. Thus courage is the midpoint between cowardice and foolhardiness, the generous man is neither miserly nor spendthrift, prudence is opposed both to meddlesome cleverness and to folly, and so on through the catalogue of virtues and vices.

3. The germination of every seed involves three motions: the downward motion of the root into earth, the upward motion of the seed leaves toward light, and the unfolding motion of growth in the center, which holds both in balance.

IN THE ORDINARY SOCIETY of every age, and more especially in that of our own nation and time, the commonplaces of exoteric thought imagine the world principally in terms of opposites. Thus arise thoughts of God and devil, good and evil, life and death, truth and falsehood, liberal and conservative, domestic and foreign, and the like in every branch of study and every subject of conversation, from the most insignificant and casual to the most passionate and profound.

It is the teaching of the Druids, and likewise of the Mysteries more generally, that this division into two commonly conceals far more than it reveals. Thinking in terms of twofold oppositions makes it difficult to notice the existence of options other than the two proposed. In politics, for example, it is often assumed that one is either a liberal or a conservative, and thus in favor of either one or the other of the assortment of personalities and policies that happen to be assigned to these two labels at the present day. The existence of other viewpoints—perhaps located in the space between these two alternatives, perhaps not—is obscured by such thinking.

In the language of the Druidical Mysteries, a twofold opposition of this kind is termed a binary. The two poles of a binary may be likened to two of the Three Rays of Light, requiring the third to resolve them into balance. A threefold pattern, which possesses the balance a binary does not, is called a ternary. The following practice will be found useful in beginning to explore the relationship between binaries and ternaries.

WHEN YOU READ THE morning paper, watch for binaries in the news of the day. You will find many of them, sometimes stated in so many words, sometimes concealed. Choose one—let it be, for the sake of example, a debate between liberal and conservative politicians—and consider it in as much detail as you feel is appropriate until you feel you understand both sides of the binary. Do not pass judgment on either of the two sides; instead, try to see whatever wisdom exists in both points of view.

When you have finished this phase, find a third point of view different from either of the first two. It may be a moderate stance that embraces the middle ground between the two contending parties or an option further to one side or the other than the binary itself goes or an opinion that identifies some common feature in the two poles of the binary and opposes itself to this and thus to the binary as a whole. Develop this third point of view in as much detail as seems appropriate until you can see its strengths as well as its weaknesses relative to the two poles of the binary.

The same exercise can be done with binaries from any other source. In popular fiction and the theater, for example, binaries are as common as they are in the newspaper and may be transformed into ternaries in the same way. Here, let us say, we have the heroine of a novel, faced with a choice between two courses of action. Find a third option for her, and try to determine, when you have finished the novel, what would have happened to her and to the other characters had she chosen it.

This exercise should be made part of your habitual patterns of thought during the time you spend in this grade.

Second Knowledge Lecture.

1. THE ART OF alchemy was among the attainments of the ancient Druids and was cultivated by an inner circle of the Druidical Order whom later Welsh documents call by the name of Pheryllt. This inner circle had a stronghold upon Yr Wyddfa (Mt. Snowdon) in North Wales, which was called Dinas Ffaraon (the City of Pharaoh, alluding to the Egyptian origins of their alchemical lore) before the coming of Merlin Ambrosius, and Dinas Emrys (the City of Ambrosius) after his time.

Alchemy may be understood as the art by which material forms are rendered capable of expressing more fully the spiritual forces that create and sustain them. This definition should be carefully studied and explored in meditation.

The alchemy taught among the Druids differed in part from the more famous Arabian alchemy of later centuries in that it took the vegetable creation, rather than the mineral, for its principal subject. The noted Rev. William Stukeley, who in his time was chief of the Mount Haemus Grove near London, was a keen alchemist and recovered a part of the ancient Druidical lore of alchemy.

2. THE TWO GREAT principles of Druidical alchemy differ from those of the earlier Arabic alchemy, though they came into use in European alchemy in its last great age—in the sixteenth and seventeenth centuries of our era. They are niter $\oplus$ and salt $\ominus$.

Niter is the active principle, and salt is the passive principle. They are the active and passive manifestations of the universal fire, or anima mundi—the first created existence, or One Thing of alchemy, from which all other things come into being.

Niter and salt are symbolized by the red and white dragons of Druidical legend, and also the winged and wingless dragons of alchemical lore. They are likewise:

⦶	⊖
Acid	Alkali
Heaven	Earth
Spirit	Body
Father	Mother
Sperm	Ovum
Active	Passive
Fire	Water
Air	Earth
Steel	Magnet
Hammer	Anvil

Niter is born in the heavens and descends to the earth, where it is materialized and becomes salt; salt is born in the earth and ascends to the heavens, where it is spiritualized and becomes niter. By this process niter and salt nourish all of the mineral, vegetable, and animal creation. With the light of the sun—itself a direct expression of the universal fire, or anima mundi—niter and salt form the Triad of Life.

3. **THE FOUR SACRED** animals of Druidical tradition are:

The Hawk of May—Air
The White Stag—Fire
The Salmon of Wisdom—Water
The Great Bear—Earth

These are invoked as emblems of the elemental creation.

4. **THE SACRED PLANTS** of Druidical tradition are primarily the oak, the mistletoe, and the vervain. Each of these have several meanings in Druid lore.

THE OAK, for its enduring strength, is a symbol of duration and time; it was also a symbol of kingship long before the future Charles II sought shelter from his enemies among its boughs. In Druidical symbolism, the Tree of Life is generally imaged as a great oak. It is associated with the whole cycle of the year.

THE MISTLETOE grows on several forest trees in Europe, most commonly on apple but very rarely on oak. The "golden bough" of the ancients, it represents the presence of the Timeless perceived amid Time: all knowledge that ever was or will be, seen in a single glance, as Einigan the Giant did on beholding the Three Rays of Light. It is associated with the winter solstice.

THE VERVAIN is an herb beneficial to the eyes, and it also confers the gift of inner vision. It is associated with the summer solstice.

Other plants were held to be sacred to the Druids on account of their use in healing, which was one of the special studies and privileges of the Ovate Grade. A paper on this subject is appended to the present knowledge lecture.

5. THE FIGURES OF geomancy are these:

• • • • • **Mab** (Boy)	• • • • • • **Colled** (Loss)	• • • • • • • **Gwyn** (White)	• • • • • • • • **Pobl** (People)
• • • • • • **Bendith Fawr** (Great Blessing)	• • • • • • **Cyswllt** (Joining)	• • • • • **Merch** (Girl)	• • • • • • • **Coch** (Red)
• • • • • • **Elw** (Gain)	• • • • • **Carchar** (Prison)	• • • • • • • **Tristwch** (Sorrow)	• • • • • • **Llawenydd** (Joy)
• • • • • **Llosgwrn y Ddraig** (Dragon's Tail)	• • • • • **Pen y Ddraig** (Dragon's Head)	• • • • • • **Bendith Fach** (Little Blessing)	• • • • **Ffordd** (Road)

The origins of the art of geomancy are not known. It was practiced until recently in all the nations of Europe as well as further abroad, and the names of the sixteen figures were translated into many languages. The figures are emblems of the relationships of the four elements. Their uses in divination and magic are manifold.

6. THE TREE OF Life imaged as an oak has its roots in the heavens while its branches descend to earth. The last and lowest of the ten stations, or spheres, is Naf, the material world, which is the furthest extension of the Tree; it and, more generally, the four lowest spheres are in Abred; the three spheres of Gwynfydd are its middle section; its roots are in Celi, Perydd, and Dofydd, the three spheres of Ceugant.

The gap between Perydd and Ener, and between Dofydd and Modur, is equivalent to the surface of the soil, dividing those parts of the oak that are visible to us from those parts that are hidden. Thus the Tree is always a Three and a Seven, the Three being concealed and the Seven manifest.

The Tree of Life may also be understood as an expression of the Three Rays of Light, as shown in the diagram on the facing page. Each of the rays has its own meanings, and these meanings and their relationships may usefully be compared to the meanings and relationships of the two alchemical principles already given.

The Left-Hand Ray	*The Central Ray*	*The Right-Hand Ray*
Knowledge	Peace	Power
Salt	Sunlight	Niter
Mother	Child	Father
Spirit Below	Spirit Within	Spirit Above
White Dragon	Staff of Merlin	Red Dragon
Gwron	Alawn	Plennydd

These three last names are included in the Lesser Ritual of the Pentagram. According to exoteric tradition, they are the names of the three primary Bards of the Island of Britain; the name Gwron is said to mean "virtue," Alawn "harmony," and Plennydd "light." Esoterically these are the names of the Three Rays of Light / | \.

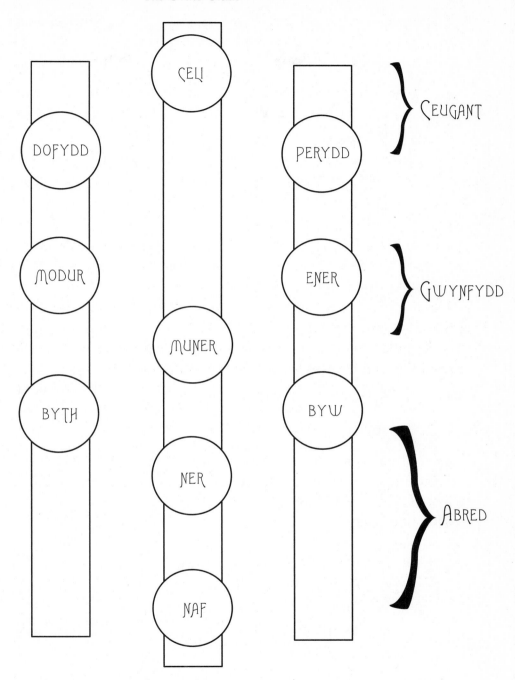

Tree of Three Rays

7. THE THREE CIRCLES are reflected in the human soul and the objects of its experience in the following manner:

> **TO ABRED** corresponds the material body and, more generally, the material plane of experience, which has weight and other physical properties, and is perceived by the five material senses of sight, hearing, touch, taste, and scent.

> **TO GWYNFYDD** corresponds the aetherial body, and more generally to the aetherial plane of experience, which is perceived in forms borrowed from those experienced by the five material senses, such as those of the imagination and memory. The aetherial plane has also been termed the astral, sidereal, or imaginal plane in various writings; its subtle substance is what modern French occultist Éliphas Lévi has called the Astral Light.

> **TO CEUGANT** corresponds the intellectual body and, more generally, the intellectual plane of experience, to what is perceived directly by the understanding without sensory form. The intellectual plane should not be confused with the ordinary functioning of the unawakened mind, which is a sorting and combining of forms, images, and similitudes belonging entirely to the aetherial plane. The intellect is the capacity of understanding through or beyond forms. Many people have had the experience of learning something by rote and then at a later date understanding the principle behind it; this latter shows the first stirrings of the intellectual body.

A word exists on each of the three planes simultaneously. The spoken word as sound or the written word as an object of sight belongs to the material plane; the word as a representation in the mind belongs to the aetherial plane, and the word as meaning belongs to the intellectual plane.

8. CERTAIN DIVINE NAMES are attributed to the ten spheres of the Tree of Life:

> **TO CELI,** OIV or OIW, representing the holy concealed name. (This is pronounced by repeating the names of the three letters.)

> **TO PERYDD,** Hu Gadarn (pronounced "HE GA-darn"), Hu the Mighty, the principal masculine divinity.

TO DOFYDD, Ked ("KEHD") or Keridwen ("KEHR-ud-wen"), the principal feminine divinity.

TO ENER, Beli ("BEY-lee") or Belinus ("BEH-li-noos"), the lord of the heavens.

TO MODUR, Taran ("TAH-ran") or Taranis ("tah-RAN-is"), the bull god of the earth.

TO MUNER, Esus ("EH-sis") or Hesus ("HEH-sis"), the chief of tree spirits, who sits in the first fork of the oak.

TO BYW, Elen ("ELL-en"), the goddess of the old straight track.

TO BYTH, Mabon ("MAH-bon"), the magical child.

TO NER, Coel ("CO-el"), the god of the life force, and Sul ("SIL"), the goddess of the healing springs.

TO NAF, Olwen ("OL-wen"), the goddess of springtime and renewal.

The double attribution to Ner is necessitated by another of that sphere's correspondences, which is the genital center in the human body and, more generally, the sexual energies. As that energy center and those energies take two forms, male and female, so the divine force embodied in that sphere likewise takes two forms. The application of these forms will be explained in detail in a later grade.

Second Meditation

LET THE OVATE TAKE a stone of any convenient size, wash it in clean water to remove all dirt from it, and allow it to dry. Let the stone then be taken as a theme for meditation, considering particularly its origins and history. Should the Ovate be unaware of these matters, let him read a popular work on geology beforehand so that his reflections may be guided by accurate knowledge.

Let him then consider the history of the stone in meditation, from its source either in molten lava from the earth's heart or in sediments deposited by the flow of ancient waters, through its separation from the parent mass and the long cycles of erosion and deposition that brought the stone to the place where he found it. Let him then imagine the stone's future and final destiny, perhaps ages hence, when it has finally been reduced by erosion to dust and deposited in the sea, there someday to be transformed once again into stone and resume the journey as before. Concentrating his faculties on this as a focus, let the Ovate endeavor to realize the cyclic pattern of change in nature.

Begin the meditation by taking the same posture for meditation as before. Prior to commencing the Natural Breath, however, direct your attention to the crown of your head and become aware of any muscular tension that may be found there. Relax the tension there and proceed to the sides, front, and back of your head, relaxing any tensions found there also.

In the same manner, direct your attention through each part of your body, in descending order, deliberately relaxing any tension you find. If any part remains tense despite your efforts, imagine it relaxing and pass onward; this act of imagination will help further the process of relaxation, so that in time the tense part will release its tension more and more.

When this process is finished, proceed to the Natural Breath as before. After a few minutes of this, begin the meditation as already described. Afterward, make notes of the ideas and pictures that arise in your mind during the meditation.

WHEN YOU HAVE MEDITATED on the stone and its history often enough that no new insights or images return to you, proceed to the teachings conferred in this knowledge lecture. These must be thoroughly considered in meditation so that they become a firm foundation for your future studies and practices.

LET THE LESSER RITUAL of the Pentagram likewise be continued as a regular practice during the time you spend on this and all subsequent knowledge lectures of this grade. It will be found useful to perform it immediately before practicing the meditations of this grade and to perform those meditations within the space purified by the summoning or banishing forms of the ritual. Pay the closest attention to any differences you perceive in your meditations between those preceded by a Summoning Ritual and those preceded by a Banishing Ritual.

The Temple of the Ovate Grade

THE WORK OF INITIATION may be accomplished in two ways, the first being conferred by human agency within an initiatory lodge or temple, while the second comes directly from the spiritual realm and is brought about by repeated practice on the part of the aspirant. Each accomplishes the same work and achieves the same ends, and each has its advantages and its drawbacks. When the first option is chosen, however, the second must follow it; without sustained personal practice to build upon the foundation laid down by ceremonial initiation, whatever gifts and contacts may have been transmitted by the ceremony will soon lapse. For this reason, the second option is the basis of our Order's work, and the first, when it is possible to perform it, is supplementary to it.

The Ovate Grade is therefore given over in part to building up the ceremonial forms through which the initiatory work of our Order is performed, just as the Bardic Grade is devoted in part to the practice of that work and the Druid Grade to the realization of the potentials it makes available to the initiate.

Each Ovate must therefore acquire the following items:

1. An altar, which may be any small table or folding tray with a surface at least eighteen inches square.
2. A white cloth to drape over the altar.
3. Three candlesticks, of which two should be the same height and the third taller.
4. Three white candles suitable for the candlesticks.
5. A bowl, cup, or cauldron for water.
6. A bowl, censer, or cauldron half filled with sand for incense.

The remaining two items are symbolic in nature and will need to be made from thin wood or pasteboard. One is a ring five inches in diameter and one inch wide, which is painted green; the other is an equal-armed cross, five inches in length and breadth, with each arm one inch wide. The circle is painted green and the cross red; their images are shown on the following page:

Ring and Cross

These are placed at the center of the altar in positions appropriate to the grade in which the temple is open. In the Ovate Grade the cross is placed above or to the east of the circle, forming the emblem of the mysterious First Matter, or Chaos, of the alchemists.

The altar should be set up in the midst of a room or private outdoor space in such a way that there is ample room for the Ovate to move about. The altar is arranged as shown in the diagram; the top of the diagram represents the side of the altar facing east.

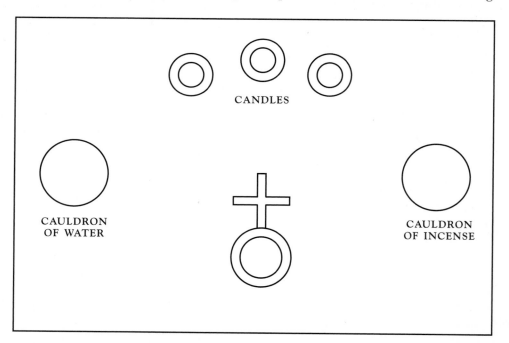

Diagram of Altar

Your first task, once you have assembled the items needed for the altar, is to familiarize yourself with ceremonial practice in the temple of the Ovate Grade. For the time being, this is best done by setting up the altar, lighting the candles and the incense, and then performing the Lesser Ritual of the Pentagram in the space surrounding the altar. The Rite of the Rays at the beginning of the ritual is performed standing at the west side of the altar, facing east; the tracing of the pentagrams is performed in the four quarters of the room or other space where you are working; after the pentagrams are traced and you have circled back around to the east, return to the west of the altar, facing east, to perform the remainder of the ritual.

This simplest form of the Ovate temple working makes a fine preparation for meditation. A chair may be set up in the west of the room or outdoor space, facing the altar; when you have finished the Lesser Ritual of the Pentagram, take your seat and proceed with your meditation.

Further expansions of the ritual work in the Ovate temple will follow in subsequent lectures. Do not neglect these first and simplest steps, however. Here, as throughout the Druidical teachings, the structure you raise, however exalted, will never be stronger than its foundation.

Concerning the Healing Art of the Ancients

THE PHYSICIANS OF MYDDFAI in Wales preserved in their manuscripts some part of the ancient Druidical healing arts, which were among the particular teachings of the Ovate Grade. Much of their lore was held in common with other healing traditions of the ancient and medieval worlds; it may reach back ultimately to Pythagoras, whose learning came originally from the Mystery Schools of Egypt and Babylon, and who, according to ancient authors, received initiation from the Druids of Gaul and is thought to have shared his own wisdom with them as well.

Ovates of our Order are expected to learn the fundamentals of the ancient healing art and are encouraged to apply these teachings to themselves. Under current laws, however, only licensed health care professionals may normally use these teachings to diagnose and treat conditions in others. Ovates are urged to consult locally applicable laws and regulations to determine what is or is not legal in the jurisdiction in which they reside.

In the human body, the four elements are represented by four conditions, which were anciently termed *humors* and guided the healing work of the wise:

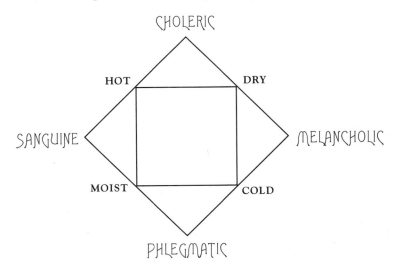

The Four Humors

Sanguine—Air (hot and moist)

Choleric—Fire (hot and dry)

Phlegmatic—Water (cold and moist)

Melancholic—Earth (cold and dry)

Every form of food and drink, every healing herb, and every other phenomenon that affects the body influences the balance of humors and thus the condition of health or illness in body and in mind. The healers of old counseled the well and sick alike to find or restore an appropriate balance among the four humors and thus maintain or recover a state of health.

Conditions opposite each other on the diagram on page 53 cannot combine with each other—thus an herb, a food, or a body cannot be at one and the same time both hot and cold, or both moist and dry, nor can a body be at one and the same time both sanguine and melancholic, or both choleric and phlegmatic.

Heat, cold, moisture, and dryness are measured in degrees, of which there are four. The first degree is mild, the second moderate, the third strong, the fourth extreme and normally harmful to the body; what is neither hot nor cold, or neither moist nor dry, is termed temperate. An herb may thus be hot and dry in the third degree, or cold in the first degree and moist in the third, or temperate (neither hot nor cold) and dry in the second, or any other possible combination. The human body in a state of health is hot and moist in the first degree, while most poisons are cold and dry in the fourth degree.

These indications comprise what healers in earlier times called the temperature of the herb or of any other substance. In addition to the temperature, each herb or other healing substance has one or more properties, which are specific effects on the body—for example, an expectorant herb is one that assists in clearing mucous from the respiratory passages, and a vulnerary is one that heals wounds. The properties of herbs may be found in such standard manuals as *J. M. Nickell's Botanical Ready Reference*.

A list of the temperatures of herbs, spices, foods and drinks, and some other substances follows. It is not necessary for the temperatures of all the items listed below to be committed to memory, but it will be found useful to learn the temperatures of those herbs, spices, and foods and drinks that the Ovate commonly uses and to note how heating, cooling, moistening, and drying substances affect the body over the short and long term.

Table of Temperatures
– Herbs –

Agrimony hot & dry 1°	Allheal hot & dry 2°	Aloe vera cold & moist 3°
Angelica hot 2°, dry 3°	Barberry cold & dry 2°	Basil hot 2°, moist 1°
Bay laurel hot 2°, dry 3°	Beech tree cold & dry 1°	Betony hot & dry 1°
Bird's-foot trefoil cold & dry 1°	Blackberry cold 1°, dry 3°	Blessed thistle hot & dry 2°
Borage hot & moist 1°	Brooklime hot & dry 2°	Bugloss temp., moist 2°
Burdock hot & dry 1°	Butterbur hot & dry 2°	Calamint hot & dry 1°
Calendula hot 2°, dry 1°	Caltrop plant cold & moist 1°	Camphor cold & moist 3°
Catnip hot & dry 3°	Cedar hot & dry 4°	Celandine hot & dry 3°
Centaury hot & dry 3°	Chamomile hot & dry 1°	Chickweed cold & moist 2°
Chicory cold & dry 2°	Cicely temp., dry 1°	Cinquefoil cold & dry 2°
Clary sage hot & dry 3°	Cleavers hot & dry 2°	Clover cold & dry 1°
Coltsfoot cold & dry 1°	Comfrey cold 1°, moist 2°	Cranesbill temp., dry 1°
Daisy, ox-eye cold 1°, moist 2°	Dandelion cold & dry 2°	Dead nettle hot 1°, dry 2°
Dill hot 2°, dry 1°	Dittany hot & dry 3°	Dock temp., dry 3°
Dock, Yellow temp., dry 2°	Elder temp., dry 2°	Elecampane hot & dry 3°
Eyebright hot 3°, dry 2°	Fennel hot & dry 2°	Fenugreek hot & dry 2°
Feverfew hot 3°, dry 2°	Figwort hot & dry 4°	Fleabane hot & dry 3°
Fumitory cold & dry 2°	Galingale hot & dry 3°	Garlic hot 4°, dry 3°
Gentian hot 3°, dry 2°	Germander hot & dry 3°	Ginger hot & dry 3°
Goat's rue temp., temp.	Goldenrod hot & dry 2°	Good King Henry hot & dry 2°
Grass, common temp., temp.	Gromwell hot & dry 2°	Ground ivy hot & dry 1°
Hawthorn hot 1°, dry 3°	Heart's-ease cold 1°, moist 2°	Hog's-fennel hot & dry 3°
Hollyhock hot & moist 1°	Hops hot & dry 2°	Horehound hot 2°, dry 3°
Horsetail cold 1°, dry 2°	Houseleek cold 3°, temp.	Hyssop hot & dry 3°
Jasmine hot & dry 1°	Juniper hot & dry 3°	Knapweed hot & dry 3°
Knotgrass cold & dry 2°	Lady's bedstraw hot & dry 1°	Lady's mantle hot & dry 2°
Lavender hot & dry 3°	Lavender, french hot & dry 2°	Lemon balm hot & dry 2°
Licorice hot & moist 1°	Lily of the valley hot & dry 1°	Linden hot & dry 2°
Liverwort cold & dry 1°	Loosestrife cold & dry 1°	Lovage hot & dry 3°
Lungwort cold & dry 1°	Marjoram hot & dry 3°	Marsh mallow hot 2°, moist 1°
Mercury, herb hot & dry 1°	Mistletoe hot & dry 2°	Moonwort cold & dry 1°
Motherwort hot & dry 3°	Mugwort hot & dry 2°	Mullein temp., dry 1°

Mustard hot & dry 4°	Nettle hot 2°, dry 3°	Oak bark cold 1°, dry 3°
Oatstraw cold & dry 1°	Oregano hot & dry 3°	Parsley hot & dry 2°
Pennyroyal hot & dry 3°	Pine temp., temp.	Plantain cold & dry 2°
Poplar cold & moist 1°	Purslane cold 3°, moist 2°	Queen Anne's lace hot & dry 2°
Raspberry cold 1°, dry 3°	Rocket hot & dry 3°	Rose cold 1°, dry 3°
Rosemary hot & dry 2°	Rue hot & dry 3°	Rush cold & dry 3°
Sage hot 1°, dry 2°	Sanicle hot 2°, dry 3°	Sassafras hot & dry 2°
Savory hot 2°, dry 3°	Saxifrage hot & dry 3°	St. John's wort hot & dry 2°
Selfheal (Prunella) hot & dry 1°	Senna temp., dry 2°	Shepherd's purse cold 1°, dry 2°
Smallage hot & dry 2°	Soapwort hot & dry 2°	Solomon's seal hot & dry 1°
Southernwood hot & dry 1°	Spearmint hot 3°, dry 2°	Stonecrop hot & dry 4°
Storax hot & dry 1°	Strawberry leaf cold & dry 2°	Sundew hot & dry 4°
Tansy hot 2°, dry 3°	Tarragon hot & dry 3°	Tea hot & dry 1°
Thyme hot & dry 3°	Tobacco hot & dry 2°	Tormentil hot & dry 3°
Valerian hot & dry 2°	Vervain cold 1°, dry 3°	Vitex hot & dry 3°
Violet cold 1°, moist 2°	Wild thyme hot & dry 3°	Willow bark cold & dry 2°
Wintergreen cold 2°, dry 3°	Wood sorrel cold & dry 1°	Wormwood hot 2°, dry 3°
Yarrow cold 1°, dry 3°		

– Spices –

Anise hot & dry 2°	Asafoetida hot & dry 3°	Capers hot & dry 1°
Caraway hot & dry 3°	Cardamom hot & dry 3°	Cayenne hot & dry 4°
Cinnamon hot & dry 2°	Clove hot & dry 3°	Coriander hot & dry 3°
Cumin hot & dry 3°	Ginger hot & dry 3°	Horseradish hot & dry 3°
Lemon peel hot & dry 2°	Mace hot & dry 2°	Nutmeg hot & dry 2°
Orange peel hot & dry 2°	Pepper hot & dry 4°	Saffron hot 2°, dry 1°
Salt cold 2°, dry 4°	Sesame hot & dry 1°	Tamarind cold & dry 2°
Turmeric hot & dry 2°		

—Food & Drink—

Ale cold 1°, dry 2°	Almond hot 2°, temp.	Apple, sour cold & dry 2°
Apple, sweet hot & moist 2°	Apricot cold & moist 2°	Asparagus temp., temp.
Banana hot & moist 1°	Barley cold & dry 1°	Beans, green hot & moist 1°
Beans, fava cold & dry 1°	Beans, kidney temp., temp.	Beef hot 1°, moist 2°
Beer cold & dry 1°	Beet hot & dry 1°	Buckwheat cold & dry 1°
Butter cold & moist 1°	Cabbage temp., moist 2°	Carrot temp., moist 1°
Celery hot & dry 1°	Cherry, pie cold 1°, dry 2°	Cherry, sweet cold 1°, moist 2°
Chicken hot & dry 2°	Chive hot & dry 3°	Chocolate (bitter) cold & dry 2°
Chocolate (sweet) cold 2°, temp.	Cress, garden hot & dry 4°	Cucumber cold & moist 2°
Currant cold & dry 2°	Date temp., temp.	Endive cold & dry 2°
Fig hot & dry 2°	Fish cold & moist 3°	Gooseberry cold & dry 2°
Grape cold & moist 3°	Grape leaf cold 1°, dry 3°	Hazel nut temp., dry 3°
Honey warm & dry 2°	Leek hot 3°, dry 2°	Lemon cold & dry 2°
Lentils temp., dry 2°	Lettuce cold & moist 2°	Melon cold & moist 3°
Milk (cow) cold & moist 2°	Milk (goat) temp., moist 1°	Millet cold 1°, dry 3°
Mushroom cold & moist 3°	Oats cold & dry 1°	Olive hot & moist 1°
Onion hot 3°, dry 2°	Orange cold & moist 3°	Parsnip temp., temp.
Pasta, wheat hot 1°, moist 2°	Peach cold & moist 2°	Pear cold 1°, dry 2°
Peas hot & dry 1°	Pine nut temp., temp.	Pistachio hot & dry 2°
Plum cold & moist 1°	Pomegranate temp., dry 3°	Pork hot & moist 1°
Potato temp., dry 2°	Purslane cold 3°, moist 2°	Quince cold & dry 2°
Radish hot 3°, dry 2°	Rice hot & dry 2°	Rye hot & dry 1°
Sesame hot & dry 1°	Spinach cold & moist 1°	Strawberry cold & moist 2°
Sugar, unprocessed temp., temp.	Sugar, refined cold & dry 2°	Sunflower temp., dry 1°
Tomato cold & moist 3°	Turnip hot 2°, moist 1°	Walnut temp., temp.
Watercress hot & dry 2°	Wheat hot & moist 1°	Wine, red hot 2°, dry 1°
Wine, white hot & dry 1°		

— Other —

Alcohol, distilled hot 2°, dry 1°	Almond oil hot & dry 1°	Balm of Gilead hot & dry 2°
Camphor hot & dry 3°	Cocoa butter cold & moist 2°	Copal hot 2°, moist 1°
Cotton hot & moist 1°	Frankincense hot 2°, dry 1°	Gum arabic temp., moist 1°
Gum benzoin hot & dry 2°	Gum tragacanth temp., temp.	Mastic hot & dry 1°
Myrrh hot & dry 3°	Olive oil hot & moist 1°	Peru balsam hot & dry 2°
Pitch hot & dry 1°	Sesame oil hot & dry 1°	Storax hot & dry 1°
Tolu balsam hot & dry 2°	Vinegar, cider hot 2°, dry 1°	Vinegar, distilled cold & dry 1°
Vinegar, wine hot 2°, dry 1°	Water cold & moist 2°	

Third Knowledge Lecture.

1. THE FOUR ELEMENTS have a vertical dimension as well as a horizontal one. Horizontally they define a circle with four quarters, or a square with four corners. Vertically they define a line or sequence extending from the lightest element to the heaviest, and from the most to the least volatile; thus:

> Fire—lightest and most volatile of the elements
>
> Air—relatively light but imperfectly volatile
>
> Water—relatively heavy but imperfectly fixed
>
> Earth—heaviest and most fixed of the elements

This order of the elements may be found in the Tree of Life:

> Fire—the three spheres Celi, Perydd, and Dofydd
>
> Air—the three spheres Ener, Modur, and Muner
>
> Water—the three spheres Byw, Byth, and Ner
>
> Earth—the final sphere, Naf

Notice that, according to this pattern, Abred is composed of earth and water together, while Gwynfydd is of air and Ceugant of fire. The diagram on the following page shows this.

2. THE SAME ELEMENTAL order may be found in the world:

> Fire—the ionosphere, or sphere of energetic particles surrounding the globe
>
> Air—the troposphere, or sphere of air capable of supporting life
>
> Water—the hydrosphere, or sphere of salt and fresh water
>
> Earth—the lithosphere, or sphere of stone and solid matter

59

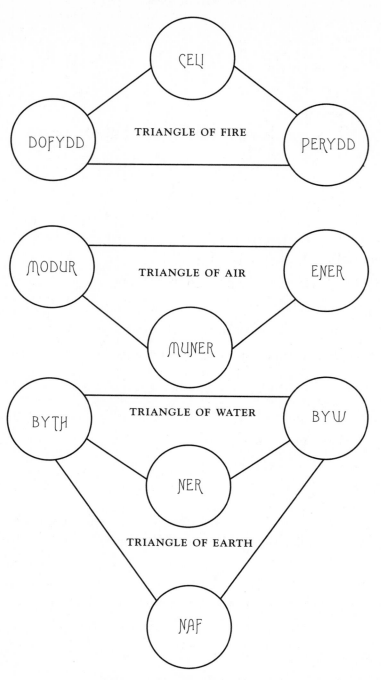

TRIANGLE OF FIRE

TRIANGLE OF AIR

TRIANGLE OF WATER

TRIANGLE OF EARTH

Tree of Life Triangles

The same order of elements, finally, may be found in each human being:

Fire—the spiritual essence or primal spark of the self

Air—the intellectual body

Water—the aetherial body

Earth—the material body

The spiritual order of being, the earth as a whole, and the individual human being are therefore reflections of one another. This is the basis of the law of the macrocosm and the microcosm, one of the central teachings of all Mystery Schools: a common spiritual pattern, which is expressed in the Tree of Life, is reflected in both the universe and the self.

3. THE WORK OF alchemy proceeds through four stages, which may also be interpreted according to this same scheme:

THE BLACK PHASE — putrefaction, in which the bonds uniting the component essences of the substance to be transmuted are dissolved;

THE WHITE PHASE — separation, in which the component essences of the substance are removed one from another;

THE YELLOW PHASE — purification, in which each of the component essences is separately brought to a state of purity in which its innate powers are freed;

THE RED PHASE — cohobation, in which the component essences are reunited to become a new and more perfect unity, more fully expressing the innate powers of the parts as well as of the whole.

The first of these is earth, the second water, the third air, and the fourth fire.

It is on account of the role of separation and reunification in alchemical practice that the vegetable work central to the alchemy of the Druids was in later years called spagyrics. This word comes from two Greek words, *spaō*, meaning "to divide," and *ageirō*, meaning "to join." The same principle underlies the great alchemical maxim *solve et coagula*—that is, "dissolve and coagulate." To this the work of initiation has a hidden but important correspondence.

4. THE GEOMANTIC FIGURES also reflect this same order of the elements in the four lines of points that compose them. A single point represents the element as present and active—in the language of alchemy, niter; while a double point represents the element as latent and passive—in the language of alchemy, salt.

Taking the figure Mab as an example:

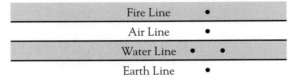

Fire Line	•	
Air Line	•	
Water Line	•	•
Earth Line	•	

An Analysis of Mab

The figure Mab therefore denotes any situation in which fire, air, and earth are active forces, while water is not. It thus represents the boy or young man whose spirit, conscious intellect, and physical body are developed, but to whom the inner intuitive life and the subtle connections that connect him to the community and the world are as yet a closed book. In the language of the Arthurian legend, the young knight possesses the crown or helm of spirit, the sword of mind, and the shield of physical matter, but he must seek the Grail cup of the inner life and the feminine to achieve completeness.

Each of the geomantic figures, interpreted along similar lines, reveals its essential meaning as a glyph of elemental relationships. It is on the basis of the understanding thus gained that the figures may be used for practical divination, magic, and clairvoyance.

5. THE ROMAN AUTHOR Pliny describes, as a high festival of the Druids, the cutting of the mistletoe when it was found growing upon the oak, the most sacred of trees in Druidical lore. (The oak does not often play host to mistletoe, which is much more commonly found on apple trees.) In his description, on the sixth night after the new moon, two white oxen without blemish were brought to the foot of the tree, where they would later be offered up in sacrifice; the Archdruid climbed the tree and, with a golden sickle, cut the mistletoe, which fell into a white cloth stretched out to receive it by the assembled Druids waiting below. Once the mistletoe was cut, the oxen were offered in sacrifice to the gods, and the mistletoe was made into a medicine that would heal all diseases.

All this is symbolic in nature. The oak is the Tree of Life; the golden crescent of the moon and the golden crescent of the Archdruid's sickle flank the mistletoe, and these three represent the three highest spheres thereof, corresponding to the triangle of fire. The Archdruid in his perch amidst the oak branches represents the triangle of air. The cloth spread to receive the falling mistletoe, as a vessel or receptacle, represents the triangle of water, and the two bulls beside the base of the oak, and the roots of the oak itself, represent the triangle of earth. The Ovate should visualize this scene and meditate upon its meaning in detail.

6. **THE MOON IN** its waxing and waning is emblematic of the two sides of the Tree of Life, and both the waxing and waning crescents may be found in the symbolic picture just described. The waxing crescent ☽ bends toward the right-hand ray of the Tree, the ray of the red dragon, of niter, and of expanding energy; the waning crescent ☾ bends toward the left-hand ray of the Tree, the ray of the white dragon, of salt, and of contracting energy. The first of these is the six day's crescent moon; the latter is the Archdruid's sickle. The mistletoe between them is imaged forth in the full moon, round and pale like the berries of the plant.

7. **CERTAIN FIGURES OF** geometry are important in Druidical teaching and may be found to this day in ancient monuments, either carved upon stones or traced by the positions of stones upon the ground. "The ancients wrote it in the earth."

The Cross

The cross represents the four elements of nature. It is not exclusively a Christian symbol, having been known and used many millennia before the time of Jesus. The form used in Druidical teaching is that with four arms of equal length.

The Circle

The circle represents the wholeness of spirit or essence from which the elements emerge by a process of division.

The Cross and Circle

The circle and cross combined in various manners thus represents the elements arising from spirit and is therefore the emblem of creation. The relative positions of circle and cross determine the relation between them.

The cross above the circle, the emblem of the Ovate Grade, represents the emergence of the elements from spirit. Other relationships of these two primary symbols have other meanings, which will be explored in later knowledge lectures.

These symbols play an important role in the Druidical tradition of alchemy and in some later traditions. Their meanings should be the subject of careful meditation at this stage in your studies so that the expressions and combinations of these symbols that will occur later on will communicate their meaning to you.

8. THE SQUARE AND equilateral triangle, two of the most basic figures of the old sacred geometry, derive from the cross and circle respectively. The square is created from a cross by drawing a line around from extremity to extremity of the cross, as shown below:

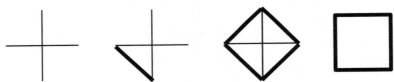

Genesis of the Square

The equilateral triangle is created from two circles overlapping so that the center of each is upon the circumference of the other, a figure called the vesica piscis:

Genesis of the Triangle

The cross, square, octagon, and other figures created from them form the basis of one of the two great schools of sacred geometry, called *ad quadratum* ("by the square") in the Middle Ages. The circle, triangle, hexagon, and other figures created from them form the basis of the other great school, called *ad triangulum* ("by the triangle") in the Middle Ages. Both schools date from long before the medieval period; a little work with straight-edge and compasses, for example, will show that Stonehenge was laid out according to the *ad triangulum* system.

Third Meditation

LET THE OVATE TAKE such opportunities as may be available to him to observe water as it appears in the natural world, whether in streams, rivers, lakes, or seas, or falling as rain, snow, or dew. Let him read in books of natural science concerning the water cycle, by which water vapor rises from the seas to fall upon the land and flow back to the seas from which it came. Let him learn the source of the water he uses for drinking, bathing, etc.; the route taken by that water from its source to his home; and the route taken by water discharged from his home until it again reaches the sea.

Let him then, in meditation, consider the multifarious forms taken by water throughout the natural world: in the mineral creation as ice, liquid water, and vapor; in the vegetable creation as the saps and juices of the plants; in the animal creation as blood and other bodily fluids. Let him imagine a single molecule of water as it passes through all these forms, moving from state to state, life to life, form to form. Concentrating all his faculties upon this as a focus, let the Ovate endeavor to realize the unity of all things in nature.

Begin the meditation by taking the same posture as before and performing the relaxation exercise given in the second meditation, beginning from the top of your head and descending through your body, releasing as much tension from your body as you can. When you have finished the relaxation exercise, proceed to the Natural Breath, but add to it the following visualization:

Imagine yourself surrounded by and immersed in an ocean of pure colorless light that extends out an infinite distance in all directions. As you breathe in, let light as well as air flow into you, and imagine that light filling every part of your body. As you retain the breath, perceive your body as luminous, radiant, and filled with light. As you breathe out, let the light flow outward with the breath, and let it take with it any impurities and imbalances that may exist in your body. Repeat this visualization with each breath. After a few minutes of this, clear your mind of the imagery of light and begin the meditation as already described. Afterward, make notes of the ideas and pictures that arose in your mind during the meditation.

WHEN YOU HAVE MEDITATED upon the water and its transformations often enough that no new insights or images emerge from the practice, go on as before to meditate on the teachings presented in this knowledge lecture and to seek to integrate them with the teachings you have already received. The sixteen geomantic figures and their meanings when interpreted as symbols of elemental relationships should receive particular attention here. As abstract as some of the symbols and teachings may seem at first glance, each of them has its practical application in the work of the higher grades, and careful attention to them at this stage of your training will yield abundant dividends later on.

Purifying the Ovate Temple

AN IMPORTANT PART OF the work of this grade, and an even more substantial portion of that assigned to the grades still to come, is done within a consecrated temple. As with the work of initiation discussed in the previous knowledge lecture, the establishment of a consecrated temple may be done collectively or individually, and as with the work of initiation, in turn, our Order has found it most useful to make the individual mode of work central to its instructional program and practical work, with the collective mode filling a supplementary role.

Among the reasons for this is the simple fact that the ritual actions needed to consecrate a temple, to perform work therein, and to return the temple and those within it to their ordinary unconsecrated state involve skills that must be learned and mastered through repeated practice. The realities of life in the world of the present day make it difficult to rent a room for temple work, at a time and place suited for members to attend, often enough to allow for a sufficient degree of regular practice, while it has been found relatively easy for individuals working alone to find the time and space to practice the same workings by themselves.

The items you were requested to obtain for your Ovate temple while pursuing the work of the previous knowledge lecture are the essential furnishings of a temple of our Order when open in the Ovate Grade. Now that you have acquired them and familiarized yourself with their places on the altar and with the rudiments of practicing ritual and meditation in their presence, the next steps toward Druidical temple work may be taken.

As in previous practices, then, set up your altar in the midst of a room or private outdoor space of sufficient size that you are able to move around the altar freely. A chair may be placed in the west, facing east, for meditation. Have clear water in the cauldron of water and any suitable incense burning in the cauldron of incense; light the candles, and then perform the Lesser Ritual of the Pentagram in its summoning mode. The Rite of the Rays is to be done at the west side of the altar, facing east, while the tracing of the pentagrams is done around the periphery of the room or outdoor space.

When you have finished the summoning ritual, take up the cauldron of water in both hands, still facing east, and raise it high above the altar. Say: "Let this temple and all within it be purified with the waters of the sacred well."

Next, carry the cauldron of water to the eastern quarter of the space. Holding the cauldron in your right hand, dip the fingers of the left hand into the water, and then flick droplets of water off your fingers three times—once down and to your right, once down and to your left, and once straight down. This pattern represents the Three Rays of Light / | \.

Carry the cauldron around to the southern quarter and repeat the same action, sprinkling droplets of water three times in the same way. Proceed to the western quarter, and then to the northern quarter, repeating the same action in each so that the four quarters have been cleansed and purified with water in the sign of the Three Rays of Light. Return to the eastern quarter, completing the circle; raise the cauldron of water in both hands and say: "The temple is purified." When this is done, return to the west side of the altar, facing east, and replace the cauldron in its proper place on the left side. You may then take your seat in the west and perform your meditation there.

When you have finished, return to the altar, take up the cauldron of water, and repeat the purification of the temple in exactly the same way. When you have finished, return the cauldron to its place, and then perform the Lesser Ritual of the Pentagram a second time, this time in the banishing mode. This completes the Ovate temple working.

This working should be practiced regularly at least until you are able to perform it correctly and smoothly from memory. Notice the effect the cleansing with water has on the space where you perform it and any difference that this effect may have upon your meditations.

A Note on the Lesser Ritual of the Pentagram

A summoning ritual is always performed to begin a temple working and a banishing ritual to end the same working. The former establishes connections between the temple and the subtle realms of power that make temple ritual more than a collection of empty forms, while the latter closes down those connections so that magical influences do not continue to spill over into everyday life. Within the specific context of temple work, the two forms of the pentagram ritual are used in this way, and in this way alone.

Outside that context, however, the pentagram ritual has other applications. By this time your regular work with the two forms of the ritual will have acquainted you with their differing effects, and you may already have begun to apply these effects in your daily activities. The summoning ritual, for example, may be used at any time when you notice a lack of energy or vitality in a place or on yourself. A certain "deadness," or devitalized quality, commonly features in many of the situations produced by modern life, and this may be countered effectually by the use of the summoning ritual, which brings into play the vital powers of the elements.

The banishing ritual, correspondingly, has its place whenever an excess of energy, or of some particular energy that is unhealthy or unbalanced, is present in a place or in yourself. It will be found particularly useful when the atmosphere of a place has been colored by grief, fear, anger, or acts of violence, or when you are yourself the target of strong hostility or some other unwelcome passion on the part of some other person—this is very often what is behind the phenomenon of so-called psychic attack and need not involve any knowledge, skill, or deliberate intent to harm on the part of the attacker. In all such cases, the repeated and regular performance of the banishing ritual will bring much relief and, in most cases, a complete cessation of the negative influence.

The Druid Wands

LET THE OVATE OBTAIN four straight and flat pieces of wood, each being four to eight inches long, one-half inch to one inch wide, and of any convenient thickness. They may be made as simple or as ornate as the Ovate may desire.

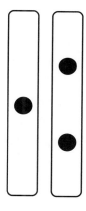

Druid Wand

Upon one side of each piece of wood, let him paint or otherwise provide a single circle or other similar mark, and let two circles or similar marks be on the other side of each piece. The marks on the first piece, or wand, should be red; on the second, yellow; on the third, blue; and on the fourth, green. The image on this page may be used as a model. Once they have been marked, any good varnish or other protective coating should be applied to the wands so that the marks may not be worn away through use.

These Druid wands, as they are called, allow the geomantic figures to be cast quickly and easily for the purpose of divination. The Ovate will find it most convenient to have a cloth upon which they may be cast. All four wands are cast at the same time and allowed to tumble in the same manner as a tossed coin; the four wands determine the fire, air, water, and earth lines, respectively, of the figure that results.

Before the Druid wands are used for the first time, they must undergo a simple con-secration. This is done by placing the four wands upon the altar, which is otherwise arranged as previously described for the Ovate Grade, and having also a silk or linen cloth available. The temple is opened and purified in the fashion outlined in the previous section of this knowledge lecture, with the Lesser Ritual of the Pentagram followed by the purification by water. Incense of any convenient kind should also be burning in the cauldron of incense. When the opening of the temple is completed, dip your left hand in the cauldron of water and sprinkle water three times over each wand in turn, saying, "I purify this Druid wand with the water of the sacred well."

Then take each wand in turn and hold it in the smoke of the incense so that every part of it comes into contact with the smoke, saying, "I consecrate this Druid wand with the smoke of the sacred fire."

Take each wand in turn, then, and breathe three times upon it, with the intention of establishing a link between the wand and your own life; when you have done this, say, "I empower this Druid wand with the breath of life. Let it be sealed unto me as a sacrament of wisdom and a sign of (here name its element)."

This concludes the consecration. The wands are then wrapped in the silk or linen cloth and the temple closed as described earlier, with the purification by water and the Lesser Ritual of the Pentagram. Once your Druid wands are consecrated, they should be kept wrapped in cloth except when taken out for use. No other person should touch them.

A single geomantic figure may be cast using the four Druid wands for a simple divination. Four figures are cast using the Druid wands and combined in a special manner for use in the complete form of geomantic divination. The method of doing so will be covered in a later knowledge lecture.

Concerning the Healing Art of the Ancients—2

THE TEACHINGS OF THE Druids as passed down through the physicians of Myddfai placed much emphasis on the elemental condition of the patient. They pointed out that if two patients with the same illness are treated with the same remedy, the same results cannot be expected; one may recover promptly, while the other may remain ill or die. The reason is that medicines affect the whole patient, not simply the illness, and the illness cannot be treated without regard to the inborn nature and current state of the patient.

They distinguished four aspects to the state of health of each person: constitution, habit, condition, and illness.

CONSTITUTION refers to the inborn state of health and balance of elemental influences each person inherits from his parents. A person's constitution cannot be changed by any medical means, although changes in habit and medicine can help to balance out any undesirable effects.

HABIT refers to the long-term effects on health and elemental balance that personal choices and repeated activities have on the balance of the body. Just as a habit is established slowly, it must be changed slowly by altering the conditions that brought it into being. Medicine and other methods can help balance its unwelcome effects over the short term.

CONDITION refers to the balance of the elements in the body at any given time, as an effect of the influences of the present and recent past. As it is created by immediate factors, it can be changed relatively quickly by changing those factors, though its unhealthful effects may require medicine to prevent damage to the body.

ILLNESS refers to specific health conditions that unfold from constitution, habit, and condition, and in turn affect the balance of elements in the body.

Six external factors were likewise held to influence the state of health:

AIR — including its purity, temperature, and humidity

FOOD AND DRINK—including their kind, purity, and elemental character

SLEEP AND WAKING—including when and for how long sleep is taken

EXERCISE AND REST—including the intensity and type of both

FULLNESS AND EMPTINESS—including the amount and timing of food, drink, and excretions

AFFECTIONS OF THE MIND—including thought, emotion, and will

Good health depends on moderation in all these and in their proper relationship with the natural balance of elements within the body. When these are persistently out of balance, medicine will bring little long-term benefit. During illness, however, sudden changes in the six external factors will place added strain on the body and make a cure more difficult; changes of this kind should be made gradually and, if possible, in a time of relative health.

Each time of day, each phase of the moon, each season of the year, each direction of wind, and each place on the earth's surface has its own balance of elements. The Druid healers of old paid close attention to all of these.

In each person, constitution and habit combine to yield a natural state of temperament, or elemental balance, and departure from this state will normally mark the arrival of an illness. There are traditionally four temperaments:

Hot and Moist: SANGUINE (Air)	Body full-fleshed, pink, and soft
	Veins and arteries large, with full and solid pulse
	Sleeps much, with pleasant dreams
	Good digestion
	Profuse sweat, urine, and stool
	Urine reddish and dense
	Becomes merry when drunk
	Generally upbeat but with volatile emotions

Hot and Dry: CHOLERIC (Fire)	Body lean, muscular, and hard
	Veins and arteries moderate, with strong, rapid pulse
	Sleeps little, with active or violent dreams
	Fair digestion but tends toward constipation
	Urine yellow and clear
	Becomes angry when drunk
	Quick-tempered, with sharp voice and strong opinions
Cold and Moist: PHLEGMATIC (Water)	Body plump, soft, and pale
	Veins and arteries narrow, with slow, soft pulse
	Sleep excessive, with vague, diffuse dreams
	Weak digestion, easily disturbed
	Urine pale and thick
	Becomes gullible when drunk
	Placid, inert, and easily moved to tears
Cold and Dry: MELANCHOLIC (Earth)	Body bony, thin, angular, and hard
	Veins and arteries small and hard, with little pulse
	Subject to insomnia and frightening dreams
	Slow and poor digestion
	Urine thin and watery
	Becomes sleepy when drunk
	Stubborn, morose, and prone to hold grudges

Few people fall precisely into any one of these temperaments. More common is a blending of two sharing a common quality—for example, a person whose temperament is principally sanguine might also have features more common in a phlegmatic temperament, since these two temperaments share the common quality of moisture. There is also a middle ground in which heat balances cold and moisture balances dryness; those who approximate to this temperate constitution in one degree or another show a mix of features and tend to suffer from fewer illnesses than those of less balanced temperaments.

FOOD AND DRINK PLAY an important role in this ancient way of healing. While medicines, and particularly herbs, were used to treat illnesses, changes in the six external factors, and particularly food and drink, were used to prevent them. This does not mean, however, that the old Druids succumbed to the modern "fad diet" custom of identifying some one foodstuff or ingredient in foods as the source of all illness. Rather, foods of all kinds were eaten, provided that they were relatively pure (i.e., not adulterated). It was an excess of any one food, any one kind of food, or any one element or quality that was considered to put the patient's health at risk.

Each person thrives best on a diet that approximates his own elemental balance; thus a choleric (warm and dry) person is most healthy when eating a diet that overall approximates a warm and dry temperament. Changes in the seasons, weather, and state of health will affect this balance. When more than one person dined together, unless all shared the same temperament, the meals served in times past would include foods belonging to all four temperatures so that by taking differing amounts from each dish, each diner could meet his own needs.

The diversity of individual needs and capacities in relation to food makes it unwise to assign a single diet to all, since in every case some will find that diet healthful and others will not. Nearly all vegetarian diets, for example, are relatively cold and dry. Those people who have cold and dry temperaments tend to thrive on them, while those with warm and moist temperaments do very poorly on such diets. Most people will thrive best on a balanced diet containing all commonly eaten kinds of food in moderate quantities.

Many of the subtleties of the method came to be part of ordinary custom, as the teachings here presented were common to most of the ancient nations and remained in common use until the end of medieval times in many countries. Beef, for example, contains a great deal of crude moisture, rendering it somewhat difficult to digest. To bring proper balance to a dish of beef, a warming and drying seasoning is best, and beef is thus customarily served with mustard or horseradish—both of which are warm and dry, and both of which also have an astringent and cleansing property. Many traditional recipes contain dietary common sense of this kind.

The pleasure of a good meal is also an important part of the Druid way of healing, which did not impose a rigid and artificial distinction between mind and body. A delicious meal will improve a sick person's condition no matter what its balance of temperature may be, while insisting that a patient eat food he dislikes will do him little good. The old texts recommend giving a sick person "comfort foods" and then using other foods to balance out any inappropriate temperature.

EVERY ILLNESS ALSO POSSESSES its distinctive temperament. Many common categories of disease, however, are associated with more than one imbalance of temperament—for example, a cold can be hot and moist (running colds with fever), hot and dry (stuffy colds with fever), cold and moist (running colds with chills), or cold and dry (stuffy colds with chills). It is for this reason that a knowledge of temperament is useful to the healer.

Each imbalance of temperament, at the same time, may be associated with many different diseases—for example, a cold and moist distemper may express itself through runny head colds, certain kinds of headache, asthma, chronic upset stomach, constipation with soft stools, impotence, skin problems, and many other symptoms and conditions. It is for this reason that a knowledge of the properties of herbs and other medicaments is at least as important as a knowledge of temperament.

Many things commonly described as illnesses, according to the traditional lore, are attempts by the body to cleanse itself of imbalances and toxins. Any apparent illness that consists primarily of one or more bodily discharges—most colds, "stomach flu," and the like—should be treated by bed rest, plenty of fluids, and gently warming herbs and foods without attempting to stop the body's natural cleansing process. Only if the illness goes on for more than a few days, develops a significant fever, or worsens over time should the symptoms be countered by medicine. It is never wise to override the body's natural cleansing processes for no better reason than that their timing is inconvenient; the toxins and imbalances that remain in the body now may cause serious disease later, which will be far more inconvenient.

To treat an illness, the physicians of Myddfai—and thus, it is believed, the Druid healers from which a part of their lore descended—used herbs of an opposite temperament from the disease. For a hot and dry illness, they used cold and moist herbs and treatments; for a cold and moist ailment, they used hot and dry, and so on. They also measured the potency of their treatments by the severity of the illness, using mild herbs for mild illnesses and more powerful herbs only for serious illnesses. The four degrees of each quality are useful guides in this context.

Before turning to herbs, however, the Ovate in training will find it most useful to explore the healing properties of foods, using the tables given in an earlier knowledge lecture as a guide. Eating warming foods to counter a cold illness or drying foods to counter a moist one will often provide as much relief as is needed, so long as the illness is minor and responds readily to the treatment. Eating also has an effect along these lines, since the process of digestion warms the body; the old adage "feed a cold and starve a fever" has its basis in this fact, for fasting for short periods can help some hot illnesses, while large meals of warming foods are invaluable for cold illnesses.

Finally, the Ovate is again reminded that ordinary common sense as well as the law of the land prohibits those who do not have professional training from attempting to diagnose and treat diseases in other people. The healing material communicated in these lessons is meant to assist Ovates in gaining an understanding of their own states of health and illness, thus bringing their bodies into a state of general health and balance that will assist them in their journey toward initiation.

Fourth Knowledge Lecture.

I. THE FIGURES OF geomancy have the following significations:

MAB (Boy, pronounced "MAB") represents the archetypal masculine—rash, energetic, passionate, and insensitive, rushing ahead into whatever deed it sets itself. It is unfavorable in most questions other than those of love or conflict. In it fire, air, and earth are active, and water is passive.

COLLED (Loss, pronounced "COL-led") represents loss in all its forms, from losing one's money to losing one's heart. It is favorable in questions of love and health, and whenever it is desirable to lose or give up something, but is very unfavorable for gain. In it fire and water are active, and air and earth are passive.

GWYN (White, pronounced "GWIN") represents the workings of mind in all their variety; clarity, intelligence, communication, and profit are highlighted in it. It is good for beginnings of all kinds and for every question in which gain is desired. In it water is active, and fire, air, and earth are passive.

POBL (People, pronounced "POB-l") represents the thought and feelings of the populace—the passive and collective background out of which the mind of the individual emerges. It is favorable with favorable figures and unfavorable for unfavorable ones. In it all the elements are passive.

BENDITH FAWR (Great Blessing, pronounced "BEN-dith VOW-r") represents strength, power, blessing, health, and success through one's own efforts. It is favorable in any question in which gain or victory may be hoped for. In it water and earth are active, and fire and air are passive.

CYSWLLT (Joining, pronounced "CUSS-oolh-t") represents connection, interaction, conflict, and generally all the modes by which one existence comes into relation with another. It is favorable with favorable figures and unfavorable with unfavorable ones, and it tells of the return of things that have been lost. In it air and water are active, and fire and earth are passive.

MERCH (Girl, pronounced "MAIR-kh") represents the archetypal feminine—calm, receptive, emotional, and sensitive, attentive to and influenced by surroundings and context. It is favorable in most questions other than those concerning conflict. In it fire, water, and earth are active, and air is passive.

COCH (Red, pronounced "KOKH") represents the workings of the body in all their variety; passion, intoxication, confusion, and deception are manifested in it. It is unfortunate in all things that are generally considered good, and fortunate in those considered evil. In it air is active, and fire, water, and earth are passive.

ELW (Gain, pronounced "ELL-oo") represents gain in all its forms, from gaining a fortune to gaining a burden or an illness. It is favorable in any question involving profit or gain but unfavorable whenever it is desirable to give up or lose something. In it air and earth are active, and fire and water are passive.

CARCHAR (Prison, pronounced "CAR-khar") represents restriction, containment, limitation, and withdrawal. It is unfavorable in most questions but favorable in questions of land or real property, or whenever restraint is desired. In it fire and earth are active, and air and water are passive.

TRISTWCH (Sorrow, pronounced "TRISS-tookh") represents downward movement of all kinds, from low spirits to the establishment of firm foundations. It is unfavorable in most questions but favorable when stability or secrecy are desired or when planting crops. In it earth alone is active, and fire, air, and water are passive.

LLAWENYDD (Joy, pronounced "lha-WEN-uth") represents upward movement of all kinds, from high hopes to the uprooting of fixed conditions. It is favorable in almost all questions except for those in which secrecy is desired. In it fire alone is active, and air, water, and earth are passive.

LLOSGWRN Y DDRAIG (Dragon's Tail, pronounced "LHOS-goorn uh THRAY-g") represents conclusions, fulfillments, and departures. It is favorable with unfavorable figures, and unfavorable with favorable ones, but it promises well for endings and losses. In it fire, air, and water are active, and earth is passive.

PEN Y DDRAIG (Dragon's Head, pronounced "PEN uh THRAY-g") represents beginnings, origins, and arrivals. It is favorable with favorable figures, and unfavorable with unfavorable ones, and it promises well for gain or whenever something is to be begun. In it air, water, and earth are active, and fire is passive.

BENDITH FACH (Little Blessing, pronounced "BEN-dith VAKH") represents influence, swiftness, subtlety, cleverness, and success through another's help or through circumstances rather than through one's own power. It is favorable for all questions in which swiftness is needed. In it fire and air are active, and water and earth are passive.

FFORDD (Road, pronounced "FORTH") represents change, movement, transition, solitude—the departure from the collective and the beginning of individuality. In its effects on other figures it is an unfavorable influence, but it is favorable for journeys and for change of any kind. In it all four elements are active.

2. THE CONCEPT OF nature was understood by the ancients in two complementary ways:

The first was usefully described by philosophers during the Middle Ages as *natura naturans* (literally speaking, "nature naturing") and corresponds to niter in alchemy. It is nature understood as a unity from which individual forms are born and to which they return.

The second was described by the medieval philosophers as *natura naturata* (literally speaking, "nature being natured") and corresponds to salt in alchemy. It is nature understood as a multiplicity of individual forms from which unity arises and to which it may be reduced. The science of our present time makes room in its thinking for this aspect of nature but neglects or even denies the existence of the previous one.

The word *nature* was borrowed into English, as well as into the Celtic languages, from the Latin word *natura*, which comes from a root meaning "to give birth" (also found in "natal" and "nativity," as well as *Nadolig*, the Welsh word for Christmas). Nature is birth, or that which is born. *Natura naturans* thus also means "what is born that gives birth," and *natura naturata* also means "the birth that is being born." These concepts should be carefully considered and explored in meditation.

3. IN THE LANGUAGE of alchemy, nature also refers to the One Thing from which all other things take shape. In the words of the *Aurea Catena Homeri,* or *Golden Chain of Homer*, the most complete surviving textbook of alchemical philosophy:

> Nature comprehends the visible and invisible creatures of the whole universe. What we call nature especially, is the universal fire, or anima mundi (soul of the world), filling the whole system of the universe, and therefore is a universal agent, omnipresent, and endowed with an unerring instinct, and manifests itself in fire and light. It is the first creature of Divine Omnipotence.

The Ovate who contemplates these words may understand more fully what light it was that burst forth in three rays at the birth of the dawning universe.

4. THE ART OF sacred geometry, as it is now called, was much practiced among the ancient Druids, as among other schools of the Mysteries in the ancient world, such as the

Greek Pythagoreans and the priesthoods of Egypt. What distinguishes sacred geometry from the more ordinary forms of the geometrical art is the recognition that the relations of geometrical figures to one another, being woven into the nature of things and discovered rather than invented by the human mind, reflect important truths of the spiritual side of reality.

The genesis of the triangle from the circle, and that of the square from the cross, express in compact form two of the fundamental patterns of sacred geometry and gave rise, as previously mentioned, to two schools of sacred geometry. The Ovate who is also a Freemason, or who has in some other way been exposed to Masonic instruction, will recognize at once that the sacred geometry of the Masonic tradition is predominantly from the *ad quadratum* school; it is for this reason that Freemasons famously "meet upon the square."

The sacred geometry of the Druids, by contrast, was predominantly from the *ad triangulum* school, as shown in the importance of triads and threefold symbolism in Druidical tradition, and the place of the square in Masonic symbolism is among the Druids taken by the circle or the vesica piscis, or symbol made by two overlapping circles. Just as Freemasons join the compass to the square, representing the need to balance the two fundamental patterns, so upon the altar of your Druid temple the circle is always to be accompanied by the equal-armed cross.

5. **THE TREE OF** Life is likewise an expression of sacred geometry, and the geometries that underlie it unfold from the vesica piscis and follow the patterns of the *ad triangulum* school. The construction of the Tree of Life using straightedge and compasses, the traditional tools of the geometer, is shown on the following page.

FIRST, using the straightedge, draw a line AB.

SECOND, using the compasses, draw a circle with its center on AB at C.

THIRD, leaving the width between the compass points unchanged, draw a second circle of the same size on AB with its center at D where circle C cuts across AB.

FOURTH, with the width between the compass points still unchanged, draw a third circle of the same size on AB with its center at E, where circle D cuts across AB.

FIFTH, with the width between the compass points still unchanged, draw a half circle of the same size on AB with its center at A, where circle E cuts across AB.

Smaller circles representing the ten spheres or stations of the Tree may then be drawn with points A, F, G, E, H, I, D, J, K, C, and B as centers.

This drawing should be constructed several times, until the Ovate can do so without having to refer to the instructions just given.

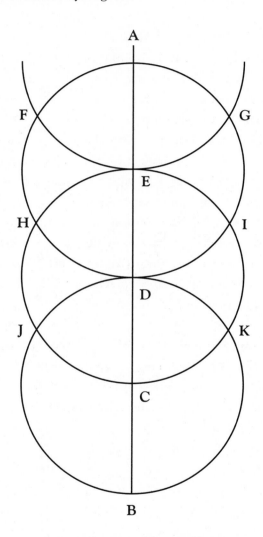

Geometry of the Tree of Life

Fourth Meditation

LET THE OVATE TAKE such opportunities as may be available to him to observe the heavens, the clouds, the winds, and all the other phenomena of air as they come to his attention in the course of his daily life. Let him read in books of natural science concerning the structure of the atmosphere, the cause of wind and weather, the shapes and significations of clouds, the cycle of the seasons and the climate of the region in which he lives. Let him, as often as he may, go to a high place from which as much as possible of the sky may be seen, in all weathers and at all times of day, and let him gain an acquaintance with the panorama of the sky, so rarely noticed in these times. Let him also pay attention to his breath.

Let him then, in meditation, consider the multifarious transformations of the sky through the day, the year, and the changing weather, and the equally diverse roles of air in his own life and the life of every being in the world of matter. Let him consider how the changes of the sky and the cycles of breath affect different beings, from the greatest to the smallest, in different ways. Concentrating all his facilities on this as a focus, let the Ovate endeavor to realize the diversity and variety of all things in nature.

Begin the meditation by taking the same posture as before, and perform the relaxation exercise given earlier in these knowledge lectures, beginning from the top of your head and proceeding to the soles of your feet, releasing as much tension from your body as you can. When you have finished this exercise, proceed to the Natural Breath with the visualization of the ocean of colorless light, but reshape it in the following way:

As you begin to breathe in, drawing in pure light along with the air, imagine that you are drawing in air and light not through your nostrils alone but through every pore in your body. As you breathe in, imagine every pore in your skin opening wide like a tiny mouth to draw in its share of the air and light, which both fill your body from top to bottom. As you retain the breath, perceive your body as luminous and filled with light, as before. As you breathe out, imagine the pores opening wide once again so that each may breathe out its share of the air and light, and with them any impurities and imbalances that may have been present in your body. Repeat this with each breath. After a few minutes of this breathing through the pores, clear your mind of the imagery and begin the meditation as already described, imagining yourself breathing normally through your nostrils. After you have finished the meditation, make notes of the ideas and images that arose in your mind during the session.

WHEN YOU HAVE MEDITATED upon the air and the diversity of its manifestations often enough that no new insights or images emerge from the practice, go on as before to meditate on the teachings presented in this knowledge lecture, and trace the connections that link them to the teachings you have already received. The sixteen geomantic figures should, again, receive the closest attention during the time you spend on this knowledge lecture.

Consecrating the Ovate Temple

AS IN PREVIOUS PRACTICES, set up your altar in the midst of a room or a private outdoor space of sufficient size that you are able to move around the altar freely. A chair may be placed in the west, facing east, for meditation. Have clear water in the cauldron of water and any suitable incense burning in the cauldron of incense; light the candles, and then perform the Lesser Ritual of the Pentagram in its summoning mode. The Rite of the Rays is to be done at the west side of the altar, facing east, while the tracing of the pentagrams is done around the periphery of the room or outdoor space.

When you have finished the summoning ritual of the pentagram, go on to purify the temple with water in the way you learned in the previous knowledge lecture. When you have done this and returned the cauldron of water to its place on the altar, take up the cauldron of incense in both hands, standing at the west of the altar, facing east, and raise it high above the altar. Say, "Let this temple and all within it be consecrated with the smoke of the sacred fire."

Next, carry the cauldron of incense to the eastern quarter of the space. Holding the cauldron in your left hand, use your right hand to wave the smoke upwards from the cauldron three times—once up and to your left, once up and to your right, and once straight up. This pattern represents the Three Rays of Light in their invoking form \ | /.

Carry the cauldron around to the southern quarter and repeat the same action, directing the incense upwards three times in the same way. Proceed to the western quarter and then to the northern quarter, repeating the same action in each so that the four quarters have been blessed and consecrated with incense in the sign of the Three Rays of Light. Return to the eastern quarter, completing the circle; raise the cauldron of incense in both hands, and say, "The temple is consecrated."

When this is done, return to the west side of the altar, facing east, and replace the cauldron in its proper place on the right side. You may then take your seat in the west and perform your meditation there.

When you have finished, return to the altar, take up the cauldron of water, and repeat the purification of the temple. When you have finished, return the cauldron to its place, and then perform the consecration of the temple in the way you hae just learned, followed by the Lesser Ritual of the Pentagram in the banishing mode. This completes the Ovate temple working.

This working should be practiced regularly at least until you are able to perform it correctly and smoothly from memory. Notice the effect the blessing with incense has on the space where you perform it, and any difference that this effect may have upon your meditations.

Ovate Tree Working

IT IS A POINT much discussed in the literature of alchemy that humanity and the vegetable creation exist in much the same relation as the winged and wingless dragons of old alchemical emblems, each of which devours the tail of the other. Plants produce the food that humanity needs for its survival, and when that food is fully digested, what is excreted by humanity provides plants with the food they need in their turn. In the same way, humanity—like other members of the animal creation—draws in oxygen with each breath and breathes out carbon dioxide as a waste product; plants, in turn, draw in carbon dioxide and breathe out oxygen as a waste product. Each produces what the other needs to live and lives upon what the other produces.

The same principle applies in subtler realms. The life force of many trees, though not all, is healthful for humanity, and the life force of humanity is healthful for many, though not all, varieties of trees. By entering into energetic contact with appropriate trees, the Ovate may improve his own health while simultaneously benefiting the tree. The following points will be found useful in doing this.

First is the selection of the proper kind of tree. Large, old, healthy trees are best able to handle the energy of human beings, which is at once very intense and often unbalanced. The traditional lore has it that cone-bearing trees such as pine, fir, cedar, and their kin are among the very best for this work, both because of their innate strength and because their energy is peculiarly beneficial for human health. Next in order of preference are hardwood fruit trees such as apple, quince, pear, and peach, and below these, but still valuable in this work, are such stout hardwoods as oak, ash, maple, and holly. The following trees are not recommended, as for a variety of reasons their energies do not blend well with those of humanity: willow, hawthorn, blackthorn, elder, and yew.

Second is the selection of the specific tree. Individuals among trees vary as much as do individual human beings, and have their likes and dislikes. To determine whether an individual tree is compatible with your energy and willing to work with you, simply approach the tree, mentally frame a courteous request to work with the tree, and listen for an answer. It will most likely take the form of a feeling, either welcoming or the opposite. If the former, you may proceed; if the latter, seek another tree and repeat the process as many times as may prove necessary until you find a tree that reacts favorably to your presence.

Third is the choice of bodily position. The two sides of your body, front and back, have different energetic relationships determined by the placement of nerves and organs. The back surface of the body is the realm of the central nervous system; the front half is the realm of the viscera, and there is a polarization between these two. Some persons have an excess of nervous influence, which shows itself in tension, overactive thoughts, difficulty in sleeping, and the like. Others have an excess of visceral influence, which shows itself in mental and physical sluggishness, passivity, excessive sleep, and the like.

Those with the first condition will benefit from placing their back against a tree, either by sitting at its base with their spine against its trunk or by standing against it, the legs a little away from the base, so that the body leans against the tree from the tailbone to the back of the skull. Those with the second condition will benefit from placing the front of their bodies against a tree; this is best done standing, with the feet slightly back from the base of the tree, the hips forward, the whole front of the body from pubic bone to fore-head resting against the trunk, and the arms raised and crossed loosely above the head, so that the forearms are supported by the tree.

Once either of these positions has been taken, the Ovate simply relaxes his body, allowing it to rest against the tree as fully as possible, and breathes slowly and deeply, without strain. The mind should be quieted and allowed to rest, without concentration on any particular object. The exercise should be continued for several minutes; normally a sense of restlessness, or more simply an awareness that the exercise has done its work and may be ended, signals that the Ovate's body has exchanged as much energy with the tree as is beneficial for both. When this occurs, all that is needed is to break the physical contact with the tree. It is traditional to thank the tree, either aloud or silently, at the conclusion of the exercise.

Regular practice of this tree working will energize and balance the subtle energies of the body and mind, rendering both more serviceable to the work of an initiate of the Druidical Mysteries. It should be performed at least once a week, and once each day would not be excessive.

Concerning the Healing Art of the Ancients—3

TO MAKE USE OF herbs and other medicinal substances to treat illnesses, according to the way of healing passed down from the ancient Druids through the physicians of Myddfai, it is necessary to make the temperature of the medicine balance the disordered temperament of the patient. This is not difficult when a single herb—in the language of the time, a "simple"—is used for healing, so long as the temperature of the herb and the temperament of the patient are appropriate to one another.

The Ovate is reminded here again that he should not attempt to diagnose and treat other people using these traditional methods, and should he choose to test them on himself, he should restrict these tests to such mild illnesses as are commonly treated at home, and be alert to any worsening of his condition that would cause any reasonably prudent person to seek medical attention.

A person suffering from an ordinary chest cold, for example—with chills and drowsiness, phlegm in the chest, and a productive cough—is suffering from a cold and moist imbalance. An appropriate treatment according to the traditional method would be plenty of bed rest, gentle warming and drying foods familiar to the patient, plenty of warm beverages, and two to three cups per day of elecampane root tea. Elecampane is hot and dry in the 3°, and its properties are pectoral and expectorant—that is, it acts primarily in the chest and assists in expelling phlegm.

It often happens, however, that more than one herb is indicated for an illness or that the herb best suited by property to a particular illness is of a temperature unsuited to the patient's temperament. For example, elecampane's pectoral and expectorant properties are of advantage in any chest cold, but if the patient suffers from a fever, warming herbs are undesirable. In this case, if another herb suited to the specific case cannot be identified or obtained, it becomes necessary for the healer to compound herbs to a specific temperature.

This requires a form of mathematics called proportional mathematics, which has been entirely forgotten in modern times, though it was a commonplace of elementary education in centuries past. Proportional mathematics, as the name suggests, is the art of determining the parts or proportions of different factors or ingredients that participate in a common whole. Architects in the Middle Ages and Renaissance relied upon it constantly, while modern architects rarely know of its existence; this is among the reasons why old buildings are so often beautiful and modern ones so often ugly.

Proportional mathematics are as easy as addition or subtraction; indeed, every schoolchild in the days of Elizabeth I could do them. Two simple methods taught in sixteenth-century herbal manuals and mathematics textbooks can be used for working out the proportions of heat, cold, dryness, and moisture in a blend of herbs.

METHOD I: *Compounding to a Particular Temperature*

This first method is used when you have two or more herbs you wish to compound and need the resulting mixture to have some particular temperature. It is rarely possible to specify the exact degree of heat or cold and the exact degree of dryness or moisture at the same time, so it will be necessary to choose the one that is most important for the case.

For example, we will suppose that you wish to treat a feverish chest cold with abundant phlegm. The herbs you have selected for their properties are elecampane, which is a pectoral and expectorant, hot and dry in the 3°, and yarrow, which is a febrifuge (an herb that reduces fever), cold in the 1° and dry in the 3°. Because of the fever, you wish the resulting blend to be neither hot nor cold—in the traditional terminology, temperate with respect to heat—but at least somewhat drying. The degree of heat is the more important factor.

> Example: Elecampane hot and dry 3°
>
> Yarrow: cold 1°, dry 3°
>
> Desired temperature: temperate

Begin by converting the degrees of hot or cold (or dryness or moisture, depending on which is more important to determine) into a number from 1 to 9, using the following table:

Cold/ Moist:	4°	3°	2°	1°	Temp.	1°	2°	3°	4°: Hot/Dry
	1	2	3	4	5	6	7	8	9

Example: Elecampane: hot 3° = 8

Yarrow: cold 1° = 4

desired temperature: temperate = 5

The next step is the one where beginners generally make errors. The difference between the number assigned to each ingredient and the number assigned to the desired temperature is the number of parts of the *other* ingredient. Thus:

Example: Elecampane 8 – 5 (desired temp.) = 3 parts of yarrow, and

Yarrow: 5 (desired temp.) – 4 = 1 part of elecampane

Thus a blend of three parts yarrow to one part elecampane will be temperate with respect to heat. Since both ingredients are dry in the 3°, the final blend will also be dry in the 3°.

If you wish to make a blend containing more than two ingredients, divide them into pairs, with one of each pair on each side of the desired temperature. If you wish to make a medicine containing St. John's wort, ground ivy, yarrow, and comfrey, for example, and wish the final blend to be temperate with respect to heat, you might pair the St. John's wort (hot in the 2°) with the comfrey (cold in the 1°) and the ground ivy (hot in the 1°) with the yarrow (cold in the 1°), work through the process just explained with each pair, and then simply add the totals together:

Example: St. John's wort: hot 2° = 7   1 part

Comfrey: cold 1° = 4   2 parts

Yarrow: cold 1° = 4   1 part

Ground ivy: hot 1° = 6   1 part

It would be equally appropriate to pair the St. John's wort with yarrow and the ground ivy with comfrey, and get the same desired temperature. The important point is that each pair should include one member on each side of the desired temperature.

If you have an odd number of ingredients or more on one side of the desired temperature than on the other, you can pair more than one ingredient on one side with one on the other. For example, if you wished to combine St. John's wort and yarrow with cleavers (hot in the 2°) in a single medicine, and wished the resulting blend to be hot in the 1°, you would do the following:

Example:	St. John's wort: hot 2° = 7	2 parts
	cleavers: hot 2° = 7	2 parts
	desired temp.: hot 1° = 6	
	yarrow: cold 1° = 4	(1 + 1) = 2 parts

Any herb in a blend that is already of the correct temperature may be used in whatever amount you wish without changing the temperature of the finished blend. You may also take any of the pairs of herbs used in the calculations just shown and multiply or divide them by any amount you wish without changing the temperature of the finished blend—for example, in the blend of St. John's wort, ground ivy, yarrow, and comfrey, you could double the amounts given for the ground ivy and yarrow while leaving the other two unchanged—and the temperature would remain the same; the proportions in this case would be one part St. John's wort, two parts comfrey, two parts ground ivy, and two parts yarrow.

In the blend of St. John's wort, yarrow, and cleavers, equally, you could reduce the St. John's wort by half and adjust the yarrow accordingly; the proportions, in this case, would be one part St. John's wort, two parts cleavers, and one and a half parts yarrow; the part of the yarrow that balances the cleavers would remain unchanged, while the part that balances the St. John's wort would decrease in the same proportion as the St. John's wort.

METHOD II: *Calculating the Temperature of a Compounded Medicine*

In order to check your work with the above calculations, or if you need to find the temperature of an existing blend, another method of proportional mathematics can be used. To do so, you will need to know the temperature (in degrees) and the amount (in parts) of each ingredient.

Example: 4 parts elecampane, hot and dry 3°

2 parts chamomile, hot and dry 1°

2 parts yarrow, cold 1°, dry 3°

Divide the temperature of each ingredient into its two parts (hot or cold and dry or moist) and multiply by the number of parts of the same ingredient.

Example: elecampane – hot 12 (3° x 4 parts), dry 12 (ditto)

chamomile – hot 2 (1° x 2 parts), dry 2 (ditto)

yarrow – cold 2 (1° x 2 parts), dry 6 (3° x 2 parts)

Add up separately all the hot, all the cold, all the dry, and all the moist. Then subtract the larger of hot and cold from the other, and the larger of dry and moist from the other.

Example: hot 14 (12+2) – cold 2 = hot 12

dry 20 – moist 0 = dry 20

Finally, divide each of the two numbers by the total number of parts in the whole mixture, rounding down if the result is a fraction. This yields the temperature of the complete mixture.

Example: hot 12 ÷ 8 (total number of parts) = 1.5 → hot in 1°

dry 20 ÷ 8 = 2.5 → dry in 2°

You will find it useful to practice both these methods of proportional mathematics until you can do them easily; an ability to calculate the correct proportions for a blend of herbs will be necessary for your Ovate examination.

Fifth Knowledge Lecture.

I. THE GENESIS OF the elements according to the teachings of alchemy proceeds in the following manner:

FIRE is the first creation and the Soul of the World. In its original and universal state, invisible and immaterial, it pervades the whole of existence. When agitated by motion it becomes light and, when further agitated, light and heat; when concentrated and agitated by violent motion it becomes a burning flame, but this is only in the presence of a fit material basis.

From fire proceeds vapor and the first generation of substance. The immaterial fire or Soul of the World has the capacity to densify into essential humidity or vapor, which is the principle of elemental **AIR**. Air is thus the vehicle of the Soul of the World and the first manifestation of substance, and air is thus a mediator and bridge between soul and matter. In all ancient languages the word for spirit or life force was also the word for air.

WATER is born from moisture by concentration into material form. Vapor or essential humidity concentrated upon itself enters into material existence in the form of liquid water, which is therefore the first principle of material existence. All matter is water centrally; a range of mountains, eternal as it seems to our eyes, differs from a wave of the ocean only in that the stone rises and crests more slowly than the sea. From light and moisture, which are fire and water, all material things come into being.

EARTH comes into being by putrefaction in the body of water. Putrefaction is the hidden fire or Soul of the World acting within material form, and it is always furthered by warmth and moisture. By putrefaction the bonds within a substance are released to permit new combinations to form, thus bringing about earthly substance in all its tremendous variety.

All the elements are therefore fire originally and centrally. This central or Secret Fire is what accomplishes all the works of alchemy; the visible, outward fire of the alchemical furnace simply furthers the work and permits it to be accomplished more quickly; what nature by her own means accomplishes in years or centuries, and in small and secret places hidden within the web of green and growing things, the alchemist accomplishes in weeks or months, visible to the eyes within a vessel of glass.

2. IN THEIR PRACTICAL application, the four elements have the following significances:

FIRE represents the influence of energy in all its manifestations. In the life of the individual, fire is the will, which is the core creative force in each human soul; more generally, fire is all those aspects of the self that are wholly internal and that relate to the essence of the individual in its own inner solitude. In social life, fire represents politics and leadership of all kinds, as well as celebrities, those persons in a society whose lives and actions make them the leaders of the collective imagination. In the life of nature, fire is energy—more particularly, what descends to earth from the sun.

AIR represents the influence of form in all its manifestations. In the life of the individual, air is the mind, which is the form-making and -perceiving power in each human soul; more especially, air is the intellectual powers of the individual, however great or little they may be. In social life, air represents the creative and intellectual realm, including the churches, the press, schools, booksellers, writers, artists, musicians, and all other means by which words, ideas, and mental forms flow through the social fabric. In the life of nature, air is information of all kinds, from the messages passed on by a bird's song to the structure of the unborn plant lying coiled within the seed.

WATER represents the influence of substance in all its manifestations. In the life of the individual, water is the emotions, passions, and vital forces, which are the substantial basis for personality and action in the human soul; more generally, water is all those aspects of the self that orient toward others in the relationships of life. In social life, water represents the population as a whole—its moods and convictions, its relationships and dynamics that provide the substance upon which the impetus of leadership and the forming influence of creative minds work. In the life of nature, water is substance of all kinds cycling through the body of the world as the water cycle, nitrogen cycle, etc.

EARTH represents the summation of the three other elements as they appear in particular manifestations, not as energy or form or substance in general but as the combination of these in an individual existence in all its specificity. In the life of the individual, earth is the body, which provides the basis of manifestation for the will, mind, and passions. In social life, earth is the material surroundings—from the land itself and the climate and other properties thereof through the built environment of structures, roads, etc., to all the products of human art and industry. In the life of nature, earth is the particular assemblage of plants, animals, etc., in a given place or region supported by the energy, information, and substances in that place or region.

Fire has for its keynote direction; air, complexity; water, flow; and earth, particularity. The relations just described will be found particularly useful in the practice of divination and magic.

3. THE NUMBERS FROM one to ten also relate to the elements in a subtle manner. Each of the first four numbers has a special application to one of the elements, as follows:

ONE is the number of fire, which is the first element, the unity from which all creation emerges, and the unity toward which all creation strives. In fire are all things made one.

TWO is the number of air, which is the element of polarity and polarization, always expressing itself in twofold form.

THREE is the number of water, which is the element of resolution and harmonization, seeking balance, as water always seeks its own level.

FOUR is the number of earth, which is the element of stability and manifestation, firmly based as a square of four sides and four corners is firmly based.

Add these numbers together, and you have the Tree of Life: $1 + 2 + 3 + 4 = 10$. This implies a correspondence of the elements to the spheres of the Tree different from the one you have already been taught. In this correspondence the first sphere, Celi, corresponds to fire; the second and third, Perydd and Dofydd, correspond to air; the fourth, fifth, and sixth—Ener, Modur, and Muner—correspond to water; and the remaining four—Byw, Byth, Ner, and Naf—correspond to earth. To these also correspond the four classes of geometrical form, as shown in the diagram below:

•

The point to Celi;

———————————————

The line to Perydd and Dofydd;

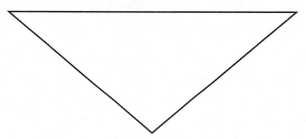

The plane to Ener, Modur, and Muner;

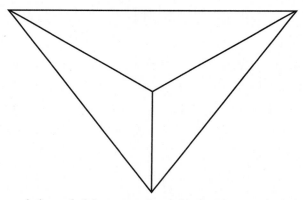

and the solid figure to Byw, Byth, Ner, and Naf

The Geometrical Tree of Life

4. **FROM THESE CONSIDERATIONS** unfolds an additional symbolism relating to the Tree of Life and its stations:

> CELI represents the universal fire, or Soul of the World. This is the One Thing of the alchemists, the source of everything in existence. More generally it represents the universe conceived of and experienced as a unity.

> PERYDD represents niter, the active principle of Druidical alchemy, and Dofydd represents salt, the passive principle of Druidical alchemy. More generally these two represent the universe conceived of and experienced as a binary.

> ENER represents the right-hand ray of the Three Rays of Light, Modur represents the left-hand ray, and Muner represents the central ray. More generally these three represent the universe conceived of and experienced as a ternary.

> BYW represents fire, Byth represents air, Ner represents water, and Naf represents earth. More generally these four represent the universe conceived of and experienced as a quaternary. These last elemental correspondences, in turn, differ from the two already presented to you, and it will be of value for you to explore in meditation the meaning and purpose of these apparently contradictory correspondences.

5. **THE FIGURES OF** geomancy display a curious and important symbolism when applied to the Tree of Life. At the lowest level, the five spheres from Naf up to Muner form the geomantic figure Merch, or Woman. This represents nature as the Great Mother and corresponds to the lives of those who remain entirely within the bosom of material nature and have not yet made the effort of awakening that leads to higher things.

One level higher upon the Tree, the six spheres from Ner to Ener form the geomantic figure Elw, or Gain; this represents all those things that are gained by raising the awareness from the material plane, the plane of effects, to the realm of causes and subtle influences that lie behind the material. It therefore corresponds to the lives of those who engage in those simple magics, common in every age of the world, that seek material and emotional benefits for the practitioner but do not pass beyond this to the threshold of the Mysteries.

A second level higher upon the Tree, the seven spheres from Byth to Perydd form the geomantic figure Gwyn, or White. This represents the purity that is required of the initiate, as well as "the light that was before the worlds" that shone down in the Three Rays, the emblem of creation and initiation. To this corresponds the lives of those who seek and find initiation in the Mystery Schools.

A third and final level higher upon the Tree, the six spheres from Muner to Celi form the geomantic figure Carchar, or Prison. This represents the unattainable realm of Ceugant, the "Empty Circle" that only divinity can traverse, and serves as a reminder that however high any initiate of the Mysteries is able to ascend, height upon height rise infinitely further above.

Fifth Meditation

LET THE OVATE LIGHT a candle and carefully observe the flame, noting its colors, shapes, intensities, and movements. Let him consider likewise the sun, being careful not to gaze upon its too-bright form directly but instead observe its rays where they fall upon the earth. Let him read in books of natural history concerning the role of sunlight in sustaining all earthly life, so that he may learn to trace the flow of sunlight from the heavens to the leaves of plants, and from thence to animals, and through all the cycles of life; and likewise from the heavens to the leaves of plants whose kinds have vanished from the earth, from thence underground where coal, petroleum, and the like are formed, and to the fuel that heats his home and provides other services to him. Let him also, when circumstances permit, expose his body to the rays of the sun as fully as possible.

Let him then, in meditation, consider the presence of light, heat, and the potential for flame in all things. Let him generalize from these reflections to consider the hidden influences and potencies concealed within material things, and see these as the manifestations of a single principle. Concentrating all his faculties upon this as a focus, let the Ovate endeavor to realize the presence of power within all things in nature.

Begin the meditation in the same way as before, taking the same posture and performing the relaxation exercise in order to release as much unwanted tension from the body as possible. When you have reached the completion of this stage of the work, proceed to the Natural Breath with the visualization of the ocean of colorless light, but reshape it in the following manner.

As before, as you breathe in imagine that the air and light enter your body through every pore, but this time as you breathe out imagine that the light remains. Breathe in again, repeating the process so that the incoming breath brings in more light, and breathe out again, retaining the light. Do this a total of seven times, accumulating the light in your body each time so that at the completion your body is filled with a great intensity of light and shines like the sun.

Thereafter, repeat the process in reverse. Breathe in, drawing air through your pores but no light, and breathe out air and light, allowing one-seventh of the light within your body to dissipate and to take with it any impurities and imbalances that may have been present in your body; breathe in air again, and breathe out air and light; repeat this until you have done it a total of seven times and all the light has left your body. At this point clear your mind of the imagery and begin the meditation as already described. After you have finished the meditation, make notes of the ideas and images that arose in your mind during the practice.

WHEN YOU HAVE MEDITATED upon fire and the presence of power in nature often enough that no new insights or images come to you, go on as before to meditate on the teachings presented in this knowledge lecture, and trace the connections that link them to teachings that you have already received.

Circumambulating the Ovate Temple

IT IS AN ANCIENT custom of the Celtic peoples, as of many other peoples around the world, to walk in a circle around holy shrines and other sacred places. This has often been interpreted as a mere gesture of respect, and nowadays it is often performed in this spirit. In ancient times, however, a deeper significance was attributed to this practice and to many other seemingly superstitious observances preserved among country folk.

If you take a piece of hard steel and touch a magnet to it, the whole steel will act for the moment as though it was a magnet. Remove the magnet, and the effect vanishes at once. Stroke the magnet along the steel, being careful always to hold the magnet in the same way and stroke in the same direction, and after many repetitions the magnetic property will be transferred to the steel; it will have become a magnet itself and can then communicate the same property to another piece of steel.

The same principle may be seen in those subtle energies to which an earlier generation of occultists gave the name "magnetism" and which by us is recognized as the Secret Fire or Soul of the World. An action repeated many times in the same manner, like the stroking of magnet upon steel, leaves a trace within the Soul of the World, and this trace draws other manifestations of the same Secret Fire into it or into motion in harmony with it. In turn, a deliberate movement in harmony with some established pattern of motion will draw force from the established pattern. These two principles are the foundations of ritual and should be contemplated at length.

To any dweller upon earth, the pattern of motion that is most firmly established of all is that circle traced by the apparent movement of the sun through the sky. To circle any sacred thing, moving in the same direction as the sun, is to impart to it some echo of those influences the sun imparts to the earth. More, it is to create and define a world. To circle the same thing thereafter, moving in the opposite direction, is to dispel the influences brought into play by the earlier action, and to dissolve the world thus created.

For this reason it is customary in the Celtic lands never to walk in a circle around a sacred thing against the sun, or, as we would say, counterclockwise. In a Druidical temple, by contrast, it is desirable to dissolve the pattern of energies created by ritual once the ritual is completed, and for this reason it is customary to circumambulate—that is, to walk in a circle—in a clockwise direction around the altar during the opening of the temple, and to do the same in a counterclockwise direction around the altar during the closing.

As in previous practices, therefore, set up your altar in the midst of a room or a private outdoor space, with ample room all around for movement, and a chair in the west for meditation. Have clear water and burning incense in the cauldrons, light the three candles, and then perform the Lesser Ritual of the Pentagram in its summoning mode. When this is finished, purify the temple with water and consecrate it with fire, as you have already been taught to do.

When you have finished, and are standing at the west side of the altar facing east, go around the north side of the altar to the east and begin to circle the altar, keeping it always on your right side. As you pass the east, cross your arms upon your chest, right arm over left, and bow your head, without stopping or breaking the rhythm of your pace. Circle the altar in a clockwise direction, from east to east, three full times, and then circle back around to the west side of the altar and face east. You may then take your seat in the west and perform your meditation there.

When you have finished, return to the altar, and then proceed to purify the temple again with water and consecrate it with fire, exactly as in the opening. When you have finished, and are again standing to the west of the altar facing east, go around the south side of the altar to the east and begin to circle the altar, keeping it always on your left side. As before, cross your arms upon your chest and bow your head as you pass the east. Circle the altar in a counterclockwise direction, from east to east, three full times, and then circle back around to the west side of the altar and face east. Proceed to perform the Lesser Ritual of the Pentagram in its banishing mode. This completes the Ovate temple working.

This working should be practiced regularly at least until you are able to perform it correctly and smoothly from memory. Notice the effect that the circumambulations have on the space where you perform it, and any difference that this effect may have upon your meditations.

Geomantic Divination—1

IN PREVIOUS KNOWLEDGE LECTURES you have been instructed in the structure and meaning of the sixteen geomantic figures and taught how to make a set of Druid wands. The figures of geomancy have many applications in our work, but one of the more important is their value as tools for the art of divination.

Divination is not at all the same thing as fortunetelling of the vulgar sort. The fortuneteller claims to be able to know what will happen in advance and presents it as a fate to which the client must submit or adapt. If there is any justification for this view of things, it is that the majority of people take no active steps to shape their lives but simply drift from birth to death, submitting at every turn to the sway of blind chance and the choices of those few around them who take an active role toward their own lives.

The initiate of this or any other Mystery School, however, knows that life is what the individual makes of it within the limits imposed by material reality and the purposes of those great and primal powers whom the nations of the world call gods and goddesses. In the hands of the initiate, accordingly, fortunetelling gives way to divination, which is the art of determining the subtle influences at work in any given situation so that an intelligent choice can be made regarding that situation. Geomancy, being founded on the lore of the four elements, is particularly useful in this regard for divination concerning the affairs of everyday life.

Casting a geomantic reading using the Druid wands is done in the following way:

1. Spread a cloth upon the table or other surface where you will be casting the reading, and have paper and a pen nearby. Unwrap your Druid wands. Holding all four together in your joined hands, concentrate briefly but intently on the subject on which you seek guidance or the question to which you desire an answer. Then cast the wands upwards so that they fall onto the cloth at random.

2. Note down the figure thus created, remembering that the red (fire) wand gives the first or uppermost line, the yellow (air) wand the second, the blue (water) wand the third, and the green (earth) wand the fourth or lowermost line. Thus

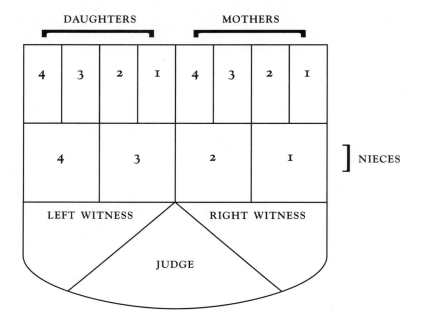

Geomantic Chart

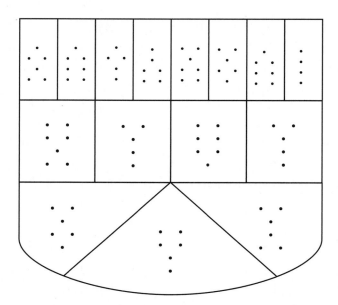

Geomantic Reading

if each of the wands lands with one point upwards, the figure formed is Ffordd. Write the first figure in the upper-right portion of the chart, as shown.

3. Gather up the Druid wands, and cast three more figures in the same manner, noting each figure on the chart to the left of the one previously cast. The four figures you have cast will thus be in order from right to left and will all be upon the upper-right portion of the chart. These figures are called the Four Mothers of the reading.

4. You have already learned that the first line of each figure is the fire line, the second the air line, and so forth. The Four Daughters, the next figures created in the chart, are formed from the Four Mothers by taking the lines of the elements in order from each of the Mothers. Thus the fire line of the First Mother becomes the first line of the First Daughter, the fire line of the Second Mother becomes the second line of the First Daughter, the fire line of the Third Mother becomes the third line of the First Daughter, and the fire line of the Fourth Mother becomes the bottom line of the First Daughter. The remaining Daughters are formed from the Mothers in the same way, the Second Daughter being formed from the air lines of the Four Mothers, the Third Daughter from their water lines, and the Fourth Daughter from their earth lines. The Four Daughters are placed in line with the Four Mothers and to their left, proceeding from right to left as before.

5. Here a new process enters into play. Any two geomantic figures may be added together to yield a third figure; this is done by adding the points in each of the four lines in order, marking down a single point if the result be odd and a double point if the result be even. The addition of Elw and Bendith Fawr thus yields Cyswllt:

$$\cdot\cdot \quad + \quad \cdot\cdot \quad = \quad \cdot\cdot \qquad (2 + 2 = 4;\ \text{two points})$$

$(1 + 2 = 3;\ \text{one point})$

$(2 + 1 = 3;\ \text{one point})$

$(1 + 1 = 2;\ \text{two points})$

This is done with the First and Second Mothers to yield the First Niece; with the Third and Fourth Mothers to yield the Second Niece; with the First and Second Daughters to yield the Third Niece; and with the Third and Fourth

Daughters to yield the Fourth Niece. (These figures are called "Nephews" in some of the old texts, but the feminine nature of earth suggests that those sources that call them "Nieces" are more correct.) They are written below and between the figures that are added to produce them.

6. In the same way, the First and Second Nieces are added to produce the Right Witness, the Third and Fourth Nieces are added to produce the Left Witness, and the two Witnesses are added to produce the Judge, which is the final figure in the reading.

Once this is done and all fifteen figures are written down, the reading may then be interpreted. This is a process that requires practice, a knowledge of the lore, and some degree of intuition.

The most basic meaning of the reading is provided by the Judge and may be interpreted in general according to the meanings of the figures given in the fourth knowledge lecture. To this is added, as an additional level of interpretation, the meanings of the two Witnesses. Of these, the Right Witness always represents the querent—that is, the person for whom the divination is performed, be it the Ovate or another person—and the Left Witness always represents the quesited (that is, the subject of the divination, the thing or matter enquired about).

There are further levels of interpretation that may be brought into play once some facility with the basics has been achieved, but for the beginner, careful attention to the Judge and Witnesses is a suitable approach and will provide clear answers to most questions.

The best way to gain skill with geomancy or any other divinatory art is to cast a reading each morning, inquiring about the events and influences one will encounter in the course of the day. At the end of the day, review the reading and try to see how the figures you cast reflect the experiences of the day. Any student who does this regularly will quickly learn what the geomantic figures are trying to communicate and thus gain ever-increasing facility in casting and interpreting geomantic readings.

Assume for the sake of instruction that the Ovate who cast the completed chart on page 110 hopes to gain access to a certain book of Druidical instruction from the last century, which is nowhere available in the libraries and bookstores known to him. He casts the chart in the manner described above and considers the Judge and Witnesses as guides to the situation.

The Right Witness in this chart is Cyswllt, or Joining, and represents connection and interaction of all kinds. This figure represents the querent and suggests that the Ovate would be well advised to make an extra effort to seek out others who might have knowledge of the whereabouts of a copy of the book he desires, whether among Druids, in the book trade, or elsewhere. The Left Witness, representing the quesited, is Elw, or Gain, and predicts success in the search, as indeed does the Judge, Bendith Fawr, or Great Blessing, the most favorable of the geomantic figures and an indication of good fortune. Our Ovate may therefore proceed with his search with high hopes of success.

A second level of interpretation, reinforcing the first, is drawn from the elemental structure of the three figures under discussion. Cyswllt has air and water active, while fire and earth are passive; air corresponds to communication and the intellect generally, while water corresponds, among other things, to the social ties that connect people to one another; the figure thus advises that our Ovate would be wisest to concentrate on these elemental patterns in his search and leave fire and earth alone. Air is the one active element common to the two Witnesses, and it refers to the querent's desire for the knowledge that is to be found in the book; water is the one active element shared by the Right Witness and Judge, and it suggests that it is by means of his social and personal contacts with other people that his quest will succeed.

When you cast each daily geomantic reading, explore its meaning along the lines of the example just given, noting the meaning and elemental structure of the figures. With practice you will learn to extract many details and much helpful guidance from these sources and be prepared for the more extensive interpretive methods to come.

Introduction to Vegetable Alchemy

THE ALCHEMY OF THE ancient Druids, as you have already learned, took the vegetable creation rather than the mineral as its principal subject. This was partly because the Druid alchemist, or Pheryllt, had as his most common work the production of herbal medicines to maintain the health of the people, and partly because Druidry found in green and growing things a key to the secrets of nature. This key was likewise grasped by alchemists of a later era: "The philosopher's stone is produced by means of the greening and growing Nature," wrote Salomon Trismosin in his famous handbook of alchemy, *Splendor Solis*.

You have likewise learned that the vegetable alchemy of the Druids was by later alchemists termed *spagyrics*, which was created from Greek words meaning "to separate" and "to combine." It is the art of separation and combination, applied to healing herbs, that brings into being the secret remedies of the Druid healer.

In order to separate and combine, it is necessary to know what it is in a plant that may be separated and what it is that may then be combined.

The fundamental principles of Druidical alchemy are niter ⨁ and salt ⊖. These are not quite identical to the physical substances now bearing the same names—or, more precisely, those physical substances are examples, or archetypal forms, of the broader concepts expressed by the alchemical terms.

Niter in alchemy represents the volatile part of each compound substance—that is, the part which may be converted to vapor by heat and returned to its liquid or solid state by cooling, without any loss of substance or change of properties. Salt in alchemy represents the fixed part of each compound substance—that is, the part which resists the action of heat and cannot be converted to vapor without undergoing chemical change but may readily be dissolved in water or some other appropriate fluid and returned to its original state by drying. Thus niter is best extracted by fire, and salt by water.

These principles are present in vegetable matter in a matrix composed largely of fluid sap and solid substances that are neither volatile nor soluble. The simplest way to extract the niter and salt of a plant is as follows. First, the plant is dried and ground into a fine powder to open it to the action of the extractive process. Then the ground plant is macerated—that is, soaked for a period of weeks or months in at least three times its quantity of pure alcohol from a vegetable source, while a gentle heat is applied to it—until the niter of the plant passes into the alcohol and gives it the plant's characteristic color and scent. Next, the mixture is strained; the tincture, as the mixture of alcohol and plant niter is called, is set aside, and the residue of herb, which still contains the salt locked up inside it, is burnt and, by the application of continued heat, reduced to a fine white ash. The ash is then ground to powder, added to the tincture, and left to macerate again for at least a week while the tincture extracts the salt from the ash. Finally, the result is strained to remove the insoluble remnants of the ash, and the resulting alchemical tincture, containing the niter and salt solution in alcohol, may be used as a medicine.

Alcohol is the most common menstruum (dissolving fluid) used in spagyric alchemy because it is itself the product of an alchemical process applied to the vegetable creation. It represents the completed or perfected form of the sap of plants. The vegetable alchemy of the Druids worked almost exclusively with alcohol, water, or blends of these two substances, as pure water and relatively pure alcohol could easily be made using the simple chemical apparatus of the ancients, and both may be taken internally by the human body. Certain more recent systems of spagyrics make use of other menstrua such as ether; the toxic nature of most of these menstrua, and a variety of other risks involved in using them, suggests that here, as in much else, the old Druids may well have been wiser to embrace their simpler and safer path.

Even within the limits of that path, though, the operation just outlined is only the simplest of a range of processes. The next step along the path is to purify the salt before it is added to the tincture. This is done by taking a great deal of dry herb, three times or more that which was used to make the tincture, and reducing it to fine white ash; the ash is then dissolved in distilled water, the water is filtered, and the filtered water placed in a shallow vessel and exposed to gentle heat, so that the water evaporates. As it does so, the salt crystallizes in the vessel. The salt may then be scraped out of the vessel, powdered, and added to the tincture, or if an even stronger medicine is desired, the process of dissolving and evaporating may be repeated once or several times, yielding a snow-white salt of great purity, which is then added to the tincture.

Another dimension is brought into play when the art of distillation is added to the alchemist's set of tools. Distillation of the tincture has the same purifying effect upon the niter of a plant that dissolution and evaporation has upon its salt, and this distillation may likewise be performed once or several times for increased purity; the careful management of the heat, so that the subtler fractions of the niter predominate in the distillate and the water and waste products remain behind, is a skill best learned through much practice. Distillation may be used in place of straining and filtering to extract the tincture from the macerated herb, and the distilled tincture may then be poured back upon the herb once or repeatedly to extract those fractions of the niter that resist extraction by ordinary maceration.

Circulation, in which the distillation apparatus is arranged so that the distillate flows back into the distilling vessel and is continually redistilled, is a delicate but powerful way to accomplish this same more complete extraction. There are further processes yet more advanced, but it is needless to discuss them here.

The practical details of the processes already outlined will be studied at a later time. The Ovate must always keep in mind two details while learning the elements of Druidical alchemy: first, that a firm and detailed understanding of herbs, their temperatures and properties, and any dangers that may attend their use is the essential foundation for work in spagyrics; second, that the skills taught in these lectures are to be used only in accordance with the laws of the country and community in which the Ovate happens to dwell.

Sixth Knowledge Lecture.

I. THE GOLDEN CHAIN of Homer, or *Aurea Catena Homeri*, among the most profound of alchemical texts, conceals the central work of alchemy in the following ten symbols:

♁ Chaos and confusion

☉ Volatile incorporeal spirit of the earth

⦵ Corporeal acid spirit of the earth

⊖ Corporeal alkaline fixed spirit of the earth

⊕ Immediate prime matter of all elemental bodies

⊖ Animal kingdom

⊕ Vegetable kingdom

⊖ Mineral kingdom

☉ Fixed concentrated spirit of the earth or pure extract of chaos

♀ Consummate perfection or universal quintessence

Each of these symbols are formed by adding the cross, either in whole or in part, to the circle. The reflections on these two figures in an earlier lecture should be consulted, and the symbols themselves studied with this in mind, in order to elucidate their meaning. They may also be related to the ten spheres of the Tree of Life, as shown in the diagram on the following page.

Certain of the terms used to describe these symbols have specialized meanings in alchemy. Chaos is the original substance out of which all things emerged, spiritual as well as material. The Spirit of the Earth, or *spiritus mundi*, is the subtle substance out of which dense substance, or matter, is condensed and is in some sense identical with Life, as the Soul of the Earth, or *anima mundi*, is in some sense identical with mind. Quintessence, the "fifth essence," is that aspect of nature that transcends the four elements. You have already been taught the meaning of the terms *fixed* and *volatile*.

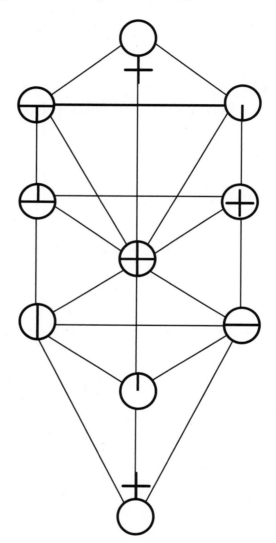

Golden Chain Tree

2. THESE FIGURES ARE further explicated in the following terms:

☿ After the chaos is divided, a volatile fire is separated.

☉ This is named the Spirit of the Earth; dew, hail, rain, snow, and all that comes from the atmosphere are its faithful companions. Here is hidden the volatile sperm of the world from the upper regions when it descends into the lower, out of which it takes a body and appears visible and palpable before our eyes.

☉ Niter is known to the whole world, but where is he that can enumerate its virtues? What is in niter can fabricate all things. The lower regions are subject to it; the upper regions cannot be without it. It is niter which generates all nature. Here is the father of all things, who causes the foundations of the earth to tremble.

Its power has been given to it by the creator; its dominion is over the skies, the earth, and the sea. It is the Adam of all things, out of which the Eve originates. The end will be obtained when the earth has been fertilized, when Adam has been fixed and no longer fulminates, and Eve sits alongside him.

Sun and moon, the motion of the sea and the earth moving continually, convert Adam into Eve.

⊖ Through heat and cold and the tides of the sea, the earth respires; this is named common salt and alkali, feeding the children of nature with its blood.

⊕ When the male and female meet, a perfect fruit is engendered; the double acid and alkaline salt gives a flavor to every dish.

⊕ The volatile animal kingdom demonstrates this.

⊕ The vegetable hermaphrodite, which is between the volatile and the fixed, shows also from whence it proceeds.

⊕ The fixed earths, stones, and flints prove that they belong to niter and salt. Air, water, and earth demand the active principle from niter.

☉ When now the noble sperm of the world has been fixed, and from vapor and water has been converted into the fixed earth, then is accomplished what the wise esteem most.

♀ The volatile must become fixed, and from vapor and humidity must become earth and a dry, red blood; then it is the treasure of the world and the highest blessing—a perfect perfection which expels poverty and diseases.

These passages are likewise from the *Aurea Catena Homeri* or Golden Chain of Homer, that work of the more recent alchemy that most closely approaches the workings of the ancient Druids.

3. THE FIGURES OF geomancy may be arranged in pairs according to a set of symbolical and mathematical relationships:

	Boy (left) and Girl (right)			Loss (left) and Gain (right)	
	White and Red			The Crowd and the Lonely Path	
	Greater and Lesser Blessing			Union and Separation	
	Sorrow and Joy			Beginning and End	

Paired Geomantic Figures

These pairings should be carefully considered in meditation and the results incorporated in your divination practice. The elemental relationships implied by the single and double points of each figure will be particularly important for you to explore. You may also find it useful to consider what third factor resolves the binary established by each pair of figures.

4. THE PATHS OF the Tree of Life are of great importance in the practical work of initiation. In Druidical practice they are counted from the bottom rather than from the top; the Tree begins from Celi and descends to Naf in the process of creation, but the initiate begins from Naf and ascends step by step along the paths to Celi.

Certain of these paths can be traversed while dwelling in the circle of Abred and incarnate in a physical body, while others cannot. Those that play a direct role in the process of Druidical initiation are those that relate to the lowest four spheres of the Tree, which correspond to Abred: the paths from Naf to Ner, Byth, and Byw; the paths from Ner to Byth, Byw, and Muner; the paths from Byth to Byw and Muner; the path from Byw to Muner; and, in a certain sense, the path from Muner up to Celi, which brings the lower reaches of the Tree into contact with the highest. Each of these possesses a special symbolism and meaning, which are communicated in a higher grade of our order, and those below and up to Muner may be traversed with the aid of ceremonial initiation.

The paths that relate to the three central spheres of the Tree—Ener, Modur, and Muner—are those that correspond to Gwynfydd. They may be traversed by the advanced initiate, but here formal symbolism and ceremonial initiation are of no avail; these higher paths must be traversed by the individual initiate working alone, using methods that will be revealed in a yet higher degree. Nor may these paths be fully traversed by one who remains in the circle of Abred and physical incarnation. The paths that relate to the three highest spheres of the Tree—Dofydd, Perydd, and Celi—may not be fully traversed by any created being.

If these limitations seem burdensome, recall that all the heights and depths of ordinary human experience and attainment in this world do not rise above the sphere of Naf, and that there are four higher spheres to enter and experience, each as vast and complicated as this material world we inhabit, before the work of ceremonial initiation is truly complete. The craving for what is beyond the reach of incarnate humanity is, by and large, a form of egotism. Within the realms open to you right at this moment are powers, marvels, and challenges enough for a hundred lifetimes and more.

Sixth Meditation

LET THE OVATE RECOLLECT the meditations that he has heretofore been assigned in this grade—on the presence of life within all things and on the four elements of earth, water, air, and fire. Let him likewise consider such realizations as may have come to him in previous meditations concerning the presence of life, cyclic change, unity, diversity, and power within all things in nature, and seek to perceive these presences as manifestations of One Thing, which is identical with the force or phenomenon that we call nature.

Let him then, in meditation, consider all things as expressions of the One Thing, and the One Thing as the common factor in all things. Let him recognize in this One Thing what has been called spirit in many faiths and philosophies. Concentrating all his faculties upon this as a focus, let the Ovate endeavor to realize the presence of spirit within all things in nature.

Begin the meditation in the same way as before, taking the same posture and performing the relaxation exercise in order to release as much unwanted tension from the body as possible. When you have reached the completion of this stage of the work, proceed to the Natural Breath with the visualization of the ocean of light and the drawing in, concentrating, and releasing of the light in the body through pore breathing. Now, however, you will work with the light of the four elements in the following manner.

In place of the ocean of colorless light, you will visualize an ocean of light of one of the four elemental colors—red for fire, yellow for air, blue for water, or green for earth. The first time you practice this meditation, breathe in fire; air the second; water the third; and earth the fourth; then repeat the sequence as you proceed with the meditations. As before, you will draw this light into your body with seven breaths, accumulating it in your body, but as you do so, you will feel not only the pressure of the light but one of four qualities corresponding to the four elements.

With the red light of fire, that quality is power; you will experience yourself as being filled with immense and vibrant strength. With the yellow light of air, that quality is lightness; you will feel yourself light, nimble, and skillful. With the blue light of water, the quality is fluidity; you will feel fluid, graceful, and responsive. With the green light of earth, the quality is stability; you will feel unshakably steady and immovably calm.

After you have breathed in the elemental quality with seven breaths, breathe it out again with seven breaths, allowing the elemental light to dissipate one breath at a time and allowing the quality of the element to dissipate as well. When you have breathed all of the elemental light and quality out of your body, clear your mind of the imagery and begin the meditation as already described. After you have finished the meditation, make notes of the ideas and images that arose in your mind during the practice.

WHEN YOU HAVE MEDITATED on the One Thing and the presence of spirit in nature often enough that no new insights or images come to you, go on as before to meditate on the teachings presented in this knowledge lecture, and trace the connections that link them to teachings that you have already received.

Opening and Closing the Ovate Temple

"BY NAMES AND IMAGES," says a traditional maxim of the Mysteries, "are all powers awakened and reawakened." The work of awakening the powers of the Ovate temple using names and images has occupied you now since you began work with the first of these knowledge lectures. The Lesser Ritual of the Pentagram, the essential ritual practice of the Ovate, began that work, and you have added to it step by step, assembling the physical requirements of the temple and then learning to purify with water, consecrate with fire, and circumambulate the temple. With this lecture the remaining portions of the Ovate temple opening and closing for solitary work will be provided you, so that in the final lecture of this grade you may be taught how to perform your own initiation into the Ovate Grade and perform that initiation in a properly opened temple.

The additions that complete the opening and closing of the temple in this grade are a commencement of the rite, an invocation, an opening proclamation, a License to Depart, and a closing proclamation.

As in previous temple practices, therefore, set up your altar in the midst of a room or a private outdoor space with ample room all around for movement and a chair in the west for meditation. Have clear water and burning incense in the cauldrons, light the three candles, and then stand on the west side of the altar, facing east. Raise your right hand, palm facing toward the east, and say, "In the presence of the holy powers of nature I prepare to open this temple in the Ovate Grade. Let peace be proclaimed with power, throughout this temple and the hearts of all who stand herein."

When you have done this, go on to perform the Lesser Ritual of the Pentagram in its summoning mode. When this is finished, purify the temple with water and consecrate it with fire, and circumambulate the temple with the sun (or, as the term is nowadays, clockwise) three times, as you have already been taught to do. When the circumambulation is finished, return to the west side of the altar and face east. Extend your arms out to your sides and downward, palms forward, as though forming the image of the Three Rays of Light, and say, "I invoke the rising of the eternal spiritual sun! May I be illumined by a ray of that Golden Dawn."

As you do this, imagine before you, in the east, the first brilliant flash of the rising sun. As you watch, it slowly emerges from below the horizon, great and golden, its rays flooding the temple with light and life. Visualize the rising sun until it has cleared the horizon and appears whole before you. When this is done, say, "In the light of the Golden Dawn and the presence of the holy powers of nature, I proclaim this temple open in the Ovate Grade."

You may then take your seat in the west and perform your meditation there.

When you have finished, return to the altar and purify the temple again with water and consecrate it with fire, exactly as in the opening. When you have finished and are again standing to the west of the altar, facing east, circumambulate the temple against the sun (or, as the term is nowadays, counterclockwise) three times, then return to the altar. Standing again at the west side of the altar, facing east, say, "In the name of Hu the Mighty, great Druid god, I set free any spirits who may have been imprisoned by this ceremony. Depart unto your habitations in peace, and peace be between us."

Then perform the Lesser Ritual of the Pentagram in its banishing mode.

Finally, standing at the west of the altar facing east, raise your right hand, palm facing the east, as you did in the opening. Say, "In the presence of the holy powers of nature, I proclaim this temple closed."

This completes the Ovate temple working. It should be practiced regularly at least until you are able to perform it correctly and smoothly from memory. Diligent practice of the opening and closing ritual will not only increase the magical and spiritual effect of your upcoming initiation but will also bring added power to the initiatory work of the Bardic Grade and the magical attainments of the Druid Grade to come, for these dimensions of our work take their start from the work you have been carrying out in this grade. To the nearest approximate metaphor, the labors of this grade are the planting of seeds; in the Bardic Grade those seeds will sprout, and in the Druid Grade they will flower and bear abundant fruit.

Geomantic Divination—2

THE GEOMANTIC CHART, as you have already learned to cast it, is the foundation on which all the divinatory methods of geomancy are raised. You will not need to learn any more complex method of casting a chart; instead, the more advanced levels of geomantic practice are attained by learning subtler methods of interpreting the chart. It is to these that we now turn.

The Four Triplicities

The Judge of a geomantic chart is the product of the two Witnesses and should be understood in any reading as resulting from the influences brought to the subject of the reading by the Witnesses—the Right Witness representing the influences of the querent and the Left Witness those of the situation in which the querent finds himself. The Druidical philosophy of the Three Rays of Light is always to be kept in mind here, for the Witnesses are the two rays to left and right, forming the binary, and the Judge is the central ray, resolving it into a ternary.

The same principle can be applied to four other ternaries in the geomantic chart—those formed the four Nieces and the figures that create them. These are called the Four Triplicities. The diagram on the following page shows how the Triplicities appear on the chart. Each of them has a specific meaning:

> **THE FIRST TRIPLICITY,** formed of the First and Second Mothers and the First Niece, represents the querent. Of these, the First Mother represents the querent's personality and nature; the Second Mother represents his childhood circumstances and background; and the First Niece represents the querent's habits, beliefs, opinions, and outlook on life.

> **THE SECOND TRIPLICITY,** formed of the Third and Fourth Mothers and the Second Niece, represents the events and influences that shape the querent's life. Of these, the Third Mother represents influences from the querent's past; the Fourth Mother represents influences from the wider world that surround the

querent's life; and the Second Niece represents the querent's situation at the time of the reading.

THE THIRD TRIPLICITY, formed of the First and Second Daughters and the Third Niece, represents the querent's home and physical surroundings at the time of the reading. Of these, the First Daughter represents the querent's home; the Second Daughter represents other places where the querent spends time regularly; and the Third Niece represents the neighborhood or surroundings in which the home and the other places are located.

THE FOURTH TRIPLICITY, formed of the Third and Fourth Daughters and the Fourth Niece, represents the other people in the querent's life. Of these, the Third Daughter represents the querent's own family and friends; the Fourth Daughter represents the querent's spouse, lover, love interest, or closest friend; and the Fourth Niece represents other people with whom the querent associates, such as fellow employees, neighbors, local businesspeople, and the like.

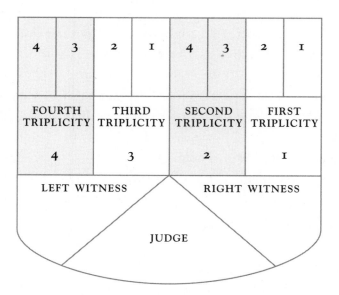

Geomantic Triplicities

The triplicities influence a geomantic reading in several ways. First, it is always wise to pay attention if the geomantic figures that appear as Judge and Witnesses also appear somewhere in the triplicities. When this happens, it indicates the presence of a connection between the Judge or Witness in question and the facet of the querent's life indicated by the figure in the triplicity. In a divination about difficulties at work, for example, if Coch is the Left Witness and also appears as the Fourth Niece, this suggests that one of the querent's fellow employees may be secretly stirring up the trouble; in a divination about a health problem, if Elw is the Judge and also appears as the First Daughter, something in the querent's home may be contributing to the problem; in a divination about a personal difficulty, if Tristwch is the Right Witness and also appears as the Third Mother, sorrows from the querent's past are placing an additional burden upon him at this time.

More generally, the meanings of the four triplicities may be factored into any divination in which the part of life they represent plays a significant role. In any divination about love, for example, the figure that appears as the Fourth Daughter will reveal much about the nature of the person the querent loves, and the other figures in the fourth triplicity will likewise have lessons to teach about the reaction of other people in the querent's life to the love affair. Very few divinations in the course of everyday life leave the correspondences of all four of the triplicities entirely untouched. It also happens in certain cases that a querent wishes a reading concerning all his affairs, and in this case all four triplicities should be read, and figures appearing in more than one place in the chart—even if they do not appear as Witnesses or Judge—should be read as noting a connection between the corresponding parts of the querent's life. If the figure that is the Fourth Daughter also appears as the Second Daughter, for example, the querent can expect to encounter a potential love interest in one of the places he normally frequents.

Another use of the four triplicities is in conjunction with the Way of Points, another of the advanced tools of geomantic divination.

The Way of Points

This is a tool for finding the hidden root or unrecognized causative factor in a reading. It begins with the Judge, and then only when the Judge has a fire or topmost line consisting of one point. When the Judge has two points in its fire line, the Way of Points cannot be formed, and this indicates that the situation facing the querent is exactly what it seems to be and there is no hidden factor at work.

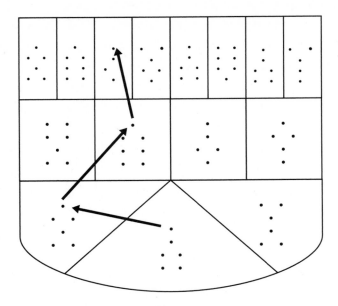

Way of Points

If the Judge has a fire line consisting of one point, on the other hand, the Way of Points can be formed. The Way proceeds from the Judge to whichever of the two Witnesses has a single point for its fire line, then to whichever of the Nieces that gave birth to that Witness has a single point in its fire line, and then to whichever of the Mothers or Daughters that gave birth to that Niece has a single point in its fire line. That uppermost figure represents the hidden root of the reading.

The diagram shows the formation of the Way of Points. The Judge in this chart, Bendith Fach, has a single point in its fire line, so the Way can be formed. The Way passes from the Judge to the Left Witness, Colled; from there to the Third Niece, Llawenydd; and from there to the Second Daughter, Mab. The exact significance of the Way depends on the question being asked, but a hidden cause of the subject of divination will be found to be related to a place where the querent spends time outside the home, which corresponds in some way to the nature of Mab—perhaps a tavern or a place associated with gambling or athletics.

During the time you spend working on this knowledge lecture, experiment with adding these two advanced techniques to your geomantic readings, and explore their uses.

On the First Work of Spagyrics

IN PREPARATION FOR YOUR initiation into the Ovate Grade, you will need to make a spagyric tincture of vervain, one of the sacred herbs of the Druids. This tincture must be prepared by yourself using the following method so that it will be attuned to your own subtle energies and essence.

You will need to obtain the following items. All but the grill should be set aside wholly for your spagyrics work.

1. Four ounces of dried vervain (*Verbena officinalis*)
2. One pint of grain alcohol or brandy, being at least 75% alcohol (150 proof)
3. Two glass containers of one pint capacity each with airtight lids (canning jars may be used)
4. A porcelain mortar and pestle for grinding the herb
5. A small glass or plastic funnel and filter paper or a coffee filter
6. A small iron pan and an iron rod for stirring
7. A gas or charcoal grill

Begin by performing the Lesser Ritual of the Pentagram in its banishing form in the room in which you will be working. Then take approximately one ounce of the vervain and grind it into powder with the mortar and pestle. Even if you have not used these before, you will find the knack easy to acquire; the herb is placed in the bottom of the mortar, and the pestle moved in circles, exerting a gentle pressure against the herb. Do not allow your mind to wander while grinding the herb; treat the grinding as a meditation, and focus your mind on the work you have done in preparation for your Ovate initiation. Keep grinding until the whole ounce is reduced to a fine powder, a process which should take perhaps twenty minutes.

Then place the powder in one of your glass jars and pour in alcohol, filling the jar no more than half full. Seal the jar tightly; if you use a canning jar, a piece of plastic wrap placed across the mouth of the jar before the lid is tightened on it will make for a better seal. Then shake the jar gently and put it in a warm place where it will receive no direct or indirect sunlight; if this is difficult to obtain, place the jar in a brown paper bag to keep the sun's rays from it.

Leave it to soak—or, as alchemists say, macerate—for at least one week, shaking the jar gently several times a day. By the end of the week the alcohol will have taken on a deep greenish color. Then pour the mixture through filter paper to separate the alcohol from the herb, allowing the colored alcohol to drain into the other jar; seal this tightly and put it in a place away from sunlight.

Take the other three ounces of dried vervain and add just enough alcohol to dampen them thoroughly. Add the herb residue from the maceration; put the resulting mass into the iron pan and take it outside on a windless day. Placing the pan on a fireproof surface, light the damp herb on fire and stir it with the iron rod while it burns, until all the alcohol has burned off and the vervain is burnt black; it will emit a great deal of smoke.

Then, having lit the gas or charcoal grill, place the iron pan in the hottest part of the flame and continue stirring with the iron rod; the vervain will blacken further, then appear to boil and seethe, then glow red, and finally be reduced to a white or gray ash. When this stage has been reached, remove the pan from the flames and allow it to cool until it is quite cold.

The ash should then be scraped into the mortar and pestle, crushed to a fine powder, and added to the jar containing the alcohol you earlier extracted from the herb. Return the mixture to a warm place where it will not be touched by the sun's rays, putting it in a brown paper bag if needed, and leave it there for one week, shaking it gently several times a day. Finally, when the week is done, filter the mixture to extract any part of the ash that is not capable of dissolving, and bury this in the ground or add it to a compost bin, should you have one. The filtered fluid is your spagyric tincture of vervain, properly prepared for your initiation into the Ovate Grade. You will need only a small portion of the tincture for the initiation; the rest should be stored in a cool, dry place for future use.

Understanding the Process

As you have previously learned, every herb contains principles known to Druid alchemists as niter and salt. A spagyric tincture is an extract of the niter and salt of an herb in alcohol or water. Grinding the herb into a fine powder in the mortar and pestle, followed by a long maceration in alcohol under gentle heat, causes the niter of the herb to pass over into the alcohol, while the salt remains behind in the mass of undissolved herb. To get at the salt, it is necessary to burn the herb, reduce it to ash, and again subject it to maceration under gentle heat; when this is done, the salt passes over into the alcohol, and the two principles, in purified form, are ready for use. Their proper use will be explained in the following knowledge lecture, the last of this grade.

Seventh Knowledge Lecture.

I. THE GEOMANTIC CHARACTERS, which are derived from the geomantic figures and are used in magical and initiatory work, are as follows:

Mab	Colled	Gwyn	Pobl
Bendith Fawr	Cyswllt	Merch	Coch
Elw	Carchar	Tristwch	Llawenydd
Llosgwrn y Ddraig	Pen y Ddraig	Bendith Fach	Ffordd

The Mystery Schools of other nations, such as the Hebrews and the Greeks, used the letters of their respective alphabets for certain mystic purposes in their symbolic and practical work. The ancient Druids, though they were acquainted with the Greek alphabet and used it for ordinary business, refused to countenance the use of letters in their Mystery Teachings. The symbols they used in place of letters were lost in the persecution of the Druidical faith in later centuries, but the geomantic characters were brought into use in medieval times and have taken the place of the lost originals. Their uses will be presented in higher grades. Learning them by heart and practicing drawing them so that they may be written on paper or traced in the air at need is valuable preparation for this later work.

2. THE GEOMANTIC FIGURES and characters may be attributed in a special sense to those portions of the Tree of Life that are accessible to dwellers in Abred. Five of the figures correspond to the five spheres of the Tree of Life from Naf up to Muner; the remainder correspond to the paths connecting the four lowest spheres to one another and to the higher influences and realms shown upon the Tree. The correspondence, beginning from Naf and ascending the Tree, is shown on the following page and tabulated below:

Naf: Carchar

First Path, Naf to Ner: Pen y Ddraig

Ner: Cyswllt

Second Path, Naf to Byth: Ffordd

Third Path, Ner to Byth: Mab

Byth: Elw

Fourth Path, Naf to Byw: Pobl

Fifth Path, Ner to Byw: Merch

Sixth Path, Byth to Byw: Bendith Fach

Byw: Colled

Seventh Path, Byth to Modur: Tristwch

Eighth Path, Byth to Muner: Coch

Ninth Path, Byw to Ener: Llawenydd

Tenth Path, Byw to Muner: Gwyn

Eleventh Path, Ner to Muner: Llosgwrn y Ddraig

Muner: Bendith Fawr

These correspondences should be studied, committed to memory, and explored in meditation, so that they may be used in the practical work of the grades to come.

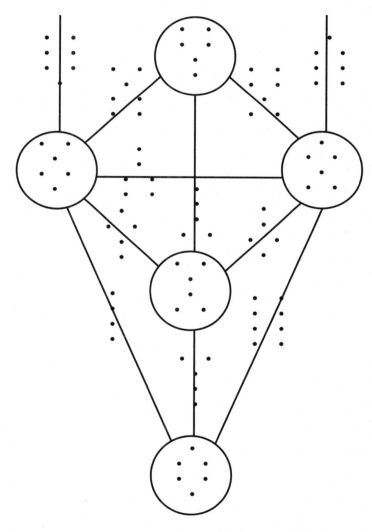

Geomantic Tree of Life

3. **THE SPHERES OF** the Tree of Life relevant to the work of the initiate in Abred also correspond to the five so-called Platonic solids, those figures of three dimensions that alone can be made with equal identical faces, edges, and vertices. (Though named after Plato, these solids were known long before his time, and stone copies of the Platonic solids have been found in ancient British graves of megalithic date.)

The correspondences are as follows:

THE CUBE composed of six squares corresponds to Naf.

THE ICOSAHEDRON composed of twenty triangles corresponds to Ner.

THE OCTAHEDRON composed of eight triangles corresponds to Byth.

THE TETRAHEDRON composed of four triangles corresponds to Byw.

THE DODECAHEDRON composed of twelve pentagons corresponds to Muner.

Note that this arrangement gives an additional geometrical symbol for the three levels of human experience: material, aetherial, and intellectual. The material level, which predominates in the lowest sphere of Naf, is represented by the square; the aetherial level, which predominates in the next three spheres rising up from Naf, is represented by the triangle; and the intellectual level, which exercises its influence on the lower spheres through Muner, is represented by the pentagon.

To each of these, in turn, a class of geometrical relationships are assigned, and each class is governed by what geometry outside the Mystery Schools terms an irrational proportion. The name is poorly given, for these represent not irrational but transrational relationships—not below the thinking mind, but above it. They are as follows:

$1:\sqrt{2}$, one to the square root of two, which is the relationship between the square and its diagonal and the governing proportion of the *ad quadratum* system of sacred geometry;

$1:\sqrt{3}$, one to the square root of three, which is the relationship between the width and the length of the vesica piscis, and the governing proportion of the *ad triangulum* system of sacred geometry;

$1:\Phi$, the Golden Proportion, the precious jewel of sacred geometry, which requires any of several subtle constructions to produce but which may be found throughout the world of nature in countless forms.

These relationships and the geometries that unfold from them will be an important aspect of your studies in higher grades.

4. **THE TWO DRAGONS** of Celtic legend have precise equivalents in the literature of alchemy. In the *Aurea Catena Homeri*, or Golden Chain of Homer, an image of a winged and a wingless dragon biting each other's tails appears above the following lines, which deserve careful study and meditation:

Whenever the dragon meets an enemy, they fight.

The volatile must become fixed, vapor and water must become earth.

Fire must become corporeal, or no life can enter into the earth.

The above must become below, and vice versa.

The fixed becomes volatile, the earth becomes water, vapor, air, and fire,

Whilst fire returns to the center of the earth. Heaven—that is, fire—

Must be converted into a fixed earth. The dragon with wings

Kills the dragon without wings, and the latter destroys the former.

Thus is manifested the quintessence and its power.

Seventh Meditation

LET THE OVATE REVIEW the knowledge lectures he has received so far in this grade and read through the notes he has made on his meditations and practices. Let him note any common themes or concepts that seem to be present throughout. Let him likewise consider what reasons induced him to seek initiation as an Ovate, and the changes in his own thinking and awareness that have taken place during the course of his journey through the Ovate Grade. Let him strive to understand, from his own point of view, what lessons the Ovate Grade has attempted to teach him and how well he has learnt them.

Let him then, in meditation, consider the nature of initiation in general and of the Ovate initiation in particular. Concentrating all his faculties upon this as a focus, let the Ovate endeavor to realize the nature and purpose of the work he has done in preparing for the initiation ceremony he is about to perform.

Begin the meditation in the same way as before, taking the same posture and performing the relaxation exercise in order to release as much unwanted tension from the body as possible. When you have reached the completion of this stage of the work, proceed to the Natural Breath with the visualization of the ocean of light, and the drawing in, concentrating, and releasing of the light in the body through pore breathing. Now, however, you will work with the light of the four elements in the following manner.

In place of the ocean of colorless light or of any of the elemental colors, you will visualize an ocean of light that is of a pale spring green tinged with gold. In that ocean of light directly ahead of you is the symbol of the equal-armed cross surmounting the circle, the emblem of the Ovate Grade. As before, you will draw this light into your body with seven breaths, accumulating it in your body, and as you do so, you will feel not only the pressure of the light but the presence of the knowledge and awareness that has been awakened in you through your study of the knowledge lectures of the Ovate Grade.

After you have breathed in the elemental quality with seven breaths, let the imagery fade from your awareness, but do not breathe it out in the usual manner. Instead, perform your meditation on the theme above, or on the other themes discussed in this knowledge lecture, while the energies of the Ovate Grade are present within you. When you have finished your meditation, begin to breathe the pale green light out again with seven breaths, allowing the light to dissipate one breath at a time while realizing that the knowledge and awareness you have gained through this grade remains with you. When you have breathed all of the light out of your body, clear your mind of the imagery and finish the meditation, and make notes of the ideas and images that arose in your mind during the practice.

WHEN YOU HAVE MEDITATED on the lessons of the Ovate Grade often enough that no new insights or images come to you, go on as before to meditate on the teachings presented in this knowledge lecture, and trace the connections that link them to teachings that you have already received. This should be done before performing the Ovate Grade initiation.

The Examination of the Ovate Grade

THE FOLLOWING EXAMINATION SHOULD be completed by you, working unassisted and alone, before you proceed to the initiation ceremony of this grade. You may use the knowledge lectures you have received as references for the work. Nonetheless, it is important for you to be honest with yourself; if you find that any of the questions below leave you completely at a loss, you owe it to yourself to leave this examination, study the relevant material, and practice the techniques you have been taught until you can return to the examination and complete the work with confidence.

It is strongly recommended that you write out the answers to the questions below, and when you are finished, keep the test paper for future reference. You may find it useful later to review your work and see what your further studies can add to it.

*　　*　　*

1. Ener is one of the spheres of the Tree of Life. Write out the meaning of its name, the divine name, the ray of light, the elemental triangle, any other elemental symbolism, and the symbol and texts from the *Aurea Catena Homeri* that are associated with this sphere.

2. Explain briefly what the following terms mean: *Natura naturata*, Gwynfydd, binary, querent, spagyrics, anima mundi, *ad triangulum*.

3. The herbs eyebright and vervain are both traditionally used to treat eyestrain. Look up the elemental temperament of both herbs, and write out this and the element that governs each of them; then, supposing that you were to prepare a medicine containing equal parts of these herbs, calculate the elemental temperament of the finished medicine.

4. Using your Druid wands, cast a geomantic chart on any question you wish, and write out your full interpretation of the chart, using the advanced methods of interpretation given in the lecture where these are appropriate.

5. Describe briefly your experiences with the following practices: thinking in ternaries, pore breathing, the Ovate tree working, the third meditation.

6. Over the time you have spent in the Ovate Grade, describe the changes you have noticed in the effects produced by your practice of the Lesser Ritual of the Pentagram.

7. Describe in general terms any changes in yourself, your life, and your circumstances that have taken place over the course of your time in the Ovate Grade, and whether any of them seem to be related in any way to your practice of the Druidical Mysteries.

The Initiation of the Ovate Grade

THE CEREMONY THAT FOLLOWS will require you to be perfectly familiar with the opening and closing ceremony of the Ovate temple, the methods of meditation taught in previous lectures, and the art of casting and interpreting a geomantic chart using the Druid wands. More generally, the ritual gains its effect from the work that the candidate has previously performed in the grade; for one who has not done the work, the initiation will be an empty shell, conferring no power and bearing no inward gifts. You are therefore most earnestly advised if you have not performed the meditations and ritual work, studied the material presented in previous knowledge lectures, and completed the Ovate Grade Examination to the best of your ability, to return to the studies and exercises already given, and prepare yourself more fully for the initiation of the Ovate Grade.

On a more formal level, to perform the ceremony you will need all the items listed in the second knowledge lecture paper on the Ovate temple; you will also need to have provided yourself with a set of Druid wands; and you will need to have prepared, using the method presented in the sixth knowledge lecture, a spagyric tincture of vervain. All these will be needed in the course of the ceremony.

You should also provide yourself with a plain white robe and a sash of green cloth four inches wide, which is worn across your body from the left shoulder to the right hip. This represents your rank as an Ovate and will be put on at a certain point in the ceremony.

*   *   *

When you are ready to begin the initiation ceremony of the Ovate Grade, set up the temple as you have been taught to do, with the altar at the center draped in white, the three candles, the cauldrons of water and fire, and the cross and circle in their Ovate positions. Wear your white robe, but do not put on the green sash as yet. A chair should be placed in the west of the space where you will perform the ritual. Near the altar have the green sash, your Druid wands, a sheet of paper and a pen, a small bowl, a glass of water, an eyedropper, and the jar containing your spagyric tincture of vervain.

Begin the ceremony by performing the complete opening ceremony as you have been taught to do. When you have finished the opening and are standing at the west side of the altar facing east, say: "By all the powers here invoked, and in the presence of the Guardians of the Ovate temple, I present myself as one who has successfully completed the required examination and who is therefore prepared to take the obligation of the Ovate Grade."

Place your left hand on the circle and cross upon the altar and raise your right hand, palm forward, facing the east, and repeat the following obligation:

"I, (say your full name here), in the presence of the holy powers of nature and the light of the Golden Dawn, do of my own free will solemnly promise and bind myself to hold the teachings of the Druidical Mysteries in due reverence as instruments for the uplifting and enlightenment of myself and others;

"I further promise and bind myself to maintain a friendly and benevolent relation with all other students of the Druidical Mysteries, refusing under any circumstances to take part in hurtful gossip or quarrels of any kind among the initiates of this or any other Mystery School;

"I further promise and bind myself to use whatever powers I may have gained or will hereafter gain through my Druidical training for good ends alone and in the service of the living earth and the living beings upon her, and never under any circumstances or pleading any excuse stoop to use them for selfish or destructive ends;

"To all these things I pledge and bind myself, placing myself in the hands of the Guardians of the Ovate temple and the holy powers of nature, and should I ever violate this, my Ovate obligation, in any particular or under any pretense, I freely and willingly consent to the loss of any powers that may be conferred upon me by this initiation, the course of study and practice that has prepared me for it, and the further studies and practices I shall pursue in the Druidical Mysteries hereafter, in the knowledge that I will regain such powers only when by labor and suffering I shall again have proved myself worthy of them. May the holy powers of nature and the rays of the Golden Dawn uphold me in this, my Ovate obligation."

Now take the glass of water and pour a few teaspoons of water into the small bowl. Then, using the eyedropper, put seven drops of your spagyric tincture of vervain in the bowl and seven more drops into the remaining water in the glass. Put the eyedropper and tincture aside, and say, "Having taken the obligation of the Ovate Grade, I ask that I may receive the blessing and empowerment of that grade." Lift the glass with the water and tincture, holding it high as though in offering, and then lower it and drink its entire contents. Then dip the index and middle fingers of your right hand into the water and tincture in the bowl, and use the liquid to trace the sign of the Three Rays of Light / | \ on your forehead, then on the palm of your left hand; then dip the index and middle fingers of your left hand into the bowl, and use the liquid to trace the Three Rays on the palm of your right hand.

Be seated in the chair in the west of the temple; enter into meditation using the method given in this knowledge lecture, and meditate on the obligation you have taken until your forehead and palms are dry. Pay close attention to any insights you may receive and any thoughts or images that come to you during this meditation. When you are finished, stand facing east and make the following two motions.

First, sweep your arms up and out to the sides in an arc, finishing with your hands above your head, palms facing each other. Draw your hands down to the level of your ears, and as you do so, turn your palms to face forward and shift your weight slightly to your right foot. Then, in a single swift movement, project the hands forward, palms down and fingertips pointing east, while your left foot steps forward and stamps on the ground. Your weight remains back, on your right foot; your head is bowed, so that your eyes look forward on the same level as your fingertips. All your attention is forward, following the line of your fingertips and your gaze. This is the Sign of Salutation or of Projection, the first of the two signs of the Ovate Grade.

Second, in a single motion draw your right hand back to your side, and your left hand to your mouth, forming the common gesture of silence, with the index finger extended and the others closed, pressing against your lips. At the same time, draw back your left foot to its place beside the right, and stamp the ground as it reaches it place. This is the Sign of Silence or of Reception, the second of the two signs of the Ovate Grade.

Advance to the west side of the altar, facing east, and say, "Having taken the obligation and received the blessing and empowerment of the Ovate Grade, and being mindful of the responsibilities I do accept thereby, I do proclaim myself an Ovate of the Druidical Order of the Golden Dawn, and I clothe myself in the garment of that grade." You may then put on the green sash, the badge of your new grade of initiation.

At this point, say, "I now ask the holy powers of nature for an omen to guide me in my work as an Ovate." Take your Druid wands and cast a geomantic chart with them; draw up the chart and interpret it. Remember that a negative figure is as valuable a guide in this setting as a positive one; should the Judge of your chart be Llosgwrn y Ddraig, for example, this may mean that it is time for you to give up some habit or other aspect of your life that restrains your progress; should the Judge be Tristwch, this may advise that you must come to terms with the difficulties and sorrows already present in your life; and so on. The chart you cast at this time should be saved and reviewed repeatedly during your studies of the subsequent grade.

When you have finished casting and interpreting the divination, set it aside. Standing at the west of the altar, facing east, say: "In the presence of the holy powers of nature and the light of the Golden Dawn, I proclaim that this ceremony of initiation into the Ovate Grade has been duly performed, and I ask the Guardians of the Ovate temple to guide me until and unless the time may come that I pass to a grade beyond."

At this point, perform the complete closing ritual of the Ovate temple as you have been taught. This completes the ceremony of initiation.

$$*\quad*\quad*$$

After the completion of this ceremony, a choice of great importance faces you: to continue with your studies in the Druidical Mysteries as presented in these lessons or to take what you have learned in your Ovate studies and depart. In either case, your rank and initiation as an Ovate remain with you, and you may freely use the teachings you have already received in whatever way may correspond to the requirements of your Ovate obligation and your own personal decisions and needs.

The work of the Bardic Grade involves a deeper commitment to the practical work of the Druidical Mysteries. The practices are more intensive, the studies more profound; daily work becomes a necessity, and the impact of your training upon your daily life is accordingly greater. If you are not prepared to enter on this more demanding course of study, it would be better for you to leave it for another time or another life than to enter into it and stop partway through.

It is therefore strongly recommended that you take some time to glance over the lessons of the grades ahead. Be sure that you are willing and able to undertake the course of work that is before you before proceeding to the introductory lecture of the Bardic Grade.

DRUIDICAL ORDER OF THE GOLDEN DAWN

— △ —

The Bardic Grade

— ▽ —

T hrice welcome, Ovate!

You have completed your labors in the preliminary disciplines of our order, and a further realm of Druidical learning and practice now stands open before you. None of the teachings you have already learned lose their importance in that further realm; to the contrary, you will be called upon to use them at every turn in your training as a Bard. You should expect to spend at least eight months on the work in this grade, and as much more as seems useful to you. As explained in the introductory letter of the Ovate Grade, it is never a mistake to expend more time than formally required if this results in a more thorough comprehension of the teachings you will receive.

The manner in which the work of this grade is presented, however, differs from that which structures the training of the Ovate. To the Ovate is given a series of knowledge lectures that divide the disciplines of that grade into small and easily learned portions. This is proper for the newcomer to the Druidical path. At this point, however, you are no longer a beginner in our work, and the teachings you will study in your Bardic training are presented in a form suited to your greater experience.

This introductory lecture summarizes those fundamental practices that will be essential to your progress toward the Bardic Grade initiation and that should be practiced daily. Two of those practices, meditation and geomantic divination, have already been presented to you. The third, the Exercise of the Central Ray, is a further expansion and development of the Lesser Ritual of the Pentagram, which you learned and practiced in the previous grade. Also presented here are the four Elemental Rituals of the Pentagram, which will be needed for the central initiatory practices of this grade and should be learned and committed to memory at the earliest opportunity.

The lectures that follow—on the Work of Earth, that of Water, that of Air, and that of Fire, respectively—present the central initiatory practices just mentioned. These lectures should be studied and the work performed in the order just given, for they teach the student to travel in the spirit vision through those spheres and paths of the Tree of Life belonging to the circle of Abred, beginning with the tenth sphere of Naf and ascending to the seventh sphere of Byw. These paths form a tetrahedron, which may be seen from two different angles, as shown below: one forming the lower section of the Tree of Life, the other the square and diagonals of the elements. The relations between spheres remain unchanged, the difference being simply the mode of presentation.

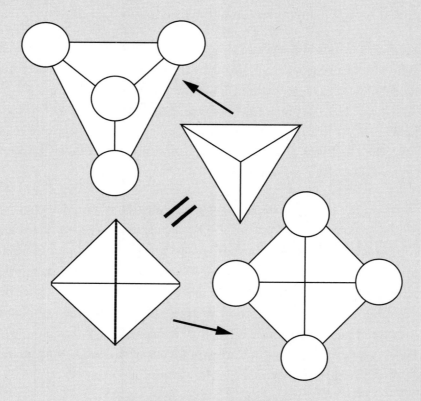

Two Views of the Elements

The Bardic Grade does not pass beyond the circle of Abred, or, to use another manner of speaking, beyond the square of the elements; the portals of Gwynfydd, the path to spirit and to the spheres above Byw, belong to the Druid Grade. In working with the elemental spheres and their connecting paths, you will find ample challenges for the time being.

In the course of meeting those challenges and accomplishing the work of this grade, you will have need of knowledge and skills that are not covered in the four lectures of the work of the elements just described. A series of additional lectures are therefore included in the material presented to you as a Bard. In them you will encounter more advanced teachings concerning the Tree of Life, sacred geometry, alchemy, geomancy, the magical properties of plants, and the subtle energies of the earth, all of which will play important roles in the work ahead of you in this and the remaining grade. You will be asked to read and study books on several of the subjects just named; as the Bards of ancient times were the custodians of the lore and knowledge of their tribes, it is your task in your studies in this grade to gain some familiarity with the wealth of lore and knowledge to be found in occult literature concerning the subjects relevant to our work and way.

It is also important to note at this time that your initiation in this grade will require a more extensive preparation than did that of the Ovate Grade. The disciplines of meditation, divination, and ritual will be of central importance, as before, but several other tasks will be assigned to you, and you will also be expected to create a set of four spagyric tinctures, using the method you have already learned, before you receive your initiation as a Bard. Details of these requirements are included in a later paper.

Meditation in the Bardic Grade

The practice of meditation, using the method in which you have already been instructed, should become a daily habit for you. Most Bards find it most effective and convenient to set aside a short period at the beginning of the day, as soon as possible after rising and before engaging in any other activity, for a daily meditation. For best results, this should be preceded by the Exercise of the Central Ray, which will be explained to you shortly.

In the Ovate Grade a series of subjects for meditation was presented to you. In this grade, out of the teachings presented to you, it will be your privilege and responsibility to select themes for meditation. Suggestions will be provided in the lectures to come, but you will find that if you pay attention to the work ahead, you will have no shortage of material to explore in meditation.

The importance of meditative work in this training program is impossible to overstate. Without it, the ritual work of the Druidical path is but empty forms and the philosophy but empty words. It may seem surprising to you that the simple process of devoting a quarter or half of an hour a day to sustained, focused thinking on the teachings of the Druidical Mysteries should be so necessary a part of your training, but long experience has shown this to be the case. It is better to meditate and do no other part of the work presented to you than it would be to do everything else and neglect your meditations. Here, as elsewhere in our work, a word to the wise is sufficient.

Divination in the Bardic Grade

You should continue to cast a geomantic chart each morning concerning the events of the day just beginning and to review the reading that evening with an eye toward how the day's events revealed themselves in the chart. You may apply the advanced techniques of interpretation covered in the Bardic Grade lecture on geomancy, once you study this lecture and when these advanced techniques are appropriate, and of course it is also entirely proper to cast additional charts to provide yourself with insight into any question or situation that may confront you in the course of your life, aside from your daily charts. Since the geomantic characters and some other aspects of geomancy have additional uses in the Bardic Grade, you will find your divinatory work enriched by new insights as you proceed. Still, the mastery of any divinatory art comes only through sustained practice in casting and interpreting readings, and the special applications of geomancy in the Druid Grade may be understood and put to use only when you have established a firm foundation in ordinary divinatory practice.

Ritual in the Bardic Grade

The Exercise of the Central Ray, which is given after this introductory letter, is practiced in conjunction with the Lesser Ritual of the Pentagram. As a method of self-development and a preparation for magical practice it is unexcelled, and therefore it should be practiced daily. Its structure and relationship to the Tree of Life will be explained to you in one of the lectures of this grade. Regular practice of this exercise will establish and charge the centers of subtle energy in your body and teach you the art of moving and directing the energies involved—an art that is central to the practice of magic.

Also provided after this letter are instructions for performing the four elemental versions of the Ritual of the Pentagram. You should learn and practice these as soon as possible, as they will be used extensively in the practical work of this grade.

With this, we welcome you again and wish you the best of success in your further work!

The Guardians of the Order

The Exercise of the Central Ray.

THE EXERCISE IS PERFORMED as follows:

FIRST, perform the Lesser Ritual of the Pentagram in the banishing mode.

SECOND, visualize the sun in its glory far above your head, and imagine a ray of light descending from the sun to form a sphere of light some eight inches across, just above your head. This sphere is white and contains the image of a golden sun. When you have formulated it, vibrate the name HU (pronounced "HE") three times.

THIRD, bring the ray of light down to your throat and there form another sphere of light of the same size. This one is pale violet and contains the image of a silver crescent moon. When you have formulated it, vibrate the name CED (pronounced "KEHD") three times.

FOURTH, bring the ray of light down to your heart and form a third sphere of light. This one is golden, and contains the image of oak leaves with light shining through them. The name vibrated here, three times, is HESUS (pronounced "HEH-sis").

FIFTH, bring the ray of light to your genital center and form a fourth sphere of light. This one is silver, the color of flowing water, and contains the image of a stone with a red dragon carved upon it under water. The name vibrated here varies depending on the gender of the practitioner; women use the name SUL (pronounced "SILL") while men use the name COEL (pronounced "KO-ell"); in either case, the name is vibrated three times.

SIXTH, bring the ray of light to your feet and form a fifth center. This one is the green of foliage and contains the image of a white flower. The name vibrated here, three times, is OLWEN (pronounced "OL-wen").

SEVENTH, return the attention to the sphere of light at the top of the head. Bring a current of white light down the right side of the head and neck, the right shoulder and arm, and the right hip and leg, down to the sphere at the feet and then back up the left leg and hip, the left arm and shoulder, and the left side of the neck and head, back to the sphere at the head. Repeat this a total of three times; if possible, synchronize with the breath, but it is more important to visualize the whole course than to make it happen within a single breath.

EIGHTH, in the same way, bring a current of white light from the sphere above the head down the midline of the front of the body to the sphere at the feet, and then back up the midline of the back of the body to the center above the head. Repeat a total of three times.

NINTH, turn the attention to the center at the feet. Breathing in, draw a current of energy up the center line of the body from that center to the center above the head; breathing out, allow it to spray like a fountain out and over the whole body, cleansing the entire aura. Do this a total of three times.

TENTH, perform the Rite of the Rays. This completes the exercise.

The Elemental Rituals of the Pentagram.

THERE ARE FOUR ELEMENTAL Rituals of the Pentagram, which differ from the Lesser Ritual in the tracing of the pentagrams, the divine names invoked with them, and the elemental powers summoned in the four directions. The Rite of the Rays at beginning and ending, and the basic pattern of movement and action, remains the same in all cases. The symbolism of the pentagrams as given here differs from other Mystery Schools.

The Ritual of the Earth Pentagram

This is performed with one or the other of the two pentagrams of earth, as shown below—the first to summon and the second to banish. The divine name that is to be vibrated in each quarter is the same, that is, **CERNUNNOS** (pronounced "ker-NOON-os"). When standing at the center (or the altar) amid the four pentagrams, you will invoke the four aspects of earth as follows:

"Before me the fertile plains, behind me the rolling hills, to my right hand the tall mountains, to my left hand the deep caverns, for about me stand the pentagrams and upon me shine the Three Rays of Light."

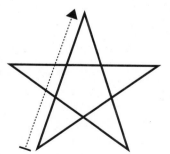 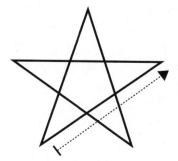

Summoning and Banishing Pentagrams of Earth

The Ritual of the Water Pentagram

This is performed with one or the other of the two pentagrams of water, as shown below—the first to summon, and the second to banish. The divine name that is to be vibrated in each quarter is the same, that is, **SIRONA** (pronounced "si-ROE-na"). When standing at the center (or the altar) amid the four pentagrams, you will invoke the four aspects of water as follows:

"Before me the dancing streams, behind me the great ocean, to my right hand the strong rivers, to my left hand the quiet lakes, for about me stand the pentagrams and upon me shine the Three Rays of Light."

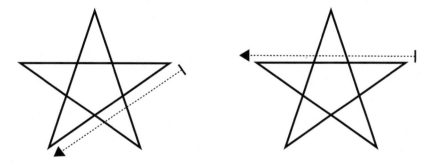

Summoning and Banishing Pentagrams of Water

The Ritual of the Air Pentagram

This is performed with one or the other of the two pentagrams of air, as shown on the next page—the first to summon, and the second to banish. The divine name that is to be vibrated in each quarter is the same, that is, **BELISAMA** (pronounced BEL-ih-SAH-ma). When standing at the center (or the altar) amid the four pentagrams, you will invoke the four aspects of air as follows:

"Before me the rushing wind, behind me the silver mist, to my right hand the shining sky, to my left hand the billowing cloud, for about me stand the pentagrams and upon me shine the Three Rays of Light."

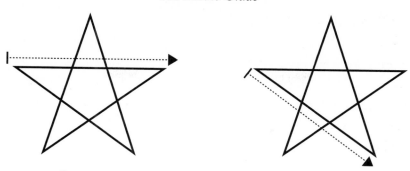

Summoning and Banishing Pentagrams of Air

The Ritual of the Fire Pentagram

This is performed with one or the other of the two pentagrams of fire, as shown below—the first to summon, and the second to banish. The divine name that is to be vibrated in each quarter is the same, that is, **TOUTATIS** (pronounced "too-TOT-is"). When standing at the center (or the altar) amid the four pentagrams, you will invoke the four aspects of fire as follows:

"Before me the lightning flash, behind me the fire of growth, to my right hand the radiant sun, to my left hand the flame upon the hearth, for about me stand the pentagrams and upon me shine the Three Rays of Light."

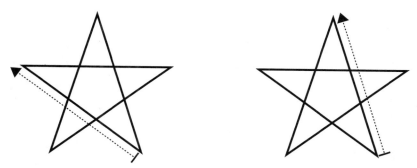

Summoning and Banishing Pentagrams of Fire

A Note on Divine Names

The names of gods and goddesses used in our Druidical Mysteries are of two forms—the first belonging to the ancient Celtic language, the second belonging to medieval and modern Welsh, one of the daughter tongues of that more ancient language. The name Belinus, for example, is in the ancient form, while Beli is the Welsh version of the same name. Not all the names of the ancient gods and goddesses are found in the later Welsh legends, however, and some of the later Welsh names cannot be traced back with any certainty to their ancient form.

Both the ancient Celtic and later Welsh names are used in practice, therefore; the names used in the elemental pentagram rituals just given, for example, are in the ancient form, while those used in the Lesser Ritual of the Pentagram are in the Welsh form. All divine names should be pronounced with due reverence, for they are formulae of great power as well as expressions of the primary creative powers of the cosmos; they should never be spoken lightly.

The Work of Earth.

AT THE HEART OF the work of the Bardic Grade, alongside the daily practices outlined in the introductory lecture already presented to you, are a sequence of workings based upon the teachings and symbolism of the four lowest spheres of the Tree of Life. These pertain, as you have already learned, to the circle of Abred and also to the four material elements. By practicing these workings, which are named for convenience after the elements themselves, you will extend your training in practical magic, learn to commune with the elemental realms, and begin the process of ascending the Tree of Life.

The first of the elemental workings you are to perform is the Work of Earth. In preparation for this work, it is recommended that you review in meditation all the symbolism of the element of earth that has been presented to you in the knowledge lectures of the Ovate Grade.

The Bardic Temple

Each of the elemental workings you will perform in this grade is to be done in a temple open in the Bardic Grade. The ritual you will use to open and close a temple in the Bardic Grade, for the time being, is the same as the Ovate Grade ritual, with three differences.

The first difference is that the arrangement of the circle and cross on the altar is not the same. The Bardic Grade is preeminently the grade of the four elements, as the Ovate Grade is preeminently that of the Three Rays of Light; in a temple of Bards, therefore, the cross is placed atop the circle, to represent the four elements as they manifest in the four directions about the temple. This is done in the usual way before the temple is opened.

Bardic Cross and Circle

Certain additional meanings of this arrangement of the circle and cross may occur to you in conjunction with the alchemical symbolism discussed in the previous grade. This is a worthwhile subject for meditation.

The second difference is that the two signs communicated to you in the initiation of the Ovate Grade, the Signs of Salutation and of Silence, are to be performed in the opening ceremony. The Sign of Salutation is made immediately after saying "May I be illumined by a ray of that Golden Dawn" and held while you visualize the rising of the spiritual sun. When the visualized sun has completed its rising and stands golden and splendid before you, make the Sign of Silence, then proceed with the words of the ritual.

The third difference is simply that when you begin, you will announce that you are preparing to open the temple in the Bardic Grade, and when the temple is declared open, you will declare it open in the Bardic Grade rather than the Ovate Grade.

Practice opening and closing your temple in the Bardic Grade until you can perform the full ceremony without referring to these or any other notes. When you have done so, you will be ready to add the next portion of the practice. This is performed in the Bardic temple after it has been opened and prior to the closing ceremony. It consists of two parts, the Calling of Earth and the License to Depart. You should learn both these parts thoroughly before proceeding.

The Calling of Earth

Begin the Calling of Earth standing at the west of the altar, facing east. Perform the Summoning Ritual of the Earth Pentagram as described in the introductory lecture of this grade. When you have finished, go around the temple with the sun—that is, in a clockwise direction, to the northern quarter, and face outwards, toward the north.

Trace a summoning pentagram of earth like those you traced in the pentagram ritual you have just completed. Imagine that you are drawing it in the air in lines of glowing green light. Point to its center and say: "In the great name **CERNUNNOS**, the Lord of Earth, Spirits of Earth, behold the rays of the Golden Dawn! Come ye forth and assist me in this work of earth."

Next, in the center of the pentagram, draw the Sigil of the Winter Solstice as portrayed below, and visualize it drawn in glowing green light. Point to its center and say: "By the great bear who guards the turning heavens and the mystical gate of the northern stars, Spirits of Earth, behold the rays of the Golden Dawn! Come ye forth and assist me in this work of earth."

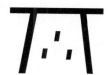

Sigil of the Winter Solstice

Now make the Sign of Earth as follows. Bring the right foot forward and place it on the ground, but keep the weight entirely back on the left foot. Raise the right hand upwards to an angle of forty-five degrees, with the wrist flexed so that the palm faces forward and the fingers point straight upwards. The left arm and left leg both remain straight and vertical. Say: "By all the powers of the northern quarter of the world, by the silence of midnight and the cold of winter, by the strength of the standing stone and the bare and leafless tree, Spirits of Earth, behold the rays of the Golden Dawn! Come ye forth and assist me in this work of earth."

Return to the west of the altar, face east, and say, "I proclaim that the powers of earth have been duly invoked." This concludes the Calling of Earth.

The License to Depart

When you have finished the Calling of Earth, or when any additional work done with the subtle forces of earth is complete, you should always proceed to the License to Depart, which releases the elemental powers you have invoked in the working.

Begin the License to Depart standing west of the altar, facing east. Proceed with the sun—that is, in a clockwise direction to the northern quarter—and face outwards, toward the north. Make the Sign of Earth and say: "With the blessings of **CERNUN-NOS** and of the great bear who guards the turning heavens, and with thanks for your assistance in this work of earth, Spirits of Earth, I license ye to depart. Go in peace, and peace be between ye and me."

Then trace the banishing earth pentagram toward the north. Return to the west side of the altar, moving around the temple with the sun, and perform the Banishing Ritual of the Earth Pentagram as described in the introductory lecture of this grade. When you have finished, proceed to close the temple with the usual ceremony.

Once you have practiced the Calling of Earth and License to Depart often enough that you can perform both ceremonies in an open Bardic temple without reference to notes, you will be ready to add the next portion of the practice, the inner grove of earth. With this stage, the focus of the work shifts from the outer world to the inner world, and you will therefore be performing the remaining aspects of the Work of Earth in a state of meditation.

The Inner Grove of Earth

Before you perform this working, place a chair in the northern part of the temple, facing inwards toward the altar. When you have opened the temple in the Bardic Grade and performed the Calling of Earth, take your seat there and enter into meditation in the way you have already learned to do, with relaxation and pore breathing. In the stage of pore breathing, the light you imagine yourself drawing into and releasing out from your body is, of course, the green light of earth; in this working, though, you do not accumulate it in your body, even for a short period. Simply draw in the light and energies of earth through your pores with every in-breath and let the light and energies of earth flow out through your pores with every out-breath, as you did with the colorless light in the preparation for the fourth meditation of the Ovate Grade.

All that follows takes place in the imagination. It is important for you to realize, as you begin this phase of your Druid training, that what exists in the world of the imagination is not, in the ordinary sense of the word, "imaginary." The human imagination is that sense organ by which we perceive the aetherial world, the middlemost of the three worlds that human beings can experience; it is also an organ of action by which we may shape the subtle substance of the aetherial world. In the practice of the four inner groves of the Bardic Grade, both these properties of imagination will be explored and trained.

Imagine, then, as you sit in your chair in the northern quarter of the temple, that you slowly open your eyes upon a different world. You are in a clearing in the forest, and it is a winter night. Dark evergreen trees surround the clearing, and there is snow here and there upon their branches. High above, the winter stars blaze in a sky as clear as crystal.

You are seated on a cubical, backless seat of stone in the northern quarter of the clearing, facing an altar of stone in the center; it is covered by a green altar cloth that falls to the ground on all sides, and on the side facing you is embroidered in silver the geomantic character of Carchar as it appears below. On the altar are the same implements you have on the altar in your temple: the three candles in candlesticks, the cauldrons of water and incense, and the cross and circle, which are arranged as in the Bardic Grade.

Carchar

The first time you enter the inner grove of earth, simply remain seated on the cubical seat of stone in the northern quarter, imagining the altar, the clearing around it, the dark trees with their sprinkling of snow, and the starry sky above all. Imagine it as clearly as you can; feel the sting of midwinter cold on your face and hands, smell the strong scent of pitch that comes from the evergreen trees all around you, listen to the vast stillness of the winter night. When you are ready, close the practice as you would close any other meditation, perform the License to Depart, and then close the temple in the Bardic Grade in the usual way.

The second and subsequent times you enter the inner grove of earth, you may remain seated on the cubical seat of stone or you may rise and move around the inner grove. When you do this, leave your physical body in its place in the chair in your temple. Simply imagine yourself rising and moving about the grove. Go to the altar, and then walk about the clearing. Notice if anything appears to have been left for you to find in the snow; sometimes signs from the inner realms of being may take this form, and if this happens, what you find should be explored thoroughly in meditation. Imagine every detail of your movements about the inner grove of earth as though you were actually walking about a physical clearing in a physical forest; the more intently you do this, the stronger and more effective the practice will become.

Finally, when you are ready to do so, imagine yourself performing the Summoning Ritual of the Earth Pentagram inside the inner grove of earth. Do this exactly as you would if you were performing the same ritual in your temple in the physical world. Imagine every gesture and word just as though you were doing them with your physical body. Do not perform the Banishing Ritual in the inner grove; the purpose of the grove is to provide you with a link to the inner energies of the element of earth by way of repeated summoning rituals, and banishing rituals performed in the inner grove will interrupt this process. The banishing rituals you will perform when you finish, in the course of the License to Depart and the closing of your temple, will do as much as needs to be done to restore you and your temple to a balanced state.

Your goal in practicing the Work of Earth at this stage of your training is to be able to open a temple in the Bardic Grade, perform the Calling of Earth, enter into the inner grove of earth, perform a Summoning Ritual of Earth there, then return to the outer world, perform the License to Depart, and close the temple in the Bardic Grade, all from memory, without any need for notes or prompts, and with a clear sense of the energies and qualities of the element of earth responding to all of the summonings and departing in response to all of the banishings. When you have achieved this you may proceed to the Work of Water, where a more advanced dimension of this practice awaits you.

The Work of Water.

LIKE THE WORK OF Earth, which you have already learned, the Work of Water is performed within a temple open in the Bardic Grade, and it consists partly of ceremonial practice and partly of work performed in the aetherial world by means of the imagination. The ceremonial portion, or Ritual of Water, is divided into two parts, the Calling of Water and the License to Depart; both these parts are learned prior to beginning work on the aetherial portion, which is the formulation of the inner grove of water.

In preparation for this work, it is recommended that you review and meditate upon all the symbolism of the element of water that has been presented to you in the knowledge lectures of the Ovate Grade.

The Calling of Water

Begin the Calling of Water standing at the west of the altar, facing east. Perform the Summoning Ritual of the Water Pentagram as described in the introductory lecture of this grade. When you have finished, go around the temple with the sun, that is, in a clockwise direction, to the western quarter, and face outwards, toward the west.

Trace a summoning pentagram of water, like those you traced in the pentagram ritual you have just completed. Imagine that you are drawing it in the air in lines of glowing green light. Point to its center and say: "In the great name of SIRONA, the lady of water, Spirits of Water, behold the rays of the Golden Dawn! Come ye forth and assist me in this work of water."

Next, in the center of the pentagram, draw the Sigil of the Autumn Equinox as portrayed on the next page, and visualize it drawn in glowing blue light. Point to its center and say: "By the salmon of wisdom who dwells in the sacred pool and the mystical gate of the western stars, Spirits of Water, behold the rays of the Golden Dawn! Come ye forth and assist me in this work of water."

Sigil of the Autumn Equinox

Now make the Sign of Water as follows. Bring the hands together in front of the body, at or just below the level of the solar plexus, with the palms facing the body. Spread the thumb apart from the fingers; place the tips of the thumbs together, and the tips of the index fingers together, to form the image of a triangle, with the point down. Say: "By all the powers of the western quarter of the world, by the peace of evening twilight and the bounty of autumn, by the power of the rolling waves and the river flowing toward the sea, Spirits of Water, behold the rays of the Golden Dawn! Come ye forth and assist me in this work of water."

Return to the west of the altar, face east, and say, "I proclaim that the powers of water have been duly invoked." This concludes the Calling of Water.

The License to Depart

When you have completed the Calling of Water, or when any additional work you have done with the subtle forces of water is complete, proceed to the License to Depart, which releases the elemental powers you have invoked in the working.

Begin the License to Depart standing west of the altar, facing east. Proceed with the sun—that is, in a clockwise direction to the western quarter—and face outwards, toward the west. Make the Sign of Water and say: "With the blessings of **SIRONA** and of the salmon of wisdom in the sacred pool, and with thanks for your assistance in this work of water, Spirits of Water, I license ye to depart. Go in peace, and peace be between ye and me."

Then trace the banishing water pentagram toward the west. Return to the west side of the altar, moving around the temple with the sun, and perform the Banishing Ritual of the Water Pentagram as described in the introductory lecture of this grade. When you have finished, proceed to close the temple with the usual ceremony.

Practice opening a temple in the Bardic Grade, performing the Calling of Water and the License to Depart, and closing a temple in the Bardic Grade until you can do the entire working by memory, without reference to notes of any kind. Once you have reached this stage of practice, you may proceed to add the next stage of the Work of Water: the inner grove of water.

The Inner Grove of Water

Before you perform this working, place a chair in the western quarter of the temple, facing inwards toward the altar. When you have opened the temple in the Bardic Grade and performed the Calling of Water, take your seat there and enter into meditation in the way you have already learned to do. Your pore breathing for this inner grove working will be blue, the color of water, and you will again simply draw in the water energies with each in-breath and allow them to flow out on each out-breath.

When you have done this for a time and feel ready to proceed, as you sit in your chair in the western quarter of the temple, imagine that you slowly open your eyes upon a different world. You are in the middle of a circle of trees, and it is an evening in autumn. Beyond the trunks of the trees you see water shimmering in every direction, for you are on a small island, an island in the midst of a vast sea. Before you the first stars are coming out; behind you the sun is setting.

You are seated on a cubical, backless seat of stone in the western quarter of the circle of trees, facing an altar of stone in the center. This latter is covered by a blue altar cloth that falls to the ground on all sides, and on the side facing you is embroidered in silver the geomantic character of Cyswllt as it appears here. On the altar are the same implements you have on the altar in your temple: the three candles in candlesticks, the cauldrons of water and incense, and the cross and circle, which are arranged as in the Bardic Grade.

Cyswllt

The first time you enter the inner grove of water, simply remain seated on the cubical seat of stone in the western quarter, imagining the altar, the clearing around it, the circle of trees, and the sea stretching in all directions around it. Imagine it as clearly as you can; see red and golden leaves begin to flutter to the ground around you, smell the salt spray of the ocean, listen to the waves splash on the beach and the wind sigh through the branches of the trees. When you are ready, close the practice as you would close any other meditation, perform the License to Depart, and then close the temple in the Bardic Grade in the usual way.

The second and subsequent times you enter the inner grove of water, you may remain seated on the cubical seat of stone or you may rise and move around the inner grove. When you do this, leave your physical body in its place in the chair in your temple; simply imagine yourself rising and moving about the grove. Go to the altar and then walk about the circle or, if you wish, pass through the ring of trees and walk on the beach that surrounds the little island. Notice if anything appears to have been left for you to find on the ground around the altar; sometimes signs from the inner realms of being may take this form, and if this happens, what you find should be explored thoroughly in meditation. Every detail of your movements and perceptions should be imagined as clearly as possible.

Finally, when you are ready to do so, imagine yourself during one or more of these workings performing the Summoning Ritual of the Water Pentagram inside the inner grove of water. Do this exactly as you would if you were performing the same ritual in your temple in the physical world; imagine every gesture and word just as though you were doing them with your physical body. As before, do not perform the Banishing Ritual in this or any inner grove.

The First Path

Once you have practiced the work given above often enough that you can open a temple in the Bardic Grade, perform the Calling of Water, enter into the inner grove of water, perform a Summoning Ritual of the Water Pentagram there, then leave the inner grove, perform the License to Depart, and close the temple—all from memory and with good effect—you may begin the next stage of the work. This involves connecting the two inner groves you have already formulated and traveling along the connection between them.

In one sense, as you have learned already, the path connecting the inner groves of earth and water passes from the north to the west of the sacred circle of the elements; in another, it is the first path of the Druidical Tree of Life, the path that ascends from Naf, the sphere of the material world, to Ner, the sphere of the fluidic energies and influences that lie behind and beyond the world of dense matter. The Bardic Grade, which is preeminently the grade of the four elements, takes the first of these as primary, but both should be kept in mind; the second will be of greater importance in the grade to come.

The training you have done heretofore in visualizing the inner groves of earth and water, and picturing yourself moving about in them, develops the skills you will need in order to traverse the first path. This journey is done using the imagination, for it is by means of the imagination that human consciousness most readily apprehends the aetherial world, that dimension of existence that extends immediately beyond the material world.

You will therefore begin your workings of the first path in the same way that you practiced the Work of Earth: by opening a temple in the Bardic Grade, performing the Calling of Earth, then seating yourself in meditation and entering into the inner temple of earth after the appropriate preliminaries and color breathing, and finally performing the Summoning Ritual of the Earth Pentagram in your imagination in the inner temple. When you have finished this and taken your seat once more upon the cubical stone seat in the north, become aware of three ghostly portals as they slowly appear before you at the southern edge of the circle of trees that surrounds the inner grove.

These portals have the shape of trilithons, like those at Stonehenge: two rough stone uprights with a lintel of stone across the top and enough space below the lintel and between the uprights that you may pass through. A cloth, like a banner or veil, hangs over the lintel and fills the space between the uprights, blocking your view of what lies beyond. There is one portal directly ahead of you, to the south, which has a red cloth; one to your left, to the southeast, which has a yellow cloth; and one to your right, to the southwest, which has a blue cloth. It is the latter alone that concerns you at this stage of your training.

When you feel ready, rise in your imagination from the cubical stone seat and walk to the portal of the southwest. As you approach it, you see that the blue cloth bears the geomantic character Pen y Ddraig, as shown on the following page, embroidered on it in silver. Stand before the portal and imagine yourself saying aloud, "In the great name of

SIRONA and all the powers of water, I seek guidance to the inner grove of water. May a true and faithful guide come to me."

Pen y Ddraig

Shortly thereafter, someone or something will pull aside the cloth. It may be a wise old Druid or a child; it may be an animal sent to guide you, or it may be something else. When it appears, whatever it may be, ask it, "In the name of **SIRONA**, will you guide me faithfully to the inner grove of water?" Wait for its answer. If the answer is affirmative, however expressed, all is well and you may then follow your guide. If the answer is negative or the apparent guide refuses to answer, say, "Depart, then, and let a true guide come to me." The entity will depart and another will come, to whom you must put the same test.

Once you have found a guide who passes this test, follow its guidance. Once you pass through the portal and the cloth falls behind you, you will see a path leading through the forest, lit by stars. Your guide will take you along this path, directing you perhaps by words, perhaps by gestures. As you follow the path you may encounter other beings, who may or may not speak to you; you may also find objects lying in the path or placed alongside it. In all cases, ask your guide what you should do, and pay careful attention to what you see and learn.

You will notice as you travel that the sky is getting lighter, but not with the gray light of dawn; rather, it is as if you are walking backwards in time, from midnight through evening toward sunset. After a certain time, the path will bring you to the shore of the sea, and you will need to ask your guide how to cross the waters. There may be a boat tied up where the path meets the shore, or a ship may come for you, or a whale; you may find yourself walking across the waves or beneath them.

One way or another, though, your guide will take you the rest of the way to your destination, the small island with the ring of trees, within which is the inner grove of water. You will enter the inner grove of water through a portal like the one you passed through in the inner grove of earth; a cloth hangs across it, bearing the geomantic figure

Pen y Ddraig, but here the cloth is green, and the portal stands in the northeast part of the inner grove. Thank your guide for the guidance and help you have received; bid him, her, or it farewell; and take your seat on the cubical stone seat in the western quarter of the inner grove. After a moment, rise in your imagination and perform the Summoning Ritual of the Water Pentagram, then return to your seat in the west.

When you are ready to finish the working, close the practice as you would close any other meditation, and then perform the License to Depart, which should be the one appropriate to the element of earth. While you have reached the realm of water on the inner levels of existence, you called on the element of earth to open the working, and so you should release the elemental spirits and powers of earth when you close; the same will apply to each of the other elements. Once this is done, close the temple in the Bardic Grade as usual.

When you have finished, write down a detailed account of what you experienced while traversing the first path. Be sure to include all the things that were said to you, as best you can recall them, and describe in as much detail as you can the things you saw and encountered. In your daily meditations thereafter, meditate on each of these things, extracting as much wisdom and knowledge from them as you can.

This is the secret to making the best and wisest use of the art of pathworking, as the exercise you have just performed is called. A pathworking that has not been explored in detail in repeated meditations is like a letter that has not been opened and read. As a general rule, a single pathworking should provide you with at least one week of daily meditations, and very possibly more.

When you have finished meditating on every detail of your first journey on the first path, repeat the process, but this time begin from the inner grove of water. The process is the same in every detail, except that you perform the Calling of Water, enter the inner grove of water, and perform the Summoning Ritual of the Water Pentagram there; the ghostly portals that appear to you are before you in the east, to your right in the southeast, and to your left in the northeast, and the one through which you pass, the portal of the northeast, has a green cloth bearing the geomantic figure Pen y Ddraig.

You will call for a guide as before, but in the name of **CERNUNNOS** and all the powers of earth, and you will test any entity who comes in response with the name **CERNUNNOS**. Your guide will then lead you to the water's edge, and you will cross the water by whatever means your guide may suggest. As you proceed, the sky will darken and the stars come out as you pass from sunset to midnight, and the journey across the water will give way to a journey down a forest path; you will again encounter beings and things, and these will most likely not be those you encountered in your first pathworking on this path. Finally, you will reach the inner grove of earth, where you will thank your guide; part company with him, her, or it; and perform the Summoning Ritual of the Earth Pentagram. Thereafter, you will close the pathworking as you would any other meditation, perform the License to Depart appropriate to water, and close the temple as usual in the Bardic Grade.

When you have meditated thoroughly on all the symbols, images, and things said to you, perform the pathworking again from earth to water in exactly the same way you did before; you will find again that the details of your experience will differ, and you may encounter a different guide as well. Repeat this, alternating the direction you travel the path and meditating thoroughly on everything you experience, until you have done a total of three pathworkings from earth to water and three from water to earth. At this point you are prepared to pass to the next stage of this aspect of your Bardic training, the Work of Air.

The Work of Air.

LIKE THE WORKS OF Earth and Water, which you have already learned, the Work of Air is performed within a temple open in the Bardic Grade, and it consists partly of ceremonial practice and partly of work performed in the aetherial world by means of the imagination. The ceremonial portion, or Ritual of Air, is divided into two parts, the Calling of Air and the License to Depart; both these parts are learned prior to beginning work on the aetherial portion, which is also twofold: the formulation of the inner grove of air and the pathworkings to that inner grove from the inner groves of earth and water.

In preparation for this work, it is recommended that you review in meditation all the symbolism of the element of air that has been presented to you in the knowledge lectures of the Ovate Grade.

The Calling of Air

Begin the Calling of Air standing at the west of the altar, facing east. Perform the Summoning Ritual of the Air Pentagram as described in the introductory lecture of this grade. When you have finished, go around the temple with the sun—that is, in a clockwise direction—to the eastern quarter and face outwards, toward the east.

Trace a summoning pentagram of air like those you traced in the pentagram ritual you have just completed. Imagine that you are drawing it in the air in lines of glowing yellow light. Point to its center and say: "In the great name of **BELISAMA**, the lady of air, Spirits of Air, behold the rays of the Golden Dawn! Come ye forth and assist me in this work of air."

Next, in the center of the pentagram, draw the Sigil of the Spring Equinox as portrayed on the next page, and visualize it drawn in glowing yellow light. Point to its center and say: "By the hawk of May in the heights of heaven and the mystical gate of the eastern stars, Spirits of Air, behold the rays of the Golden Dawn! Come ye forth and assist me in this work of air."

Sigil of the Spring Equinox

Now make the Sign of Air as follows. Raise your arms up and out to the sides, elbows and wrists bent, palms facing upwards at the level of the top of your head, fingertips pointed inward toward your head, as though you were supporting a weight above you. Say: "By all the powers of the eastern quarter of the world, by the splendor of the dawn and the renewal of spring, by the strength of the rushing winds and the everlasting sky, Spirits of Air, behold the rays of the Golden Dawn! Come ye forth and assist me in this work of air."

Return to the west of the altar, face east, and say, "I proclaim that the powers of air have been duly invoked." This concludes the Calling of Air.

The License to Depart

When you have finished the Calling of Air, or when any additional work you have done with the subtle forces of air is complete, proceed to the License to Depart, which releases the elemental powers you have invoked in the working.

Begin the License to Depart standing west of the altar, facing east. Proceed with the sun—that is, in a clockwise direction to the eastern quarter—and face outwards, toward the east. Make the Sign of Air and say: "With the blessings of **BELISAMA** and of the hawk of May in the heights of heaven, and with thanks for your assistance in this work of air, Spirits of Air, I license ye to depart. Go in peace, and peace be between ye and me."

Then trace the banishing air pentagram toward the east. Return to the west side of the altar, moving around the temple with the sun, and perform the Banishing Ritual of the Air Pentagram as described in the introductory lecture of this grade. When you have finished, proceed to close the temple with the usual ceremony.

Practice opening a temple in the Bardic Grade, performing the Calling of Air and the License to Depart, and closing a temple in the Bardic Grade until you can do the entire working by memory, without reference to notes of any kind. Once you have reached this stage of practice, you may proceed to add the next stage of the Work of Air: the inner grove of air.

The Inner Grove of Air

Before you perform this working, place a chair in the eastern quarter of the temple, facing inwards toward the altar. When you have opened the temple in the Bardic Grade and performed the Calling of Air, take your seat there and enter into meditation in the way you have already learned to do. Your pore breathing for this inner grove working will be yellow, the color of air, and you will again simply draw in the air energies with each in-breath and allow them to flow out on each out-breath.

When you have done this for a time and feel ready to proceed, as you sit in your chair in the eastern quarter of the temple, imagine that you slowly open your eyes upon a different world. You are in the middle of a circle of trees, and it is daybreak in spring. The trees around you are dressed in the pale green of springtime's new leaves, and some have already burst into flower; beyond the circle of trunks you see only blue sky and scattered clouds, and after a moment you realize that you are on the summit of a hill. The hill is surrounded by meadows of tall grass, over which the wind blows unceasingly. Behind you the sun is just rising, and the last stars are fading out ahead of you in the west.

You are seated on a cubical, backless seat of stone in the eastern quarter of the circle of trees, facing an altar of stone in the center. This latter is covered by a yellow altar cloth that falls to the ground on all sides, and on the side facing you is embroidered in silver the geomantic character of Elw as it appears here. On the altar are the same implements you have on the altar in your temple: the three candles in candlesticks, the cauldrons of water and incense, and the cross and circle, which are arranged as in the Bardic Grade.

Elw

The first time you enter the inner grove of air, simply remain seated on the cubical seat of stone in the eastern quarter, imagining the altar, the clearing around it, and the circle of trees and the grassy fields stretching in all directions around it. Imagine it as clearly as you can; see the new leaves fluttering in the wind on the trees around you, smell the scent of the flowers, listen to the wind whisper among the branches. When you are ready, close the practice as you would close any other meditation: perform the License to Depart and then close the temple in the Bardic Grade in the usual way.

The second and subsequent times you enter the inner grove of air, you may remain seated on the cubical seat of stone or you may rise and move around the inner grove. Go to the altar and then walk about the circle or, if you wish, pass through the ring of trees and walk a short distance out into the meadows. Notice if anything appears to have been left for you to find on the ground around the altar; sometimes signs from the inner realms of being may take this form, and if this happens, what you find should be explored thoroughly in meditation. Every detail of your movements and perceptions should be imagined as clearly as possible.

Finally, when you are ready to do so, imagine yourself during one or more of these workings performing the Summoning Ritual of the Air Pentagram inside the inner grove of air. Do this exactly as you would if you were performing the same ritual in your temple in the physical world; imagine every gesture and word just as though you were doing them with your physical body. As before, do not perform the Banishing Ritual in this or any inner grove.

The Second and Third Paths

Once you have practiced the work given above often enough that you can open a temple in the Bardic Grade, perform the Calling of Air, enter into the inner grove of air and perform a Summoning Ritual of the Air Pentagram there, then leave the inner grove, perform the License to Depart, and close the temple—all from memory and with good effect—you may begin the next stage of the work. This involves connecting the inner grove you have just reached with the two you have already formulated and traveling along the connections between them. As with the first path, the two paths worked in this phase of the work are traveled in the imagination by means of the art of pathworking.

The second path, which runs from the inner grove of earth to that of air, should be done before the third path, which runs from the inner grove of water to that of air. Just as you did with the first path, you will begin working the second path by opening a temple in the Bardic Grade, performing the Calling of Earth, entering into meditation and the inner grove of earth, and performing the Summoning Ritual of the Earth Pentagram in the usual way. When you are well established in the inner grove of earth, imagine the three ghostly portals appearing at the southern edge of the clearing.

This time you will be venturing through the left-hand portal, which has a yellow cloth hanging across it. Upon the cloth is embroidered in silver the geomantic character Ffordd, as shown here. Stand before the portal and imagine yourself saying aloud, "In the great name of **BELISAMA** and all the powers of air, I seek guidance to the inner grove of air. May a true and faithful guide come to me."

Ffordd

As before, a guide will come to the portal, and you should test it by asking, "In the name of **BELISAMA**, will you guide me faithfully to the inner grove of air?" If it answers affirmatively, follow your guide; if the answer is negative or the apparent guide refuses to answer, say, "Depart, then, and let a true guide come to me." The entity will depart and another will come, to whom you must put the same test.

Once you have found your true guide and begin your journey, your guide will lead you along a path through the forest. Pay careful attention, as before, to everything you encounter and anything that is said to you by your guide or any other being. As you travel you will notice that the sky is gradually turning pale and the stars are beginning to fade as midnight gives way to the small hours of the morning, and then to the gray time before dawn. After a certain point your path will lead you out of the forest and across wide meadows of tall grass, and finally you will see a low hill before you, surrounded with a circle of trees. As you approach it you will recognize it as the inner grove of air.

You will enter the inner grove of air through a portal like the one you passed through in the inner grove of earth; a cloth hangs across it bearing the geomantic figure Ffordd, but here the cloth is green and the portal stands in the northwest part of the inner grove. Thank your guide for the guidance and help you have received; bid him, her, or it farewell; and take your seat on the cubical stone seat in the eastern quarter of the inner grove. After a moment, rise in your imagination and perform the Summoning Ritual of the Air Pentagram, then return to your seat in the east.

When you are ready to finish the working, close the practice as you would close any other meditation, and then perform the License to Depart, which should be the one appropriate to the element of earth. Once this is done, close the temple in the Bardic Grade as usual. When you have finished, write down a detailed account of what you experienced while traversing the first path, and be prepared to spend the next week meditating on all the details of your experience.

When you have finished meditating on every detail of your first journey on the second path, repeat the process, but this time begin from the inner grove of air. The process is the same in every detail, except that you perform the Calling of Air, enter the inner grove of air, and perform the Summoning Ritual of the Air Pentagram there; the ghostly portals that appear to you are before you in the west, to your left in the southwest, and to your right in the northwest, and the one through which you pass, the portal of the northwest, has a green cloth bearing the geomantic figure Ffordd.

You will call for a guide as before, but in the name of **CERNUNNOS** and all the powers of earth, and you will test any entity who comes in response with the name **CERNUNNOS**. Your guide will then lead you across the meadows and, eventually, into the forest. As you proceed, the sky will darken and the stars come out as you pass from sunset to midnight; you will again encounter beings and things, and these will most likely not be those you encountered in your first pathworking on this path. Finally, you will reach the inner grove of earth, where you will thank your guide and part company with him, her, or it, then perform the Summoning Ritual of the Earth Pentagram. Thereafter, you will close the pathworking, perform the License to Depart appropriate to air, and close the temple as usual in the Bardic Grade.

As before, you should perform this pathworking three times in each direction, from earth to air and from air to earth, meditating on all the details of one pathworking before proceeding to the next. In this way you will gain the most benefit from your work. Once you have done this, you may proceed to the third path.

This path runs from the inner grove of water to that of air, and it is worked in the same way as the first and second paths. First open a temple in the Bardic Grade, perform the Calling of Water, enter into meditation and the inner grove of water, and perform the Summoning Ritual of the Water Pentagram. In your imagination, take your place on the cubical seat of stone and watch as the three ghostly portals appear before you in the eastern side of the inner grove.

The portal you will be using in this working is the central one, facing due east. A yellow cloth hangs across it, and on the cloth the geomantic character Merch, as shown here, is embroidered in silver. As you did with the second path, you will approach the portal and call for a guide in the name of **BELISAMA** and all the powers of air, and you will test any being who appears in response by the name of **BELISAMA**. Once you have found a true guide, you may follow its lead through the portal and begin your journey.

Merch

As you approach the edge of the little island on which the inner grove of water is located, your guide will indicate how you are to cross the waters. Follow its guidance, paying close attention to everything you experience and listening carefully to whatever beings you may encounter and whatever your guide may say to you. After a time the voyage will bring you to a shore, and beyond the shore, a path will lead eastwards through meadows of tall grass. You will discover as you travel that, in some mysterious way, evening has given way to morning without passing through the intervening night! You may have further encounters in the meadows, but finally you will come within sight of the low hill surrounded by trees that is the inner grove of air.

Here you will enter through the middlemost of the three portals in the west, which is veiled with a blue cloth bearing the geomantic character Merch. Thank your guide and bid him, her, or it farewell; take your place on the cubical seat of stone in the east, and then rise in your imagination and perform the Summoning Ritual of the Air Pentagram in the inner grove of air. Return to your seat in the east, and finish the working in the usual way with the License to Depart of Water, and then close the temple in the Bardic Grade.

When you have meditated thoroughly on the images and ideas that you received during the pathworking, work the same path in the other direction, beginning in the inner grove of air and proceeding to that of water. You have already learned how to work a path in the reverse direction; the same principles apply here. As before, plan on working the third path three times in each direction, from water to air and from air to water, before going on. Once you have done this, you are prepared to pass to the final stage of this aspect of your Bardic training: the Work of Fire.

The Work of Fire.

LIKE THE WORKS OF Earth, Water, and Air, which you have already learned, the Work of Fire is performed within a temple open in the Bardic Grade, and it consists partly of ceremonial practice and partly of work performed in the aetherial world by means of the imagination. The ceremonial portion, or Ritual of Fire, is divided into two parts, the Calling of Fire and the License to Depart; both these parts are learned prior to beginning work on the aetherial portion, which is also twofold: the formulation of the inner grove of fire and the pathworkings to that inner grove from the inner groves of earth, water, and air.

In preparation for this work, it is recommended that you review in meditation all the symbolism of the element of fire that has been presented to you in the knowledge lectures of the Ovate Grade.

The Calling of Fire

Begin the Calling of Fire standing at the west of the altar, facing east. Perform the Summoning Ritual of the Fire Pentagram as described in the introductory lecture of this grade. When you have finished, go around the temple with the sun—that is, in a clockwise direction—to the southern quarter, and face outwards, toward the south.

Trace a summoning pentagram of fire, like those you traced in the pentagram ritual you have just completed. Imagine that you are drawing it in the air in lines of glowing red light. Point to its center and say: "In the great name of TOUTATIS, the lord of fire, Spirits of Fire, behold the rays of the Golden Dawn! Come ye forth and assist me in this work of fire."

Next, in the center of the pentagram, draw the Sigil of the Summer Solstice as portrayed on the next page, and visualize it drawn in glowing red light. Point to its center and say: "By the white stag who dwells in the summer greenwood and the mystical gate of the southern stars, Spirits of Fire, behold the rays of the Golden Dawn! Come ye forth and assist me in this work of fire."

Sigil of the Summer Solstice

Now make the Sign of Fire as follows. Bring both hands above your face, pressing the backs of the hands to your forehead; spread the thumb apart from the fingers; touch the tips of the thumbs to each other and the tips of the forefingers to each other, forming a triangle before your head, point upwards. Say: "By all the powers of the southern quarter of the world, by the brilliant light of noon and the heat of summer, by the glory of the dancing flame and the verdant fire of life, Spirits of Fire, behold the rays of the Golden Dawn! Come ye forth and assist me in this work of fire."

Return to the west of the altar, face east, and say: "I proclaim that the powers of fire have been duly invoked." This concludes the Calling of Fire.

The License to Depart

When you have finished the Calling of Fire, or when any additional work you have done with the subtle forces of fire is complete, proceed to the License to Depart, which releases the elemental powers you have invoked in the working.

Begin the License to Depart standing west of the altar, facing east. Proceed with the sun—that is, in a clockwise direction to the southern quarter—and face outwards, toward the south. Make the Sign of Fire and say: "With the blessings of **TOUTATIS** and of the white stag who dwells in the summer greenwood, and with thanks for your assistance in this work of fire, Spirits of Fire, I license ye to depart. Go in peace, and peace be between ye and me."

Then trace the banishing fire pentagram toward the south. Return to the west side of the altar, moving around the temple with the sun, and perform the Banishing Ritual of the Fire Pentagram as described in the introductory lecture of this grade. When you have finished, proceed to close the temple with the usual ceremony.

Practice opening a temple in the Bardic Grade, performing the Calling of Fire and the License to Depart, and closing a temple in the Bardic Grade until you can do the entire working by memory, without reference to notes of any kind. Once you have reached this stage of practice, you may proceed to add the next stage of the Work of Fire: the inner grove of fire.

The Inner Grove of Fire

Before you perform this working, place a chair in the southern quarter of the temple, facing inwards toward the altar. When you have opened the temple in the Bardic Grade and performed the Calling of Fire, take your seat there and enter into meditation in the way you have already learned to do. Your pore breathing for this inner grove working will be red, the color of fire, and you will again simply draw in the fire energies with each in-breath and allow them to flow out on each out-breath.

When you have done this for a time and feel ready to proceed, as you sit in your chair in the southern quarter of the temple, imagine that you slowly open your eyes upon a different world. You are seated in the middle of a circle of trees, and it is noon in high summer. The sun blazes down from high overhead, and the trees that surround you are of kinds that are found in hot and dry countries. Out beyond the circle of their trunks, you see a desert landscape stretching away into the distance on all sides; the air shimmers with heat, and far away to one side smoke and flame rise from a distant volcano. You realize that the inner grove of fire is an oasis in the midst of this hot, dry land.

You are seated on a cubical, backless seat of stone in the southern quarter of the circle of trees, facing an altar of stone in the center. This latter is covered by a red altar cloth that falls to the ground on all sides, and on the side facing you is embroidered in silver the geomantic character of Colled as it appears here. On the altar are the same implements you have on the altar in your temple: the three candles in candlesticks, the cauldrons of water and incense, and the cross and circle, which are arranged as in the Bardic Grade.

Colled

The first time you enter the inner grove of fire, simply remain seated on the cubical seat of stone in the southern quarter, imagining the altar, the clearing around it, the circle of trees and the desert landscape stretching in all directions around it. Imagine it as clearly as you can: feel the sun's heat blazing down from above; smell the resinous scent of the trees and the dry, dusty smell of the desert air; hear the soft hissing of sand as the wind blows it from dune to dune. When you are ready, close the practice as you would close any other meditation: perform the License to Depart, then close the temple in the Bardic Grade in the usual way.

The second and subsequent times you enter the inner grove of fire, you may remain seated on the cubical seat of stone or you may rise and move around the inner grove. Go to the altar and then walk about the circle or, if you wish, pass through the ring of trees and walk a short distance out into the desert. Notice if anything appears to have been left for you to find on the ground around the altar; sometimes signs from the inner realms of being may take this form, and if this happens, what you find should be explored thoroughly in meditation. Every detail of your movements and perceptions should be imagined as clearly as possible.

Finally, when you are ready to do so, imagine yourself during one or more of these workings performing the Summoning Ritual of the Fire Pentagram inside the inner grove of fire. Do this exactly as you would if you were performing the same ritual in your temple in the physical world; imagine every gesture and word just as though you were doing them with your physical body. As before, do not perform the Banishing Ritual in any inner grove.

The Fourth, Fifth, and Sixth Paths

Once you have practiced the work given above often enough that you can open a temple in the Bardic Grade, perform the Calling of Fire, enter into the inner grove of fire, perform a Summoning Ritual of the Fire Pentagram there, then leave the inner grove, perform the License to Depart, and close the temple—all from memory and with good effect—you may begin the next stage of the work. This involves connecting the inner grove you have just reached with the three you have already formulated and traveling along the connections between them by means of the art of pathworking.

The method you will use for these three paths is identical to those you have already used. The fourth path runs from earth to fire and begins at the middlemost of the three ghostly portals on the southern side of the inner grove of earth. That portal is veiled with a red cloth that bears the geomantic character of Pobl, as shown below, in silver embroidery. You will call your guide by the name of CERNUNNOS and all the powers of earth, and test any being that appears by the name of CERNUNNOS. The fourth path begins in the forest and ends in the desert, and halfway along you will discover that midnight has suddenly changed to noon.

Pobl

The fifth path runs from water to fire and begins at the rightmost of the three ghostly portals in the inner grove of water. That portal is also veiled with a red cloth, but the geomantic character embroidered on it in silver is Mab, as shown below. You will call your guide by the name of SIRONA and all the powers of water, and test any being that appears by the name of SIRONA. The fifth path begins with a voyage across the water and ends with a journey across the desert, and as you travel it you will notice evening turning backwards to noon, as though time was running in reverse.

Mab

The sixth path runs from air to fire and begins at the leftmost of the three ghostly portals in the inner grove of air. That portal is veiled with a red cloth, like the others, but the geomantic character embroidered on it in silver is Bendith Fach, as shown on the following page. You will call your guide by the name of BELISAMA and all the powers of air, and test any being that appears by the name of BELISAMA. The sixth path begins in grassland and ends in the desert, and as you travel it you will see morning turn to noon in the ordinary way of nature.

Bendith Fach

When you return along each of these paths, you will pass through all three of the ghostly portals in the inner grove of fire, which appear before you on the northern side of the grove. The portal on the northern side, in the middle of the others, is the portal of the fourth path; it bears a green cloth embroidered in silver with the geomantic character Pobl. The portal to the northwest, on the left-hand side, is the portal of the fifth path; it bears a blue cloth embroidered in silver with the geomantic character Mab. The portal to the northeast, on the right-hand side, is the portal of the sixth path; it bears a yellow cloth embroidered in silver with the geomantic character Bendith Fach. When you approach each of these portals, you will call for a guide in the name of **TOUTATIS** and the powers of fire, and test any being that presents itself in the name of **TOUTATIS**; only when you have found a guide who passes that test will you proceed.

As with your previous pathworkings, the workings of the fourth, fifth, and sixth paths should be done in a particular order. You will begin working the fourth path from earth to fire, and after meditating on your experiences, work the same path from fire to earth; this is repeated until you have worked the path three times in each direction, meditating on everything you encounter in one pathworking before you proceed to the next. Once you have done this, begin the fifth path from the inner grove of water to that of fire, and thereafter work it from fire to water; repeat this, meditating between each working, until you have worked the path three times in each direction. The sixth path, finally, is worked first from air to fire, and then from fire to air; this is repeated until this path, too, has been worked three times in each direction. When you have completed all this, you will have finished this aspect of your work in the Bardic Grade and be properly prepared for the more advanced practices that will be encountered in the grade to come.

Additional Lectures of the Bardic Grade.

On the Tree of Life

THE TREE OF LIFE has already been introduced to you in a variety of forms in your studies in the Ovate Grade. In the Western Mystery Schools it is the most important as well as the most commonly used symbolical glyph. Its nature, symbolism, and uses will be central to much of the work before you in this and the subsequent grade, and a careful study of the material in this lecture, along with the recommended reading, will thus greatly assist your progress.

I. On the Origins of the Tree of Life

The version of the Tree of Life diagram used at present in the majority of Mystery Schools in the Western world came to those schools by way of the Kabbalah, the branch of the Mystery Teachings that belongs to the Jewish people. It was during the Renaissance that Christian initiates of the Mysteries studied the Kabbalah closely, in the hope that a better understanding of the Jewish roots of Christianity might assist them in rediscovering the inner dimensions of their own faith, of which so much had been lost in the persecutions of the Gnostics, Cathars, and Templars. In this they were not disappointed, and from this circumstance came a belief, which is still common in certain Mystery Schools, that the Tree of Life is exclusively Jewish in its origin.

This is, however, a misconception, and the diagram on the following page may help to clarify matters. This diagram is the T'ai Chi T'u, or Diagram of Ultimate Polarity, and it first appeared in the writings of the great Chinese philosopher Chou Tun-yi. Chou's diagram appears in an extensive treatise that explains, in terms of the Taoist and Confucian teachings of China, the origins of all things in the cosmos. It incorporates all the fundamental elements of traditional Chinese Mysteries—the beginning of the cosmos from Wu Chi, the Limitless; their polarization into yang and yin, the active and passive potentialities of the cosmos; the further differentiation of the five elements of Chinese magical tradition; then the coalescence of the whole into male and female creative forces and, from this, the creation of the manifest cosmos.

The similarities between this diagram and the Tree of Life are by no means superficial. Each of the elements of the T'ai Chi T'u has the same function as the corresponding part of the Tree of Life—for example, the sphere of Earth in the center is the principle of balance and harmony, just as is the sephirah Tiphareth, which occupies the same place in the Jewish version of the Tree.

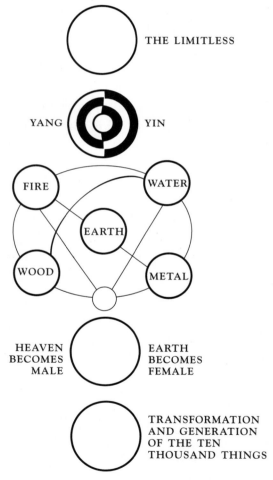

The T'ai Chi T'u, or Diagram of Ultimate Polarity

Chou lived and taught in the eleventh century of our era. The first version of the Tree of Life in the Jewish Kabbalah was created in the school of Rabbi Isaac the Blind in the city of Narbonne around AD 1150, roughly a century after Chou's time. It is thus evident that Chou was not copying a Jewish diagram, and it is no more likely that Rabbi Isaac or any of his students had knowledge of Chinese; rather, both teachers clearly drew on older teaching diagrams that were current in Mystery Schools across the Old World quite probably for some time before either of these great teachers devised their own variant on the common theme.

That common theme may well date back to classical times, and perhaps further still. The number mysticism of the Pythagorean school, which was founded in the sixth century BC, makes use of a set of symbolic attributions to the first ten numbers, and these correspond closely to the symbolism of the Tree of Life as this has come down to us. Similarly, the ten essential concepts discussed by Aristotle in his *Categories* can be assigned to the Tree of Life with a precision that suggests the great Greek philosopher was familiar with some similar pattern—perhaps one of the unwritten teachings of Plato, in whose school he studied.

It is in this sense that the Tree of Life has been adopted into the Druidical tradition in place of whatever lost diagrams might have been used by Druidical instructors in ancient times. As you have already learned, each sphere of the Tree has its own proper title, a divine name associated with it, and a number of other symbols and meanings; those correspondences form the basis for the more complex material outlined in this lecture.

II. The Ten Spheres of the Tree

Down through the centuries, the Tree of Life has become the center of a wealth of symbolism and philosophy, but at its core it is a structure of immense simplicity. It begins with pure being, the simplest and most basic attribute that can be applied to any existing thing whatsoever, and descends step by step to the full complexity of manifest existence. In this way, according to tradition, it reflects the way the cosmos itself came into being and likewise reflects the structure of the higher dimensions of existence. In this is concealed an important teaching, for creation is not a thing that took place once and for all at the beginning of time; it is a continuing process by which the cosmos is brought into being anew at every moment.

CELI, THE FIRST SPHERE, is the beginning of that process of creation and the first element of the creative triad, just as it is the highest and most abstract of the realms of existence. It is pure being without any other attribute; strictly speaking, one may say no more concerning it than IT IS. In it there is no space, time, or change, for the manifestation of each of these things requires more than one thing to exist—space can be known only by the separation between here and there, time by the difference between before and after, change by the distinction between the thing changing and the thing changed—and in Celi, there is only One Thing.

In sacred geometry it is the point, the symbol of being;

In the categories of Aristotle it is position;

In the T'ai Chi T'u it is Wu Chi, the limitless and unpolarized;

In the Kabbalah it is Kether, the crown.

PERYDD, THE SECOND SPHERE, is the next step in the process by which the cosmos comes into being, the second element in the creative triad. In the language of an ancient metaphor, pure being overflows into becoming as a still lake overflows into a river, and so change comes into existence. As yet abstract, beyond space and time, it is pure becoming, without any permanence or rest. It is the origin and first exemplar of all generation and corruption, all coming into being and passing away, and it is therefore also the source of all power, for power is the capacity to bring about change.

In sacred geometry it is the line, the symbol of extension;

In the categories of Aristotle it is action;

In the T'ai Chi T'u it is Yang, the principle of heaven;

In the Kabbalah it is Chokmah, wisdom.

DOFYDD, THE THIRD SPHERE, completes the triad of creation. It exists on the same plane of being as Perydd, and thus is shown on the same level in the diagram of the Tree of Life; indeed, these two spheres, Perydd and Dofydd, cannot exist in isolation from one another, and their equivalents in the T'ai Chi T'u are thus shown as two halves of one great circle. Where Perydd is change, Dofydd is rest; where Perydd acts, Dofydd is affected by that action. It is thus the principle of all stillness, passivity, and receptiveness, and it is the ultimate root of substance.

In sacred geometry it is the circle, the symbol of limitation;

In the categories of Aristotle it is affection (that is, being affected);

In the T'ai Chi T'u it is Yin, the principle of earth;

In the Kabbalah it is Binah, understanding.

BETWEEN DOFYDD AND THE SEVEN LOWER SPHERES lies a discontinuity, or existential distinction, known traditionally as the Abyss, which separates the circle of Ceugant from that of Gwynfydd. The Abyss lies between those realities that are pure, abstract, and absolute (which are above it) and those that are composite, concrete, and relative (which are below). The Abyss may not be traversed by any created being; only what is already above the Abyss may inhabit the realm of the creative triad. In the innermost core of each human soul is a spark of the light that is above the Abyss, and it is what makes the human soul a child of eternity and an inheritor of the power and wisdom of the eternal gods; yet this spark is latent until it be kindled into flame. Of this more will be said in a further grade.

ENER, THE FOURTH SPHERE, is the first of the spheres below the Abyss, reflecting the first sphere on the plane of manifestation, and it is thus the highest reality that may be comprehended by the human mind. It is the sphere of concrete being; that is, it establishes the capacity for individual things to come into being, exist, and pass away. At this stage in the creative process, no individual things have yet emerged; only the conditions under which they may exist have emerged, and those conditions are comprised in Ener. This sphere may most easily be comprehended under the image of space.

In sacred geometry it is the equal-armed cross, the symbol of radiation;

In the categories of Aristotle it is space;

In the T'ai Chi T'u it is the element of water;

In the Kabbalah it is Chesed, mercy.

MODUR, THE FIFTH SPHERE, is the second sphere below the Abyss and thus reflects the second sphere on the plane of manifestation. It is the sphere of concrete becoming; that is, it establishes the process by which individual things come into being, exist, and pass away. As shown in the diagram of the Tree of Life, it exists on the same level as Ener, a level on which individual things have not yet emerged; it is the principle of all the processes of generation and corruption prior to any specific manifestation of those processes. It may therefore most easily be comprehended under the image of time.

In sacred geometry it is the vesica piscis, the symbol of creation;

In the categories of Aristotle it is time;

In the T'ai Chi T'u it is the element of fire;

In the Kabbalah it is Geburah, severity.

MUNER, THE SIXTH SPHERE, is the third sphere below the Abyss and therefore completes the reflection of the creative triad on the plane of manifestation. Concrete being and concrete becoming unite here to bring individual things into existence; as it reflects the third sphere, Muner grants each such individual thing the capacity to remain itself and retain its own identity. Here, for the first time in the creative process of the cosmos, the distinction between one thing and another has meaning. Where Ener and Modur are the spheres of space and time respectively, Muner is the sphere of the individual thing, filling a certain space and existing for a certain time.

In sacred geometry it is the equilateral triangle, the symbol of manifestation;

In the categories of Aristotle it is substance;

In the T'ai Chi T'u it is the central element of earth;

In the Kabbalah it is Tiphareth, beauty.

BETWEEN MUNER AND THE FOUR SPHERES BELOW IT lies a barrier—not an existential distinction like the Abyss but a limit traced by the capacities of the uninitiated human soul—traditionally called the Veil. This is the dividing line between the circle of Abred—which represents the powers, perceptions, and capabilities that the human soul has evolved heretofore—and the circle of Gwynfydd, which represents those further powers, perceptions, and capabilities that the human soul has not yet evolved collectively but that each human being has the potential to attain. The work of initiation in which each Druidical initiate is engaged has, as its goal, the parting of the Veil, so that he may rightly claim the full birthright of humanity.

BYW, THE SEVENTH SPHERE, is the sphere of fire and represents the capacity of each individual thing to act upon its surroundings, reflecting the second sphere on the plane of individual existence. Included in Byw are all the motive forces and potentials for action present in every individual thing, from the momentum of a falling stone to the biological desires that drive the animal consciousness to action to the focused, deliberate will of the initiated human being. It is thus especially the sphere of art, for this unfolds from the active potentials of the human soul, bringing what is within the soul outward into manifestation.

In sacred geometry it is the square and its diagonal, the symbol of generation;

In the categories of Aristotle it is quality;

In the T'ai Chi T'u it is the element of metal;

In the Kabbalah it is Netzach, victory.

BYTH, THE EIGHTH SPHERE, is the sphere of air and represents the capacity of each individual thing to perceive its surroundings, reflecting the third sphere on the plane of individual existence. Included in Byth are all the means and capacities by which any individual thing can be affected by its surroundings, from the material response of a stone when struck by some object to the senses and perceptions of the animal consciousness to the finely tuned intellect and aesthetic sense of the initiated human being. It is thus especially the sphere of science, for this unfolds from the perceptive potentials of the human soul, observing what is outside the soul and understanding it within.

In sacred geometry it is the double square, the symbol of progression;

In the categories of Aristotle it is quantity;

In the T'ai Chi T'u it is the element of wood, which is also associated with wind;

In the Kabbalah it is Hod, glory.

NER, THE NINTH SPHERE, is the sphere of water and represents the union of all the capacities of each individual thing, active and passive, into a single web of relationships connecting it to the rest of the cosmos. It thus reflects the integrating and unifying power of the sixth sphere after its own fashion, and on its own plane. Included in Ner are all the connections between any individual thing and the things that surround it, near and far, obvious and subtle, from the purely physical relations that obtain between one rock and another, through the biological and emotional relations that exist between one animal and another, to the psychological and spiritual relations that develop between one human being and another. It is thus especially the sphere of magic, for the potencies of magic unfold from the connections that unite the mage with the rest of the cosmos, uniting within and without into a seamless fabric.

In sacred geometry it is the Golden Section, the symbol of harmony;

In the categories of Aristotle it is relation;

In the T'ai Chi T'u it is the sphere of generation in which heaven becomes male and earth becomes female;

In the Kabbalah it is Yesod, foundation.

NAF, THE TENTH SPHERE, is the sphere of earth and represents the coalescence of all individual things and all their relations into a single cosmos, one coherent whole. It thus represents the primordial unity of the first sphere, even as it stands at the opposite extreme from Celi's unity of pure being. Included in Naf are all the beings, things, and phenomena we encounter directly in the course of our lives—their essential being descending from Celi, their capacity for change from Perydd, their capacity for stability from Dofydd, their dimensions in space from Ener, their dimensions in time from Modur, their individual nature from Muner, their capacities for action from Byw, their capacities to receive and perceive from Byth, and their relations to all other things from Ner. It is thus especially the sphere of all ordinary activities, practical skills, and the various professions.

In sacred geometry it is the pentagram, the symbol of unity in diversity;

In the categories of Aristotle it is state;

In the T'ai Chi T'u it is the transformation and generation of the ten
thousand things;

In the Kabbalah it is Malkuth, the kingdom.

III. Patterns on the Tree

In the knowledge lectures of the Ovate Grade you were introduced to many of the basic
patterns and relationships among the spheres that define the inner structure of the Tree
of Life. These are crucial to a fuller understanding of the Tree and its many uses in the
Mystery Teachings, and they should be reviewed at this time. The patterns already introduced are the following:

In the second knowledge lecture, the Three Rays and the three circles;

In the third knowledge lecture, the four elemental triangles;

In the fourth knowledge lecture, the geomantic structure of the Tree;

In the fifth knowledge lecture, two additional elemental correspondences;

In the sixth knowledge lecture, the Golden Chain of Homer;

In the seventh knowledge lecture, the geomantic figures and the Platonic solids.

These should be studied in detail as you work with the teachings of the Bardic Grade
and should be compared with the insights you receive while meditating on your experiences with the four inner groves of the elements and the six paths connecting them.

In addition to the patterns already mentioned, a series of triadic relationships runs
all through the Tree of Life and should be the subject of sustained study and regular
meditation during the time you spend in this grade. These triadic patterns may be traced
out on the Tree by noting triangles formed by the spheres and paths. Any three spheres
connected by three and only three paths form a triad, and the three elements of each of
these triads relate to one another as a ternary, following the pattern introduced to you in
the first knowledge lecture.

The following triads may be found on the Tree of Life:

Celi, Perydd, and Dofydd

Celi, Perydd, and Muner

Celi, Dofydd, and Muner

Perydd, Dofydd, and Muner

Perydd, Ener, and Muner

Dofydd, Modur, and Muner

Ener, Modur, and Muner

Ener, Muner, and Byw

Modur, Muner, and Byth

Muner, Byw, and Byth

Muner, Byw, and Ner

Muner, Byth, and Ner

Byw, Byth, and Ner

Byw, Byth, and Naf

Byw, Ner, and Naf

Byth, Ner, and Naf

In each of these triads each pair of spheres forms a binary, which is resolved by the third into a ternary. Thus in the first triad, for example, Celi and Perydd form a binary that is resolved by Dofydd; Celi and Dofydd form a binary that is resolved by Perydd; and Perydd and Dofydd form a binary that is resolved by Celi. Time spent exploring these relationships in the light of the meanings of the spheres given earlier in this lecture will elucidate much concerning the structure of the Tree of Life and its meaning as a chart of the process whereby creation unfolds from pure being to the world of everyday experience.

IV. The Tree of Life in Practice

The Tree of Life serves the initiate in a Mystery School in much the same way as a good map serves a traveler in unfamiliar countries. The ordinary, unawakened human soul is aware solely of the tenth sphere, Naf, the endpoint of the creative process—a realm of effects rather than causes, surfaces rather than depths, appearances rather than realities. Looking around, the dweller in Naf experiences the world as a given, a fixed reality subject to change only in small details, and imagines creation as something that took place once and for all at the beginning of time. It is only those who begin to lift their eyes from this world of appearances who come to suspect that the fixity of Naf is more apparent than real, and that whole worlds of power and meaning lie behind the surfaces that confront the soul on every side.

Those who begin to make this discovery often leap to the conclusion that what lies on the other side of the world of appearances is a single world of realities, parallel to the world of Naf in every way. It is from this kind of thinking that we inherit the conventional notion of heaven or, in folklore, of an otherworld that is merely a mirror image of the world of our everyday experience. It takes time, repeated encounters with inner realities, and a willingness to revisit one's initial assumptions—not all of which are easy for the spiritual seeker to achieve—to pass beyond this overly simple model and grasp the full complexity of the inner realms that await the awakening human soul.

The Tree of Life simplifies this latter process by presenting a model of inner experience sufficiently rich and detailed to embrace the complex experiences of the soul in the early stages of initiation. By studying the Tree, the initiate comes to realize that the first glimpses he attains of the world beyond appearances may come from any of three higher spheres of being—Ner, the sphere of life, which brings wordless, intuitive perceptions of vitality and power; Byth, the sphere of mind, which brings insights, images, and intellectual understandings; or Byw, the sphere of heart, which brings emotional and aesthetic experiences. Recognizing that each of these spheres is a world unto itself, fully as rich and complex as the world of everyday experience that we call Naf, the initiate avoids a too-simple analysis of the experiences he encounters, and as these three spheres above Naf become familiar ground, he learns to recognize the first faint whispers of the spheres even further up the Tree.

One lesson that may be drawn usefully from these considerations is that there is always more than one way to relate a symbolic pattern such as the Tree of Life to the phenomena of human experience. It is never appropriate to insist that one set of correspondences are correct while all others are wrong. This is quite as foolish as the supposed argument between the Englishman, the Frenchman, and the German about whether the four-legged animal barking at all three was a dog, un chien, or ein Hund! Certain systems of correspondence have been found useful in the work of training and initiation, and each Mystery School has its own tables relating symbols to experiences; students of any school may reasonably be expected to attain a good working knowledge of the system of correspondences their school teaches, as indeed you are expected to do; yet it is a mistake, as counterproductive as it is common, to believe that the differences between one school's correspondences and another's shows that one school is right and others are wrong. As you proceed further in the work of initiation, you would do well to keep this in mind.

V. Further Study

An Introduction to the Study of the Kabalah by William Wynn Westcott is recommended for all students of the Tree of Life; while it deals principally with the Jewish Kabbalah, it does so from the point of view of modern students of the Mysteries. *The Kabbalah* by Adolphe Franck and *The Kabbalah* by Christian D. Ginsburg may also be consulted.

On the Sacred Geometry of the Druids

THE KNOWLEDGE LECTURES OF the Bardic Grade introduce the rudiments of the art of sacred geometry as it pertains to the Druidical Mysteries—the circle and equal-armed cross as essential generative principles; the equilateral triangle and square as basic figures derived therefrom; the *ad triangulum* and *ad quadratum* schools of geometry that unfold, in turn, from these; the progression from point to line to plane to solid that sets out the three dimensions in space; and the five Platonic solids and the set of proportions that may be derived from them and applied to the material, aetherial, and intellectual levels of existence.

To learn these as abstract concepts is a first step, but only a first step, in understanding the sacred geometry that formed such an important part of the studies of the ancient Druids. Even in a study as seemingly intellectual as geometry, the mind can only travel so far on its own; it must sooner or later descend into the realm of manifestation if it is to pass beyond its own limits and enter into a wider world. Thus the student of sacred geometry must sooner or later pass from contemplation to creation—the actual construction of geometrical designs—and then return to contemplation with the insights gained from the act of construction.

Mastering the art of sacred geometry requires practice and not merely study. The constructions basic to the art must be drawn in the traditional manner, not once but many times, using the classic tools of the geometer. In this the process is as important as the product, and the steps by which any given geometrical form is created have at least as much to reveal to the studious and meditative mind as does the completed form itself.

The constructions included in this paper are among the most basic in the sacred geometry of the Druidical tradition. Others may be found in books on the subject, some of which are listed at the end of this lecture.

I. The Tools of Sacred Geometry

The traditional tools of the sacred geometer are the pencil, the straightedge, and the compasses. These differ slightly from those of the ancient Druids, who, in common with other ancient peoples, used cords and wooden stakes to carry out their geometrical constructions, and the earth itself as their writing surface (*geo-metria*, "earth measure"). Every Druid should on at least one occasion lay out a construction or two on bare earth using ropes and stakes, following in the footsteps of the builders of stone circles and tumuli; still, for everyday use it is a good deal more convenient to work on paper with less cumbersome tools.

The pencil, straightedge, and compasses have symbolic as well as practical dimensions, for they represent three fundamental principles in sacred geometry. The first, the pencil, symbolizes position, which is also symbolized by the geometrical point. It is, after all, the point of the pencil that matters! The paper, before it receives its first mark, is as close a representation as can be had in the realm of geometry to the undefined and limitless void; once the pencil marks a point upon the paper, it is as a voice saying "Let there be unto the void a restriction." The pencil, therefore, is the emblem of Being, the first element of the creative triad.

The straightedge represents extension, which is also symbolized by the straight line. A point, according to the formal definition, is pure position without any other qualities. The line, by contrast, may extend to infinity in either direction, at least in an ideal sense, or it may be bounded on one or both ends by a point; in either case it has the dimension of length, which is lacking in the point. It is with the straightedge that a line may be extended in any direction, and for this reason the straightedge is the emblem of Becoming, the second element of the creative triad.

The compass represents limitation, which is also represented by the circle or the arc, that is, a portion of a circle. A circle possesses the dimension of breadth as well as that of length, and thus it exists in two dimensions, not merely one as does the line. It may be large or small, but it cannot extend to infinity without ceasing to be a circle. The compass is the instrument by which circles are drawn, and it also serves to define and limit a desired length, cutting the line at an interval determined by the distance between its points. For this reason the compass is the emblem of Limiting, the third element of the creative triad.

Exercise 1: The Three Geometrical Tools

Unless you already have experience with practical geometry, you will find it useful to explore the pencil, straightedge, and compass by using them without any particular construction in mind. Simply mark some points, draw some lines, and trace some arcs and circles upon a sheet of paper. As you do this, pay attention to the concepts represented by the tools you are using; as you mark a point, see it as a representation of being; as you draw a line, of becoming; as you trace an arc or a circle, of limiting. At the same time, you will begin the process of gaining facility with the tools; you will learn the kind and amount of pressure needed to hold a straightedge in place against the pressure of a pencil sliding along its edge, for example, and the trick of the wrist that neatly produces a circle. When you feel comfortable with your tools, proceed to the first of the constructions given below.

II. The Genesis of the Triangle

As you have already learned, the sacred geometry of the Druids belongs to the school that in later centuries was called *ad triangulum*, "by the triangle." It thus differs from the school central to modern Freemasonry and, as a result, to much of contemporary sacred geometry. Freemasons, as is commonly known, meet "on the square," while Druids gather in the circle. The philosophical and esoteric traditions that derive from a Masonic source begin with the material world, symbolized by the square and the cube; proceed from there through the modalities of inner experience that we call the aetherial realm, symbolized by the equilateral triangle and the solid figures made from it; and finally attain the intellectual realm, symbolized by the pentagon and the dodecahedron. It is thus no accident that modern science had its origins in an intellectual milieu permeated by Masonic teaching and activities.

Druid sacred geometry, and the *ad triangulum* school more generally, proceeds by a different route to the same goal. The starting point here is the individual consciousness and its inner world of experience, represented by the triangle; from there, the work proceeds to the outer world of the senses, represented by the square; and finally to the intellectual realm from which both inner and outer worlds take their origin, and which is represented by the pentagram.

Thus the practice of Druidical sacred geometry begins with the genesis of the triangle, and this starts from the primary geometrical pattern of the *ad triangulum* school, the vesica piscis.

Exercise 2: Construct a Vesica Piscis

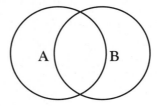

Using the compasses, draw a circle with any point A as center and any convenient distance between the compass points. Choose any point B on the circumference of circle A; without changing the distance between the compass points, draw a second circle with B as center. The space included in both circles is the vesica piscis, or "vessel of the fish."

It is important, again, not merely to read these instructions but to follow them several times, paying close attention to the details of the experience. Certain things will be learned by reflecting on even so basic a geometric construction that in no other way can be learned as effectively.

Exercise 3: Construct an Equilateral Triangle from a Vesica Piscis

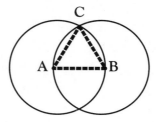

FIRST METHOD: Construct a vesica piscis using the method in exercise 2. Mark one of the two points where the circles intersect as point C. With the straightedge, draw lines connecting A and B, A and C, and B and C to create the triangle ABC as shown.

You may also use this construction to create an equilateral triangle in which every side is equal to a given line. If you begin with line AB, simply create a vesica by drawing circles or portions of circles with centers at A and B and the compasses set to the distance between A and B. Find point C by their intersection and proceed from there.

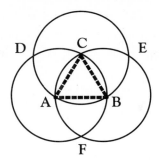

SECOND METHOD: Construct a vesica piscis using the method in exercise 2. Mark one of the two points where the circles intersect as C. Draw a third circle with C as the center and the compass points at the same distance apart you used to draw circles A and B. Connect the three points A, B, and C as shown to create the triangle ABC.

Notice that this method defines two equilateral triangles—the smaller triangle ABC and a larger triangle that may be formed by connecting the three intersections D, E, and F. The outer triangle is exactly four times larger than the inner triangle. If you then draw three more circles with centers at D, E, and F, and the distance between any two of these points as the compass setting, the outer intersections of those circles would define a third triangle, four times as large as triangle DEF; the same process may be repeated out to infinity.

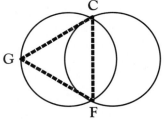

THIRD METHOD: Construct a vesica piscis using the method in exercise 2. Set the compass points to the distance between the two intersections of the circle at C and F, and then swing the compasses with either C or F as center to cut the circle at G. Connect C, F, and G with straight lines to create triangle CFG. If, with the compasses set to the distance from C to F, you draw two circles with their centers at C and F respectively, you will create a second, larger vesica with CF as its width and G as one of its points.

The threefold nature of the vesica piscis goes beyond its obvious geometrical side. If the distance across the middle of a vesica, called the minor axis by geometers—from A to B in our third diagram—is equal to 1, the distance from one point of the vesica to another, called the major axis—from C to F, in the same diagram—is √3, the square root of 3. This works out, in decimal notation, to 1.73205... and so on for an infinite number of digits.

Mathematicians refer to numbers of this kind as irrational numbers, but they might better be known as transrational numbers. In sacred geometry the various relationships that are denoted by transrational numbers, such as the 1:√3 proportion defined by the vesica piscis, represent primary spiritual principles that, in their fullness, transcend human reason. The principle that manifests in the vesica piscis and the equilateral triangle may be understood for the time being as the feminine principle, or the principle of creation; a more complete understanding of this principle may be gained through meditation on the process of constructing the forms just given.

III. *The Genesis of the Square*

The movement from the triangle to the square—or, as it may equally well be described, from the circle to the cross—begins once again from the vesica piscis, the core diagram of Druidical sacred geometry. Among the properties of the vesica is that it defines a precise right angle between its major and minor axes. Thus the vesica generates the cross, and the cross a square; from the square, in turn, unfolds the 1:√2 proportion, the governing proportion of the *ad quadratum* school of sacred geometry. In the same way, beginning with the square and its diagonal, the core diagram of the *ad quadratum* school, the 1:√3 proportion soon appears; each school thus implies and leads to each other—a binary that seeks its proper resolution in a third factor.

Exercise 4: Divide Any Line in Half

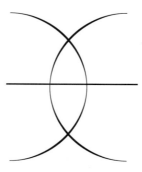

Draw a line of any length using the straightedge. Take the compass, and with the center on one end of the line and any setting of the compass that is more than half the length of the line, draw an arc to both sides of the line, as shown. Move the compass center to the other end of the line, leaving the distance between the compass points unchanged, and draw a corresponding arc, intersecting the first arc above and below the line. A line drawn between the two intersections will divide the original line in half.

To draw a line perpendicular to any line, use this same construction. The line extending above and below the original line is perpendicular to the latter.

Exercise 5: Construct a Square Within a Circle

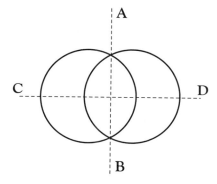

Begin with the diagram described in exercise 2. Using the straightedge, draw a line from A to B, along the minor axis of the vesica, extending it as far as you wish to either side. Again using the straightedge, draw a line from C to D, along the major axis of the vesica, again extending it as far as you wish to either side.

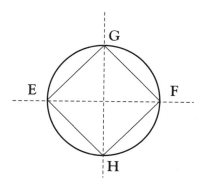

Next, take the compass, and with the center placed on the intersection of line AB and line CD, draw a circle of any convenient size. The points E, F, G, and H, where the circle intersects the two lines, are the four corners of a perfect square.

Exercise 6: Construct a Square Around a Circle

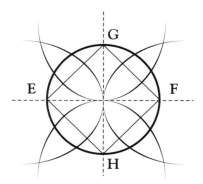

Begin with the same construction used in exercise 5. When you have finished it, place the compass center on point E and set the width between the compass points to the distance between E and the center of the circle. Draw an arc to each side of line EF, covering at least half a circle. Repeat the same process with the center of the compass on points F, G, and H. The points where the four arcs intersect with each other will be the corners of a square that exactly surrounds the circle EFGH.

This construction is also known as the doubling of the square, and it appears in this context in one of the dialogues of Plato. If you draw the entire construction and consider the two squares—the one within the circle and the one surrounding it—you will quickly notice that the one within is divided into four identical right triangles by lines EF and GH, while the one surrounding is composed of eight such triangles.

The corners of the outer square may again be used as the centers of four arcs and the construction repeated to produce a third square, which will be twice the size of the outer square and four times the size of the inner square. This process may be repeated to infinity.

Just as the vesica piscis embodies a threefold pattern that expresses itself in many ways, the square and equal-armed cross embody a twofold pattern that manifests in various forms of doubling and halving, and especially in the ratio between the side of the square and its diagonal. If the side—for example, line EG—is equal to 1, the diagonal—for example, line EF—will be equal to $\sqrt{2}$, the square root of 2, which is approximately equal to 1.4142... and so on, again, for an infinite number of digits. This principle may be understood as the masculine principle, or the principle of generation; a more complete understanding of this principle may be gained, in turn, through meditation on the process of constructing the forms just given.

IV. The Genesis of the Fundamental Roots

The square, which gives geometrical form to the principle of generation, is also unique in its ability to generate other transrational roots from itself. The relation between a square and its diagonal is the starting point for this process.

Exercise 7: Construct a Series of Root Rectangles

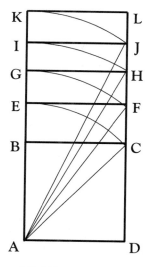

Begin by constructing a square ABCD using any convenient method—the methods in exercises 5 and 6 are suitable for this. Extend two parallel sides of the square, AB and DC, out to one side as shown in the diagram above. Set the distance between the compass points to the diagonal of the square—for example, the distance from B to D. Then, with centers at A and D respectively, draw arcs down from B and C to cut the extended lines at E and F. Draw in line EF to create the rectangle AEFD. If the sides of the square ABCD are equal to one, the long sides of AEFD are equal to $\sqrt{2}$, since the diagonal of a square is $\sqrt{2}$ times the side of the square. This is a "root two rectangle," one of the basic forms in traditional design.

Next, repeat the process, setting the compass points to the diagonal of the new rectangle and drawing another pair of arcs to cut the extended sides of the square at G and H. If the sides of the original square remain equal to one, the sides of the new rectangle AGHD are equal to √3—you may wish to construct a vesica piscis using a line equal to AD as the minor axis, then set the compass points to the length of the major axis, and compare this to the length from A to G. AGHD is a "root three rectangle" and is also much used in traditional design.

Repeat the same process a third time, using arcs drawn from the diagonal of AGHD to mark points I and J on the extended lines, and create the new rectangle AIJD. The long side of AIJD will be exactly twice the length of the side of the original square—that is, AIJD is a double square, with sides equal to √4 (which, of course, equals 2). It could be called "root four rectangle," though this term is never used in practice; "double square" is the standard term for this figure.

The diagonal of AIJD, finally, produces a "root five rectangle," with a short side equal to one and a long side equal to √5. The root five rectangle is not much used in traditional design, and the rectangles with sides even longer are rarely seen at all. The importance of this part of the diagram, rather, is that the square root of five plays an important role in opening the door to a far more important transrational ratio, the Golden Section.

V. Proportions and the Golden Section

The 1:√2 and 1:√3 ratios between them define a binary relationship that, like all binaries, naturally seeks a third factor to resolve it. The ratio that provides that third factor, transforming the binary into a ternary, comes from a different aspect of sacred geometry from those we have been discussing so far.

Any relation between two numbers—call them A and B for the present—is understood in geometrical terms as a ratio between two lengths: the height and breadth of a standing stone, for example, or the diameters of two stone circles in the same ancient temple site, as at Avebury. An identity between two ratios, in turn, defines a proportion. For example, if one standing stone is 10 feet high and 4 feet broad, and another is 15 feet high and 6 feet broad, a common proportion unites them. In modern notation, we write 10:4::15:6, "ten is to four as fifteen is to six." Any other pair of numbers in the same ratio is proportional with those already mentioned: for example, if a round barrow not far away from these stones is 20 yards across and 8 yards high, the attentive researcher will recognize that a common proportion, one doubtless meant to convey or express some particular symbolic meaning, was used by the builders. As is explained in another knowledge lecture of this grade, the proportions drawn from music and geometry have an important role in magical practice.

The type of proportion just described is known as a discontinuous proportion because it requires no continuity between the measures composing the varying ratios comprised in it. To a ratio of 10 feet by 4 feet any other pair of measures in the same relationship is proportional, be they in fractions of an inch or multiples of the earth's distance from the nearest star. The builders of earlier times, seeking more coherence within their structures, commonly made use of another type of proportion, the continuous proportion, in which a common measure unites two ratios.

Let us imagine, for example, that one standing stone is 10 feet high and 4 feet broad, and a smaller stone next to it is 4 feet high and just over 1 foot 7 inches broad. These two stones are proportional to one another, and they also share a common measure, as the breadth of one is the height of the other. In modern notation, where a discontinuous proportion may be represented by A:B::C:D, a continuous proportion may be represented by A:B::B:C, "A is to B as B is to C." In practice—whether in architecture, art, or in the magical applications of sacred geometry—a continuous proportion has stronger effects than a discontinuous one.

This fact inspired the ancient masters of sacred geometry to seek even more closely interrelated proportions and led them eventually to the ratio that resolves the binary between the 1:√2 and 1:√3 ratios. This is the Golden Section, which the great astronomer Johannes Kepler described as the "precious jewel" of sacred geometry.

A discontinuous proportion, A:B::C:D, requires four differing measures: A, B, C, and D. A continuous proportion, A:B::B:C, requires three: A, B, and C. The ancient masters accordingly sought a more than continuous proportion, A:B::B:A+B—"A is to B as B is to the sum of A and B"—and discovered, first, that only one ratio can be used to construct such a proportion, and second, that that ratio involves another transrational number, which is usually represented by the Greek letter phi (Φ). In decimal numbers, Φ works out to 1.61803... and so on for an infinite number of digits. It may more precisely be represented as $(1 + \sqrt{5})/2$; it is the square root of 5, in other words, that provides the key to the genesis of Φ, and many of the constructions that produce Φ make use of √5 in one way or another.

Φ is a number with surprising properties—for example, $\Phi + 1 = \Phi^2$, $\Phi - 1 = \sqrt{\Phi}$, and $\Phi - 1$ is also $1/\Phi$—and it appears in a remarkable range of phenomena throughout nature. Many people know that the shell of the chambered nautilus is structured according to Φ, for each chamber within the shell is Φ times as large as the chamber immediately behind it. Less commonly known is the fact that many of the proportions of the human body likewise depend on Φ; on average, for example, each joint of the human hand and arm is Φ times the length of the one farther toward the fingertips; thus the length of the last joint of each finger multiplied by Φ gives the length of the second joint, and so on, to the length of the upper arm, which is the length of the lower arm multiplied by Φ. The branches of many species of trees are arranged in a similar manner and so on through all the kingdoms of nature.

VI. The Genesis of the Golden Section

The Golden Section is easy to construct geometrically, and the constructions that follow show two ways of doing so, one starting from the vesica piscis according to the *ad triangulum* school, the other starting from the square according to the *ad quadratum* school.

Exercise 8: Construct the Golden Section from the Vesica Piscis

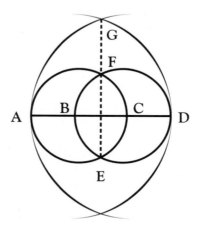

Using the straightedge, draw a line of any convenient length and mark a point to one side of the middle (B in the diagram). Using the compass, draw a circle of any convenient size with B as center; then, with the compass points at the same distance, draw another circle with its center at C, where the circumference of the first circle crosses the line. This gives you the initial vesica piscis. Mark points A and D where the two circles intersect the line outside the vesica, as shown.

Next, put the center of the compass on C, set the other point on A, and draw an arc above and below the line. Move the center of the compass to B, and draw a second arc above and below the line from D. Using the straightedge, draw a line through the points of the vesica at E and F, and extend it to the upper intersection of the two arcs at G. The line segments FG and EF are divided according to the Golden Section; if FG is equal to 1, EF will be equal to Φ.

Exercise 9: Construct the Golden Section from the Square

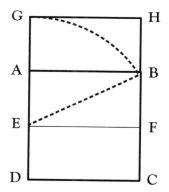

Construct a square ABCD using the method given in exercise 5 or any other convenient method. Divide two parallel sides of the square in half, at points E and F, using the method given in exercise 4. With the center of the compass on point E and the distance between the points equal to the distance from E to B, draw an arc above the square as shown (from B to G); move the center of the compass to F, and draw a second arc (which is not shown in the diagram but goes from A to H). Using the straightedge, extend the sides of the square out to intersect the arcs at points G and H, and draw in line GH to complete rectangle GHCD. If the length of the side of the square is 1, the length from C to H is Φ.

The rectangle GHCD is called a Golden Rectangle. Studies have shown that most people find a rectangle of these proportions more aesthetically attractive than any other. Like the Golden Section that defines it, it replicates itself at different scales; subtract the original square and the rectangle left over, GHBA, is also a Golden Rectangle, and their areas relate to one another in the Φ ratio; similarly, if you were to construct a square with sides that extend from G to D and add it to the long side of rectangle GHCD, the resulting rectangle would again be a Golden Rectangle, and its area would be Φ times as great as the area of GHCD.

The Golden Section also plays a central role in one of the most important geometrical figures in magic, the pentagram. Several books provide constructions that will produce a geometrically perfect pentagram; this is a construction of some complexity, however, and you should gain some facility with the more basic diagrams of sacred geometry before attempting it. In the meantime, however, since you are constructing pentagrams on at least a daily basis in your practice of the Lesser and Elemental Pentagram rituals, you would do well to understand the sacred geometry of this figure.

The diagram will explain the geometries of the pentagram:

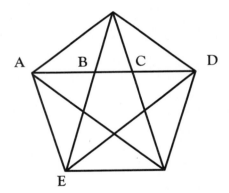

The 1:Φ ratio pervades both the pentagram and a pentagon drawn around it. If the distance from A to E in the diagram (or from A to C, which is the same) is 1, the distance from A to D is Φ. If the distance from A to B is 1, the distance from A to C is Φ, and if the distance from B to C is 1, the distance from A to B is Φ. Thus the pentagram is a geometric expression of the Golden Section and embodies its full meaning and power.

Pentagrams are of great importance in Druidical magic. Where the 1:√3 ratio is traditionally held to represent creation and the feminine, and the 1:√2 ratio generation and the masculine, the 1:Φ ratio represents regeneration and the balanced union of the polarized powers of feminine and masculine. It is the great geometrical emblem of balance and harmony. This accounts for its power in ritual work, for the work of magic is that of regeneration and of bringing the often chaotic forces of the world of manifestation into harmony. More will be said concerning this in another grade.

VII. *Further Study*

The material covered in this knowledge lecture is only a small portion of the field of sacred geometry as it has been practiced in the Druidical Mysteries and in other Mystery Schools around the world. Very little on this subject has been published to date in English; the writings of the American designer Jay Hambidge, found principally in his magazine *The Diagonal*, are a welcome addition to the otherwise meager resources, to which may also be added Fredrik Macody Lund's useful book *Ad Quadratum*.

Plants in Magic and Alchemy

THE IMPORTANCE OF HERBS, trees, and vegetation to the Druids of old is a matter of common knowledge, even among those whose understanding of Druidical matters extends only to a dim notion or two about white-robed figures at Stonehenge. Like other peoples who lived close to the earth, the ancient Celts made much use of wild plants for food, healing, and folk magic of the kind that was commonplace everywhere in the world before the rise of our present-day enlightened civilization, and it will doubtless be commonplace again around the world after that civilization is no more. Like the priests and priestesses of every ancient nation, the Druids of ancient times took the body of knowledge shared by the common people as a foundation and added to it much additional plant lore, comprising much of their magic and, according to tradition, of their alchemy as well.

It is unfortunately the case that most initiates of the Druidical Mysteries in our present age are born and raised in cities and towns, and the old intimacy with the green world of vegetation is something few ever experience and fewer still have as an ordinary part of the daily round, as was once commonplace. Time spent sitting out of doors, attentively observing the subtle displays of nature through the cycles of the seasons, is still an essential of Druidical training, and time should be made for it at least once a week. Still, it is necessary to supplement this with the kind of learning at which most people are skilled nowadays, the knowledge of names, forms, and concepts that can be communicated in a lecture of this sort.

The following notes, together with time spent in silence in nature and further research in books on the subject, will help you achieve a basic grasp of the place of the plant world in Druidical magic.

I. Plants and the Earth Spirit

It is a matter of common knowledge that the great majority of living things belong to one of two great divisions, the plants and the animals. Those who recall the biology they studied in school may remember as well that the difference between the two divisions, as understood by science, is that plants produce their own food from air, water, and sunlight, while animals cannot do this and must seek their food from plants or other animals. This is quite correct so far as the physical plane is concerned.

Above the physical plane, in that division of the cosmos we call the aetherial plane, the same difference may be found between the same two divisions, but the direction of the flow is reversed. Where, on the physical plane, energy flows into material form by the action of the plants and is released again from material form by the action of the animals, on the aetherial plane it is the animals who bring the descending current from the cosmos and the plants who return it to the cosmos by way of an ascending current.

This may be seen to be symbolically expressed in the physical forms of plants and animals respectively. The stems of plants are at their most massive where they leave the ground and rise up into the air in progressively finer branchings; the bodies of animals are generally at their most massive at shoulders and hips, well above the ground, and taper downwards from there in those progressively finer branchings we call limbs, fingers, and toes. Consider the structure of your own arm as an example: the upper arm is most massive and contains a single bone; the lower arm is less massive and contains two bones; the hand has many bones, terminating in tapering fingers. The hair upon the human head corresponds to the roots of plants—it may be noted that many mammals have extra hair upon the head, neck, shoulders, or spine, and birds and reptiles very often have crests of feathers or scales respectively in the same place, echoing the root-function of the plant.

To the eye of the Druidical initiate, then, animals—human beings among them—are vessels for a current of force that descends from heaven to earth, while plants are vessels for an equal and opposite current of force that ascends from earth to heaven. There is an important difference between the two currents, however, which is that the descending current is much less varied than the ascending one. The descending ray comes to the animal creation directly from the sun; the ascending ray comes to the vegetable creation from within the earth, influenced by all the diversity and variation of material existence.

Thus every variety of animal receives from the sky above it and transmits to the earth beneath it the same quality of aetherial force, albeit varying to some degree with the cycles of time and the movements of the various heavenly bodies. Each variety of plant, by contrast, receives from the earth beneath it and transmits to the sky above it a quality of aetherial force unique to that variety of plant, drawn from the great reservoir of the earth. It is these unique qualities of force that Druids use in their magical and alchemical work with plants.

The sum total of energies flowing through the body of the earth and rising through plants of all kinds to return to the heavens constitutes what is called the earth spirit. This is a mighty force, one of two great forces that play a part in Druidical magic; the other, equally mighty, is the current descending from the sun. The ways of working with these two great forces vary from one school of the Druidical Mysteries to another. Some schools teach students to draw the earth spirit up into their bodies, to energize and purify the aetherial form; others work with both streams of power at the same time, and even unite them in certain ways.

In the system of Druidical magic you are studying, however, we work with these two great forces in our own way. We work with the single current of energy descending from the sun by means of the exercise of the Central Ray, and certain other formulae derived from it, which you will learn in due time. We work with the infinitely diverse currents of energy rising from the earth by means of their material expressions in plant substances. The descending current provides the force, the ascending current the form, and the intention that guides the magical ceremony, whatever that intention happens to be, brings this binary into balance as a ternary and enables wonders to be performed.

II. Sixteen Herbs for Magic and Alchemy

The following sixteen herbs represent only a very small selection from the vast number of herbs, or unique magical energies, that can be put to use in Druidical magic and alchemy. You are asked to familiarize yourself with them partly for a reason that will be explained in the instructions dealing with preparation for the Bardic Grade initiation and partly because the process of learning magical herb lore must begin somewhere!

All sixteen of these herbs are readily available from herbal suppliers and, in many cases, local herb stores, and all can be used in relative safety by most people; each of them can also be assigned readily to one of the geomantic figures with which it shares certain symbolic properties. Please take the time to look up the medicinal effects of these herbs in a standard manual such as *J. M. Nickell's Botanical Ready Reference*, and consult other books on herbal magic and alchemy concerning them as well.

You will find that different books describe the magical properties of herbs in different and often contradictory ways. This has been true for thousands of years, and learning to sort through the confusion and make your own judgments is one of the basic skills required for study of herbal magic and alchemy in modern times.

Mab: Southernwood (*Artemisia abrotanum*)

Warm and dry in the third degree, southernwood is called Lad's Love by some herbalists and Maiden's Ruin by others! It stimulates the vital spirits, brings happiness, and removes sexual difficulties. The leaves are the part used.

Colled: Rose (*Rosa* spp.)

There are more than a hundred different species of rose, but all share the same elemental balance—cold in the first degree, dry in the third—and the same magical properties. They are used in love magic of all kinds. The petals are the part used.

Gwyn: Dill (*Anethum graveolens*)

A protective herb, dill is hot in the second degree and dry in the first. It banishes hostile spirits and evil influences of all kinds, and brings clarity and insight to the mind. The seeds are used.

Pobl: Rosemary (*Rosmarinus officinalis*)

Hot and dry in the second degree, rosemary strengthens the memory, clears the mind, and banishes depressed moods. Use the leaves.

Bendith Fawr: Angelica (*Angelica archangelica*)

Hot in the second degree and dry in the third, angelica has potent protective qualities; it will drive off hostile spirits and magical workings, banish bad luck, and change one's fortune for the better. The root is the portion used.

Cyswllt: Cinquefoil (*Potentilla anserina*)

Called Five Finger Grass by folk magicians, cinquefoil is cold and dry in the second degree. It has the power of strengthening any other magical herb and also grants the gift of communication and persuasion. The leaves or the root may be used.

Merch: Lady's Mantle (*Alchemilla vulgaris*)

Hot and dry in the second degree, lady's mantle is purifying and protective. Its leaves gather drops of dew, which are important in some alchemical workings. Use the leaves.

Coch: Basil (*Ocimum basilicum*)

Hot in the second degree and moist in the first, basil dispels fears and brings courage; taken in excess, it produces belligerence. Use the leaves.

Elw: Dandelion (*Taraxacum officinale*)

Cold and dry in the second degree, dandelion is among the world's most widespread plants. It has protective and visionary powers, and is used in spells to make wishes come true. The root is the part used.

Carchar: Mullein (*Verbascum thapsus*)

Temperate and dry in the first, mullein is a potent protective herb, placing firm limits on the powers of hostile spirits or evil magic. The leaves are used.

Tristwch: Comfrey (*Symphytum officinale*)

Cold in the first degree and moist in the second, comfrey is a powerful healing herb, but it also brings protection to travelers and is used in spells to help hold on to wealth. The leaves or root may be used.

Llawenydd: Lemon Balm (*Melissa officinalis*)

Hot and dry in the second degree, lemon balm dispels melancholy, restores the vital spirits, and attracts romance and new relationships. It is also much used in plant alchemy, for an interesting reason—it helps the mind understand the riddling language in which so much alchemical lore is written. The leaves are the part used.

Llosgwrn y Ddraig: Mugwort (*Artemisia vulgaris*)

Hot and dry in the second degree, mugwort is a powerful herb of magic. It is placed above doors and windows to keep evil spirits from a home, placed under the pillow to bring dreams of the future, and a sprig placed under the doorstop makes unwanted visitors go away! The leaves are the part that is used.

Pen y Ddraig: Borage (*Borago officinalis*)

Hot and moist in the first degree, borage overcomes feelings of fear and depression; "I, borage, grant courage" is an old rhyme remembered by herbal magicians. The leaves or flowers may be used for this purpose.

Bendith Fach: Chamomile (*Matricaria chamomilla*)

Hot and dry in the first degree, chamomile is an herb of protection and blessing, and is often grown in gardens to keep ill luck away. The whole herb is used.

Ffordd: Plantain (*Plantago major*)

This common roadside weed is cold and dry in the second degree, and has the power to banish nightmares and unwelcome spirits. The leaves are used.

III. An Outline of Plant Magic

The practical formulae of Druidical magic are reserved to the Druid Grade so that the necessary preparation and instruction will have been completed before the ceremonial work is attempted. Nonetheless, just as the techniques of plant alchemy were surveyed in the Ovate Grade in order to provide you with a sense of the possibilities open to you, it is not out of place here to outline the ways in which plants are used in magical practice.

AMULETS are small containers of various kinds—cloth bags are the most common—in which one or several dried herbs or other plant substances are placed and then consecrated with a ritual working. Amulets have the great advantage of holding a magical influence for an extended period of time, so that the influence remains effective long after the ritual work is completed. Once made and consecrated, an amulet may be carried on the person, worn on a string around the neck, or placed in a location where its effects are needed.

BATHS AND WASHES are strong infusions of plant substances—in effect, very strong herb teas—that are made and consecrated, then added to the water of a bath or to the bucket of water used to clean a floor or anything else. Baths may be used for any magical purpose; washes are most often a means of protective and purifying magic, used to cleanse the floor of a room or house to remove unwelcome influences and introduce favorable ones.

INCENSES are plant substances of various kinds that are placed on hot coals to produce smoke in order to fill the air with a desired influence. Incense is a powerful tool in magical practice, and nearly all magical rituals make use of it, but it requires careful study. Not all herbs smell the same when burnt as they do in other contexts; peppermint, for example, loses all trace of its familiar scent when burnt and instead produces an odor that is unpleasantly reminiscent of cat urine. Plants suitable for incense should be finely powdered in a mortar and pestle before use.

OILS are made by steeping plant substances in a suitable vegetable oil such as grapeseed oil or almond oil. The best magical oils are never heated but are steeped for months or years in a cool, dry place, then strained to remove the plant matter and consecrated. Once made, they are used to anoint parts of the body or objects that are to receive a magical influence. They should not be confused with essential oils, which are distilled from plant matter and should never be applied undiluted to the body, as many of them are strong enough to cause skin burns, rashes, and toxic reactions. When time is short, a functional magical oil can be made by adding a few drops of one or more essential oils to a vegetable oil, but oils made by steeping herbs are preferable.

OINTMENTS are identical to oils except that wax or some other thickening substance, such as a vegetable butter, is melted and then added to the oil after the vegetable matter is strained out to produce a semisolid substance that is less messy to handle than oil.

POTIONS are, for all intents and purposes, mild herb teas made in the usual manner—by steeping a single herb or a blend of several herbs in boiling water, straining out the plant matter, consecrating the potion, and then allowing the water to cool. For magical purposes, a very light tea is normally appropriate, as the power of the plant passes readily into water. A potion may be used to bathe some part of the body—this is called "laving" when done in a ritual context— or an object that is to be charged with the plant's energy; it may be sprinkled around an area like holy water to purify and bless the area or to affect it in any other way, according to the nature of the plant matter included in the potion; and it may also be taken internally, provided always that the herbs used are safe for internal use.

It should be noted that alchemical tinctures may be used in place of unprocessed plant matter in any of these contexts, with a great increase in effectiveness and power.

Many traditions of folk magic from around the world use these forms of plant magic, and most also include other forms as well—for example, in Africa and those parts of the New World settled by people of African ancestry, it is common to see folk magicians grind up plant materials into a fine powder, mix this with other substances and white clay or some substitute such as talcum powder, and use the resulting powder in magical workings. If you have the opportunity to learn the variety of folk magic practiced in the area in which you live, much can be learned by doing so; it is by attentively studying older folk traditions, in all probability, that the ancient Druids amassed much of their lore, and Druid initiates of later ages have made use of this same opportunity in replacing teachings that have been lost down through the years to persecution and the passage of time.

One additional way of using plants in Druidical magic should be mentioned at this time; though it is not available to every initiate, it is among the most powerful of all and should be explored by those who have the opportunity to do so: this is the magical garden. Living plants radiate the force of the earth spirit more powerfully than do dried herbs or even alchemical tinctures. Those students who have even a small patch of earth that can be set aside as a magical garden and who choose, plant, and tend plants there for their magical effects will find that the garden serves as a type of amulet, radiating magical influences of the kind determined by the chosen plants that grow there.

IV. Further Study

There are many books available on the folklore and magical uses of herbs, and it will be to your advantage to consult at least a few of these during the time you spend in this grade. Those specific to the region in which you live, if such can be found, will be particularly useful. One more general book that may be particularly recommended is Mrs. C. F. Leyel's *The Magic of Herbs: A Modern Book of Secrets*.

Principles of Color and Sound

AMONG THE MOST IMPORTANT tools of initiates in any Mystery School, color and sound are particular studies assigned to the Bardic Grade. The Bards of old made use of the ancient British harp, which spanned only a single octave, in studying and teaching the properties of sound, and their use of color was limited to those hues nature provided them. Students of the Druidical Mysteries today have more possibilities available, but the essential principles are still comprised in a single octave of seven distinct notes and the natural spectrum of seven distinct colors.

I. The Octaves of Sound and Light

In music, an octave may be defined as the difference between two notes, one of which is produced by a vibration twice as fast as the vibration that produces the other. Thus the note we call middle C, for example, is produced by a string, tuning fork, or other object vibrating at a rate of 256 cycles per second; the c above middle C is produced by some similar object vibrating at a rate of 512 cycles per second, and to human ears the two notes are, in some sense, "the same." This relationship between notes is not unique to Western music; it stands at the foundation of most of the known musical systems around the world and throughout time, and it has been found to be recognizable by animals as well as human beings.

Between two notes in an octave relationship other notes can be placed, and here the world's musical systems embrace almost limitless variation. The music of China is famously based on an "octave" of five notes, called in the West the pentatonic scale; in Java, an "octave" of seventeen notes is known. In the Western world we place six notes between the two ends of the octave, for a total of seven distinct notes—the two at either end, again, are heard as "the same note." The eight divisions of the scale thus established are responsible for the term *octave*, which means "a group of eight."

The colors of the spectrum of visible light follow a similar pattern to the octave of sound, though the vibrations are almost unimaginably faster. The lowest vibration of visible red light is around 400 trillion cycles per second, while the highest vibration of visible violet light is a little under 800 trillion cycles per second, yielding nearly the same octave relationship. It is worth noting that to the human eye, red and violet seem to blend into one another; it is possible that if we could see infrared or ultraviolet light, we would see the "notes" of the light spectrum repeat themselves on a lower or higher octave, as the notes of the musical octave do.

The precise divisions of the octave of sound and the spectrum of light—the notes and the colors, respectively—may be determined mathematically in several ways, many of which have their own traditional meanings and symbolism. The notes used in nearly all modern music are assigned according to a system known as equal temperament, but as recently as the eighteenth century many different systems of temperament were in use. In the same way, the exact boundaries between colors are difficult to determine, and the exact shade that should be considered "pure red," say, is a matter of some dispute. Still, it is useful in practice to make notes and colors correspond precisely to one another so that each note represents a color and each color, a musical note. This makes possible certain important magical applications of each.

a	440 cps	798 tcps	red (G#—purple)
G	391 cps	709 tcps	violet (F#—see text)
F	352 cps	634 tcps	indigo
E	330 cps	594 tcps	blue (D#—turquoise)
D	293 cps	528 tcps	green (C#—chartreuse)
C	264 cps	475 tcps	yellow
B	248 cps	446 tcps	orange (A#—flame)
A	220 cps	396 tcps	red

cps = cycles per second

tcps = trillion cycles per second

(All figures rounded to nearest whole number)

Scale of Sound and Color

The scale of sound and color shows the correspondence between these two, using one set of figures for the note values (the system called "just temperament"). The octave shown is a natural minor scale, or what was anciently known as the Aeolian mode; as its assignment to the first seven letters of the alphabet in order may suggest, it is the most basic of musical scales and the one fundamental to the Druidical symbolism of sound.

II. **The Structure of the Musical Scale**

It is necessary to cover some basic music theory to make sense of what follows. Every scale in Western music is divided unevenly, with some intervals half the size of others. Here the intervals between B and C and between E and F are half steps, while the other intervals are whole steps. In minor scales beginning with other notes, flatted or sharped notes put half steps between the second and third notes of the scale and between the fifth and sixth, as having half steps there is what produces the distinctive sound of a minor scale, the old Aeolian mode. If the half steps are between the third and fourth and the seventh and eighth notes of the scale, the result is the major scale or Ionian mode. Other arrangements produce the other five musical modes; these are rarely heard now but were once important in Western music.

A chord is a harmonious relationship between three or more notes sounded at the same time. The most common type of chord is made by sounding three notes from the same scale: a so-called tonic note, which gives its name to the chord, and the third and fifth notes counting upwards from the tonic. In the scale printed above, for example, an A chord is made by playing A, C, and E at the same time. Because the interval between the first two notes is one and a half steps—remember that B and C are separated only by a half step—this chord is a minor chord, A minor. By contrast, the chord C-E-G is a C major chord, because C and E are separated by two full steps. Even among the notes of a minor scale there are some major chords. Both minor and major chords span a perfect fifth, the strongest of the musical harmonies.

III. *Chords, Colors, and Elements*

By comparing the notes of the natural minor scale beginning with A to the spectrum of visible light and matching this with color symbolism, it is possible to find the natural musical expressions of the four elements.

The color traditionally attributed to the element of fire is red, the first or lowest note in the spectrum, and its musical note will therefore be A, the first or lowest note of the minor scale. The corresponding chord, A minor, comprises the notes A-C-E, as already explained. The colors that correspond to these notes are red, yellow, and blue. These are the three primary colors—the colors from which all other colors may be derived. Since fire is the highest and most exalted of the elements, this is quite appropriate.

The color traditionally attributed to the element of air is yellow, and its musical note will therefore be C. The corresponding chord is C major, comprising the notes C-E-G, and the colors that correspond to these notes are yellow, blue, and violet. The first two of these are primary, but the third, violet, is a secondary color—it is made by the mixture of equal parts of two primary colors, red and blue. The shift from three primary colors to two primary and a secondary marks the descent of one step in the great chain of being from fire to air.

Note also that yellow and violet, the first and last notes in the color chord of air, have a special relationship to each other. They are flashing colors—put matching shades of yellow and violet next to one another and the eyes will be dazzled, as though the two colors flash and sparkle at their mutual boundary. As you have already learned, the notes corresponding to these colors, C and G, have the interval of a perfect fifth between them. (There is also a perfect fifth between the notes at either end of the chord of fire, A and E, but the flashing effect cannot take place between primary colors such as red and blue; it requires one primary color and a corresponding secondary color in contact with one another.)

The color traditionally attributed to the element of water is blue, and its musical note will therefore be E. The corresponding chord is E minor, composed of the notes E-G-b; remember that each octave blends without a break into the octaves above and below it, so the b played here is from the next octave up. The colors that correspond to these notes are blue, violet, and orange—one primary color, this time, and two secondary colors. This marks another step down the great chain of being. At the same time, blue and orange, the two colors at the ends of the color chord of water, are also flashing colors.

The color traditionally attributed to the element of earth is green, a secondary color, and its musical note is D. The corresponding chord is D minor, composed of the notes D-F-a. The colors that correspond to these notes are green, indigo, and red. Green, as already mentioned, is a secondary color. Indigo is neither primary nor secondary but tertiary; it cannot be made by combining equal amounts of any two primary colors, as it is a blend of primary blue and secondary violet. With red, finally, the first of the primary colors, the cycle comes back around to its beginning—and green and red, again, are flashing colors.

Indigo is the odd color out in the spectrum. The human eye is least sensitive to light in the indigo portion of the spectrum; some people cannot see it at all, and many others, recognizing that it is neither a primary or secondary color, insist on that basis that it does not belong in the spectrum at all. Nonetheless, it appears as the relatively wide, dark band just inside of violet in every rainbow.

IV. Color and Sound on the Tree of Life

The Tree of Life also has its traditional color symbolism, which relates in turn to the perspectives discussed already in this lecture. The first triad of spheres—Celi, Perydd, and Dofydd—are beyond color, as they are beyond all other forms of human experience. For symbolic reasons they are assigned three grades of colorless light: Celi is pure white brilliance, Perydd is the gray formed by the blending of light and darkness in equal amounts, and Dofydd is pure darkness. The second triad of spheres—Ener, Modur, and Muner—correspond to the three primary colors. Ener is represented by the color blue, Modur by red, and Muner by yellow. The third triad of spheres, Byw, Byth, and Ner, correspond to the three secondary colors. Byw is represented by the color green, Byth by orange, and Ner by violet.

The final sphere, Naf, is represented by the color indigo. Other Mystery Schools have used different colors to represent the final sphere of the Tree, and this is wholly appropriate since it is in the nature of symbolism that symbolic structures are adaptable to the needs of individual schools. Still, in the Druidical Mysteries indigo is the color assigned to Naf, and it will be found most effective as a representation of that sphere in practical workings.

Each of these color correspondences, in turn, has its own musical equivalent. The middle triad of the Tree of Life—Ener, Modur, and Muner—is represented by the C major chord, and the individual spheres by E minor for Ener, A minor for Modur, and C major for Muner, the chords of the elements water, fire, and air, respectively. While the middle triad, belonging to the circle of Gwynfydd, is, strictly speaking, above the realm of the elements, the roots of the elements are present in these three spheres—Ener is the root of water, Modur of fire, and Muner of air.

The triad in Abred of Byw, Byth, and Ner is more complex in musical terms, just as it is in terms of the process of manifestation discussed in another lecture. The three secondary colors also form a musical chord, but it is not one of the elemental chords already introduced; rather, it is the G major chord, G-B-D, extending up from below the initial A of the scale. Naf, finally, is represented by the F major chord, F-A-C.

V. *Practical Work with Color and Sound*

Most of the practical applications of this lore are reserved to the Druid Grade, where they will play an important role in the practice of Druidical magic. One application that may usefully be added to your practices at this time, however, is chanting or singing the divine names in ritual using the notes or chords of the elements.

To learn this you will need a musical instrument that does not require the use of your mouth—for example, a piano, a harp or any other stringed instrument, or a set of tuning forks. If you do not already know how to pick out the notes from A to a, ask someone more knowledgeable to teach you or find a suitable book that explains the instrument. Also, make sure the instrument is properly tuned so that you can be sure of making the correct note.

The simplest version of this practice is to learn the four notes corresponding to the elemental colors—C for air, A for fire, E for water, and D for earth. Listen to the note and match it with your voice, going up or down one or more octaves as needed to get the note into an octave where you can produce it without straining your voice. Practice chanting or singing the name Heu'c (pronounced "HEY'k") in a steady C, and so on for the others; if possible, learn to do so without having to check your voice against the musical instrument. (Some people find this relatively easy, while others do not.) When you are comfortable doing so, chant or sing the names in your daily practice of the Lesser Ritual of the Pentagram.

The more complex and more potent version is to chant or sing the divine names to the notes of the elemental chords. Here a special rule applies: when you have traced a summoning pentagram, chant or sing the notes of the chord in their normal rising order—you are quite literally calling up the power of one of the elements, using the divine name to do so. For example, in a summoning ritual, you would sing the name Heu'c to a rising series of notes, like this:

"Heuuuuuu'c"

C......E.....G

When you have traced a banishing pentagram, by contrast, you chant or sing the notes of the chord in their reversed, descending order, like this:

"Heuuuuuu'c"

G......E......C

Unless you have musical training or a great deal of natural talent, using the chords in this way will require extensive practice. The benefits in terms of increased effect in ritual, however, are extensive, and the training will also prepare you for other forms of magical practice in the grade that is still before you.

VI. Further Study

Little has been published on the magical applications of color and sound in modern times, and the great majority of what has been published either consists of erudite works on complex systems of teaching poorly suited to the beginner in this branch of magic, on the one hand, or is of very doubtful quality on the other. Any introductory book on music theory, of the sort intended for the novice who is attempting to learn to play an instrument, would be worth studying at this point, and it will also be to your advantage to learn a little about playing a musical instrument of some kind. Serious musical study is not required of you, but the ability to pick out a simple tune and having some sense of how chords function will be helpful to your future Druidical work. You should plan on doing at least this much during the time you spend in the Bardic Grade.

Practical Geomancy

THE ART OF GEOMANTIC divination using the Druid wands is an important part of the studies assigned to the Ovate Grade, and as you have already learned, it forms one of the foundations of training in the Bardic Grade as well. The form of geomantic chart introduced in the Ovate Grade knowledge lectures is only one of several that have come into use down through the centuries, and there are also a great many other methods of casting a chart, some more cumbersome, some less. You are free to explore other methods if those interest you. Nonetheless, the form of chart and method of casting already presented to you will be more than sufficient to take you to the depths and heights of the geomantic art.

What distinguishes the novice in geomancy from the master differs not at all from the equivalent factors in any other branch of occult studies, or indeed in any other skill whatsoever. There are two such factors, and the first is the unavoidable requirement of repeated practice. The more geomantic charts a student casts and interprets, the better he will become at casting and interpreting them. With this requirement we can provide little assistance except by encouraging each student of this art to cast and interpret a geomantic chart each day—and, of course, this is something already done in the lectures of this grade.

The second factor is partly up to the individual initiate but may also be furthered by instruction. This factor is the development of a richer and more elaborate sense of the meanings of the sixteen geomantic figures, which can then be applied to the interpretation of geomantic readings. Practice, again, will provide much assistance in this; each chart that is cast and read, and then compared to the events that followed, offers new insights into what the figures in the chart will have meant; and these insights, stored in memory either consciously or in that unconscious memory that comprises the largest part of what the world calls intuition, will provide the breadth of interpretive possibilities that will assist you in developing skill at geomancy. Yet it is also possible and useful to draw upon the experience of other geomancers, especially those masters of the art in the Middle Ages and Renaissance, when geomancy was much practiced and enriched with many subtle methods of interpretation.

The notes below, drawn from classic texts on the art of geomancy, may be found useful in this regard. They should not be used to replace the meanings of the figures you have already been taught, but to supplement them. Thus, for example, if you cast a geomantic chart for a question dealing with love, and the Judge and Witnesses are favorable but the figure Elw appears three times in the chart—an unfavorable indication for questions dealing with love, as mentioned below—this does not reverse the meaning of the Judge and Witnesses; instead, it suggests that the outcome will be generally favorable but with some difficulties. The nature of the difficulties may then be determined by considering the places in the chart where the figure Elw appears, particularly with regard to the four triplicities. The same principle should govern all the indications that follow; in all cases, the basic rules already learned take precedence.

I. Fixed and Mobile Figures

The geomantic figures are divided into two groups, these being fixed and mobile figures.

> FIXED: Gwyn, Pobl, Bendith Fawr, Merch, Elw, Carchar, Llawenydd, Pen y Ddraig

> MOBILE: Mab, Colled, Cyswllt, Coch, Tristwch, Llosgwrn y Ddraig, Bendith Fach, Ffordd

A fixed figure represents a situation that is relatively stable and resistant to change; a mobile figure, one that is relatively unstable and subject to change. In interpreting the Judge in any geomantic chart, consider whether it is made from two stable figures, two unstable figures, or one of each; combine this with the stable or mobile nature of the Judge itself, and you will know whether the outcome revealed by the chart will be of long, medium, or short duration. If both Witnesses and the Judge are fixed, the situation will be of very long duration; if any two are fixed and one is mobile, of relatively long duration; if any two are mobile and one is fixed, of relatively short duration; if both Witnesses and the Judge are mobile, of very short duration.

The same rule may be applied to any other figure composed of other figures—for example, in reading each of the four triplicities, consider whether the third figure in each triplicity is fixed or mobile and whether it is made from fixed or mobile figures. This will yield an indication of the stability or transiency of the situation indicated by each triplicity.

II. *Repetition of the Figures*

As mentioned, these meanings should be seen as modifying the general meaning of the chart, not overturning the indications of the Judge and Witnesses. When any of the figures appears two or more times in a single chart, in addition to the meanings indicated by its position and relation to other figures, it has the following significance:

MAB indicates lamentations and changes; great difficulty; fornication and pleasures; barriers to journeys by land; madness, delirium, and furor; it is unfortunate in questions concerning voyages and prisoners but fortunate for questions concerning pregnancy.

COLLED indicates loss; dishonesty; empty words; disputes; the complete loss of whatever was stolen or misplaced; peace and reconciliation after war; good health during travels; clouds and wind.

GWYN indicates deception; levity; misfortune for the querent; good fortune and liberty for prisoners if it appears in the company of the figure Coch; it is unfortunate for questions concerning illness.

POBL indicates changes, disputations, and troubles of every kind but also presages healing from illness.

BENDITH FAWR indicates the recovery of things stolen, voyages to distant places, liberation from prison, and the return of those who have been abroad; it is unfortunate for questions concerning illness.

CYSWLLT indicates an abundance of words; struggle and victory; profit for conspirators and traitors; it is unfortunate in questions concerning prisoners, travel, and pregnancy.

MERCH indicates peace, passion, excessive desires, obstacles caused by fear; thieves and depredations during travel; healing from illness; an advantage for the querent; it is unfortunate for questions concerning travel and voyages.

COCH indicates prejudice and bloodshed, useless and difficult projects; in questions of health, a serious illness; in questions concerning prisoners, a long imprisonment; gain through the favor of a superior or ruler; fire, if it appears in the company of the figure Colled; thieves, if it appears in the company of the figures Bendith Fawr or Pen y Ddraig.

ELW appearing two or more times in a chart indicates gain, obstacles in travel, recovery of things lost, larceny and theft; it is unfortunate in questions concerning love, illness, and prisoners.

CARCHAR indicates peace and reconciliation between enemies, safety in travels, and release after imprisonment.

TRISTWCH indicates that whatever is predicted by the chart will come more quickly than expected; it predicts loss, and the capture of a thief; it is unfortunate in questions concerning pregnant women and prisoners.

LLAWENYDD indicates quarrels and brawls in the midst of enjoyments—for example, between friends at a dinner or drinkers in a tavern; it indicates an object desired by the querent; healing from illness; attainment of honors and official positions.

LLOSGWRN Y DDRAIG indicates losses to the querent, a change of route, liberation for prisoners, and improvement of health.

PEN Y DDRAIG indicates stability and perfect success in whatever the querent has asked about; confirmation of benefits received from superiors or rulers; it is favorable in questions concerning illness and pregnancy.

BENDITH FACH indicates disputes and illnesses, fevers, discords, envy, madness, and the loss of the thing asked about; it is unfortunate for questions concerning illness.

FFORDD indicates the postponement of anything asked about in the reading; patience and a need to plan for the long term; debauchery; and healing from illness.

Note that whenever the figure Pobl appears as the Judge, the two Witnesses will be identical, and the above notes may be used as a guide to the outcome of the question.

III. *Special Meanings of the Figures*

Each of the geomantic figures also has, alongside its general meaning and its qualities, specific meanings that should be kept in mind when a given figure appears as Witness or Judge in a given class of questions.

IN QUESTIONS CONCERNING AGRICULTURE, LIVESTOCK, AND FERTILITY, the following figures are favorable: Gwyn, Bendith Fawr, Merch, Tristwch, and Pen y Ddraig. The following figures are medium: Colled, Pobl, Cyswllt, Elw, Carchar, and Ffordd. The following figures are unfavorable: Mab, Coch, Llawenydd, Llosgwrn y Ddraig, and Bendith Fach.

IN QUESTIONS CONCERNING GAIN AND LOSS, the following figures indicate gain: Gwyn, Bendith Fawr, Cyswllt, Merch, Elw, Carchar, Tristwch, Llawenydd, and Pen y Ddraig. The following indicate loss: Mab, Colled, Pobl, Coch, Llosgwrn y Ddraig, Bendith Fach, and Ffordd.

IN QUESTIONS CONCERNING HONESTY AND DECEPTION, the following figures indicate honesty: Gwyn, Elw, Merch, Llawenydd, Pobl, Pen y Ddraig, and Bendith Fawr. The following indicate deception: Mab, Colled, Coch, Carchar, Tristwch, Llosgwrn y Ddraig, Bendith Fach, and Ffordd. The following may indicate one or the other, depending on whether it is formed by figures of honesty or deception: Cyswllt.

IN QUESTIONS CONCERNING ILLNESS, the following figures are favorable for a prompt recovery: Colled, Merch, Llawenydd, Llosgwrn y Ddraig, Bendith Fach, and Ffordd. The following predict gradual recovery: Gwyn, Bendith Fawr, and Carchar. The following predict that the illness will continue long: Pobl, Cyswllt, Coch, Tristwch, and Pen y Ddraig. The following predict that it will worsen: Mab and Elw.

IN QUESTIONS CONCERNING LOVE, the following figures indicate true love: Cyswllt, Merch, Elw, and Llawenydd. The following indicate false love: Mab, Colled, Coch, Llosgwrn y Ddraig, and Bendith Fach. The remaining figures are mixed and suggest that some genuine affection coexists with other motives, relationships, or concerns.

IN QUESTIONS CONCERNING MARRIAGE, the following figures are best of all: Tristwch and Cyswllt. The following are good: Bendith Fawr, Elw, Llawenydd, and Pen y Ddraig. The following are medium: Mab, Gwyn, Pobl, and Merch. The following are bad: Colled, Coch, Bendith Fach, and Ffordd. The following are worst of all: Carchar and Llosgwrn y Ddraig.

IN QUESTIONS CONCERNING PRISON AND OTHER DIFFICULT SITUATIONS, the following figures indicate a prompt release: Mab, Colled, Llawenydd, Llosgwrn y Ddraig, Bendith Fach, and Ffordd. The following indicate that release will not come soon: Pobl, Bendith Fawr, Elw, Carchar, Tristwch, and Pen y Ddraig. The following indicate a middle time: Gwyn, Merch, and Coch. The following may indicate one or the other, depending on whether it is formed from figures indicating a quick or slow release: Cyswllt.

IN QUESTIONS CONCERNING RECEIVING BENEFITS FROM ANOTHER, the following figures are favorable: Gwyn, Bendith Fawr, Cyswllt, Elw, Llawenydd, Pen y Ddraig, and Bendith Fach. The following are unfavorable: Mab, Colled, Coch, and Ffordd. The remaining figures are neutral.

IN QUESTIONS CONCERNING RELOCATION, the following figures favor a move: Bendith Fawr, Llawenydd, Llosgwrn y Ddraig, and Pen y Ddraig. The following figures are medium: Mab, Gwyn, Cyswllt, and Elw. The following argue against a move: Colled, Pobl, Merch, Coch, Carchar, Tristwch, Bendith Fach, and Ffordd.

IN QUESTIONS CONCERNING SEX AND INFIDELITY, the following figures indicate that the person in question is faithful to his commitments: Gwyn, Bendith Fawr, Merch, Carchar, Tristwch, Llawenydd, and Pen y Ddraig. The following indicate that he is unfaithful: Mab, Colled, Pobl, Cyswllt, Coch, Elw, Llosgwrn y Ddraig, Bendith Fach, and Ffordd.

IN QUESTIONS CONCERNING THEFT, the following figures indicate that the item inquired about has been stolen: Mab, Colled, Pobl, Cyswllt, Coch, Carchar, Tristwch, Llosgwrn y Draig, Bendith Fach, and Ffordd. The following indicate that the item has not been stolen: Gwyn, Bendith Fawr, Merch, Elw, Llawenydd, and Pen y Ddraig. The following figures indicate that the item will be recovered: Mab, Gwyn, Cyswllt, Bendith Fawr, Elw, Carchar, and Pen y Ddraig. The following indicate that it will not be recovered: Colled, Pobl, Coch, Llawenydd, Llosgwrn y Ddraig, Bendith Fach, and Ffordd. The following indicate a partial recovery or a chance but not a certainty of recovery: Merch and Tristwch.

IN QUESTIONS CONCERNING TRAVELING, the following figures indicate a safe and speedy journey: Bendith Fawr, Elw, Llawenydd, Pen y Ddraig, and Bendith Fach. The following indicate a good journey, but only if the journey is by land: Ffordd and Carchar. The following figure is good for travel, but there will be delays: Merch. The following indicate a difficult journey: Colled, Gwyn, Pobl, Cyswllt, and Tristwch. The following indicate robbery on the journey: Coch and Llosgwrn y Ddraig. The following figure indicates other dangers on the way: Mab.

IN QUESTIONS CONCERNING WAR AND PEACE, the following figures indicate war: Mab, Colled, Coch, Tristwch, Llosgwrn y Ddraig, and Bendith Fach. The following indicate peace: Gwyn, Bendith Fawr, Merch, Elw, Llawenydd, and Pen y Ddraig. The remaining figures are uncertain, suggesting that the situation could go either way depending on the choices of individuals.

IN QUESTIONS CONCERNING WORRIES, the following figures indicate there is nothing to fear: Mab, Colled, Llosgwrn y Ddraig, and Ffordd. The following offer an unfavorable indication: Gwyn, Bendith Fawr, Cyswllt, Coch, Elw, and Pen y Ddraig. The remaining figures are neutral and depend on the figures accompanying them for their meaning.

IV. The Figures as Descriptions of Persons

Each of the geomantic figures also describes a type of individual, and that description may be read on one of three levels—the level of personality, the level of physical appearance, and the level of social relations. A grasp of these correspondences is useful for identifying persons described in readings, as well as obtaining insight into one's own affairs and those of others for whom geomantic charts may be cast.

MAB on the level of personality indicates cruelty and a hot temper, a tendency for feelings to show readily on the face, a preoccupation with appearance, easily aroused passions, and a fondness for fighting and sex. On the level of physical appearance it indicates short stature, a body more thick than thin, an attractive but fleshy face, skin of a reddish or brown color with a certain reddening of the face, a sparse beard (if male), little eyes, and poor teeth. On the level of social relations it indicates constant quarrels and difficulties with society, caused by rash behavior.

COLLED on the level of personality indicates love of reputation, simplicity, dishonesty, strong passions, and a quick temper. On the level of physical appearance it indicates a height a little shorter than average, a robust constitution, a long neck, a big head, large shoulders, a round face, a little mouth, attractive eyes, large feet, plenty of hair, and sometimes a visible scar or physical deformity. On the level of social relations it indicates a habit of easily spending money but also of escaping from misfortune.

GWYN on the level of personality indicates a love of peace and quiet, confidence, charity, innocence, modesty, a habit of easily acquiring friends but little ability to retain them, and a propensity to spend more than he earns. On the level of physical appearance it indicates an apple-shaped body, larger above the waist than below; a medium height; a large head; a forehead that perspires readily; a round face; a relatively thick beard (if male); coarse skin on the face; little eyes; and a mark on one eye. On the level of social relations it indicates many social connections but repeated problems with money.

POBL on the level of personality indicates inconstancy, dishonesty, pensive and variable moods, a love of travel and of change, and affections constantly shifting from one person to another. On the level of physical appearance it indicates a moderate height tending toward tallness, an attractive and smiling face, a good complexion, a large and heavy body, a spot over one eye or one eye larger than the other, sallow skin, long teeth, a visible scar or birthmark, and a stiff gait; if male, a thick beard. On the level of social relations it indicates a tendency to drift through life under the influence of others.

BENDITH FAWR on the level of personality indicates generosity, modesty, forthright speech, a love of order and tradition, easy manners, ambition tending toward arrogance, and the love of spending and dissipating wealth. On the level of physical appearance it indicates a large build, middle to tall height, a full face, small teeth, large eyes, fine skin, one leg larger than the other, and a propensity to blush. On the level of social relations it indicates high rank and station in life and a position in a respected trade or profession.

CYSWLLT on the level of personality indicates a love of reading and learning, glibness, goodwill, a facility at acquiring many friends, generosity, a propensity to spend more than he makes, dishonesty, luxury, talent, and illegal activities. On the level of physical appearance it indicates beauty and grace, a slender and lean body, a long and attractive face, attractive eyes, a small but fine beard (if male), a small nose, and fine legs.

MERCH on the level of personality indicates vanity, strong affections, love of harmony and beauty, concern for the regard of others, easy morals, and often a certain shallowness. On the level of physical appearance it indicates beauty, plumpness, a medium height, a soft voice, attractive eyes, a long neck, a large head, a round face, and a little mouth. On the level of social relations it indicates a busy social life and a habit of spending money freely.

COCH on the level of personality indicates vehemence, passion, violent speech, and a habit of sowing discord. On the level of physical appearance it indicates an angular face with a forbidding look, a pear-shaped body that is larger below the waist than above, skin reddish or brown, often red spots or pimples on the face, a sparse beard (if male), and a menacing and loud voice. On the level of social relations it indicates a bad reputation, criminal behavior, and plenty of boon companions who are no better.

ELW on the level of personality indicates modesty, tenacity, a love of fine clothing, an innate sense of elegance, and a lack of generosity and courage. On the level of physical appearance it indicates medium height, an attractive face, a small and narrow mouth, a body slightly bent forward, small ears, a long neck, plenty of hair, large eyes turned to the ground, the forward teeth larger than those further back, and narrow shoulders. On the level of social relations it indicates plenty of money and a respected position on account of ancestry, wealth, or power.

CARCHAR on the level of personality indicates harshness, self-discipline, cruelty, and an eagerness to gain wealth combined with an unwillingness to spend it; yet, despite this, it also indicates a certain greatness of soul. On the level of physical appearance it indicates a medium height tending toward shortness, a large head, short arms, relatively dark skin, a full and attractive beard (if male), strong jaws, a large chest, some defect of the feet, coarse hair, a short and slender neck, a small mouth, and small red eyes. On the level of social relations it indicates few but loyal friends and modest wealth well managed.

TRISTWCH on the level of personality indicates a tendency to hold grudges, disrespect for the law, dishonesty, a love of solitude, a quick temper, and very little inclination to laugh. On the level of physical appearance it indicates a long and lean body, dark or sallow skin, long teeth, a long face, a stiff gait, large feet, a mark on the heel, and coarse hair. On the level of social relations it indicates few friends and a bad reputation, which is not always earned.

LLAWENYDD on the level of personality indicates intelligence, good habits, religious feelings, honesty, rashness, and a fondness for white or light-colored clothing. On the level of physical appearance it indicates an attractive and modest appearance, a tendency to look toward the ground, a good figure, large feet, a round face, large eyes, a broad forehead, coarse hair, a thick neck, a large nose, and two teeth missing from the upper jaw. On the level of social relations it indicates a good reputation and ample wealth.

LLOSGWRN Y DDRAIG on the level of personality indicates unwholesome desires and habits, a lack of concern with the opinions of others, a hot temper, and an aged quality even in earliest childhood. On the level of physical appearance it indicates a lean, long body better shaped behind than before, a long face, large jaws, long and strong legs, a large nose and mouth, and long, uneven teeth. On the level of social relations it indicates a bad reputation, many disputes, and violence.

PEN Y DDRAIG on the level of personality indicates innocence, honesty, goodwill, enthusiasm, a lack of prudence, and a childlike quality even in old age. On the level of physical appearance it indicates a medium height, attractive eyes, a round and attractive face, a large nose and mouth, long teeth, and plenty of hair. On the level of social relations it indicates many friendships and relationships but also unhappy secrets of some kind.

BENDITH FACH on the level of personality indicates audacity and arrogance yet also a surprising degree of personal modesty, strong religious feelings, and greatness of soul and generosity. On the level of physical appearance it indicates a moderately round body and a height average to short, a round and pale face, large hands, a large nose, dark eyes, fine skin, a large forehead, sparse and coarse hair, narrow shoulders, and (if male) a moderate beard. On the level of social relations it indicates many changes in life and success coming only late in life.

FFORDD on the level of personality indicates a temper slow to awaken but savage if roused, a love of travel and change, and an inability to stay in any place or with any person or situation for more than a relatively short time. On the level of physical appearance it indicates a medium height, an apple-shaped body larger above the waist than below, one eye larger than the other or a spot above one eye, small teeth, and a forehead that perspires easily. On the level of social relations it indicates poverty.

V. *Miscellaneous Symbolism of the Figures*

Several of the geomantic figures also have additional correspondences that do not fit into the categories already given. These are worth keeping in mind, for it will sometimes happen that one of these additional correspondences will add a useful detail to the interpretation of a reading.

Mab also represents justice.

Colled also represents blood and events within hours.

Gwyn also represents books, manuscripts, and all-white objects.

Pobl also represents plants, herbs, and water.

Cyswllt also represents objects of diverse colors, temperance, and events within days.

Elw also represents prudence.

Carchar also represents prisons, tombs, dark pits, and dark, dull objects.

Llawenydd also represents fortitude.

Llosgwrn y Ddraig also represents anger and quarrels, and events within weeks.

Pen y Ddraig also represents the home and herds.

Ffordd also represents trees.

VI. *Further Study*

It is unfortunate that the classic texts of medieval and Renaissance geomancy are difficult to obtain. Cornelius Agrippa's *On Geomancy* and Gerard of Cremona's *On Astrological Geomancy* may sometimes be found reprinted as part of the *Fourth Book of Occult Philosophy* attributed to the former author; those students with access to the British Library or other scholarly libraries should consult the library catalogue for works on geomancy in English or other languages.

Preparation for the Bardic Initiation.

BEFORE YOU MAY PROCEED to the examination and initiation of the Bardic Grade, as has already been mentioned to you, it is necessary for you to make certain spagyric preparations, for the initiation ritual of this grade, like that of the Ovate Grade, has an alchemical dimension. Where one spagyric tincture, that of vervain, was used in the Ovate Grade initiation, four are to be used in the initiation of the Bardic Grade— and the four herbs that are to be used as the basis for these tinctures are determined by divination.

This is the reason—or, more precisely, one of the reasons—for the assignment of sixteen herbs to the sixteen geomantic figures in the lecture on herbs in magic and alchemy given previously. When you are ready to begin preparing the tinctures, you must cast four Mother figures as though you were going to use them as the basis for a geomantic chart. Instead of constructing the chart, though, you will take each Mother figure as an indication for one of the herbs you will use to make your tinctures for the initiation of this grade. Whichever herb corresponds to the First Mother will be the basis for a tincture that, in the ritual, represents the essence of the element of fire; the herb corresponding to the Second Mother, the tincture representing air; the Third Mother, that of water; and the Fourth, that of earth.

The elemental nature of the herb itself does not influence this attribution, which applies only to this one initiation ritual. Thus, for example, if the First Mother you cast is Tristwch, the herb that will represent fire for you in your Bardic initiation will be comfrey, even though comfrey in itself is cold and moist and thus corresponds to water. The reason is simply that the Bardic Grade initiation is meant to balance and integrate the elemental forces within the initiate; if the element of fire is too strong in you already, an herb of water in the place of fire will calm and balance it so that it can relate to the other elements in a more harmonious fashion.

Similarly, it may also happen that you cast the same Mother for two or, exceptionally, more of the elements. In this case, you will make three or two or only one alchemical tincture instead of four, and use the same tincture for those elements indicated by your divination.

The method you use to create your spagyric tinctures may be the same very simple method you used to create a vervain tincture for the Ovate Grade initiation. Alternatively, any of the methods outlined in the paper on vegetable alchemy in the fifth knowledge lecture of that grade may be used.

Several weeks at least will be needed to prepare the tinctures before your initiation, so you would do well to plan ahead and begin the process of creating them before you finish the rest of the work of the Bardic Grade. When you have prepared all your tinctures, you may proceed to the Examination of the Bardic Grade. You will need only a small portion of each tincture for the initiation; the rest should be saved in a cool, dry place for later use.

The Examination of the Bardic Grade.

THE FOLLOWING EXAMINATION SHOULD be completed by you, working unassisted and alone, before you proceed to the initiation ceremony of this grade. You may use the lectures you have received and the books that you have studied as references for the work. Nonetheless it is important for you to be honest with yourself; if you find that any of the questions below leave you completely at a loss, you owe it to yourself to leave this examination, study the relevant material, and practice the techniques you have been taught, until you can return to the examination and complete the work with confidence.

It is strongly recommended that you write out the answers to the questions below, and when you are finished, keep the test paper for future reference. You may find it useful later to review your work and see what your further studies can add to it.

* * *

1. Choose one pathworking you performed during the time you spent on the work of this grade. Write it out in full, copying out the details from your practice journal, and make a list of all the symbols, concepts, and themes from the pathworking you used as subjects for meditation. Reviewing the pathworking, what did you learn from it?

2. Choose one subject for meditation from the pathworking you chose, and describe in detail one session of meditation on it. Reviewing the meditation, what did you learn from it?

3. Choose one of your daily geomantic divinations. Draw the complete chart, and then copy the full interpretation of the chart, including any indications you drew from the material covered in the Bardic Grade lecture on geomancy.

After this, note how the reading related to the events of the day. Reviewing the reading, interpretation, and events, what did you learn from them?

4. Consider your daily practice of the Lesser Ritual of the Pentagram and the Central Ray exercise, reviewing the passages in your practice journal that discuss this. Reviewing this practice and its effects, what did you learn from it?

5. Consider the five additional lectures of the Bardic Grade—on the Tree of Life, sacred geometry, plant magic and alchemy, color and sound, and practical geomancy. Which of these lectures seemed most useful and interesting to you? Reviewing your studies of that lecture, what did you learn from it?

6. In the final section of each of the five lessons just mentioned, further studies were suggested to you, including several books. List the books you read in response to this request, and choose the one you found most useful and interesting. Reviewing that book, what did you learn from it?

7. Describe in general terms any changes in yourself, your life, and your circumstances that have taken place over the course of your time in the Bardic Grade, and whether any of them seem to be related in any way to your practice of the Druidical Mysteries. Reviewing these changes, what did you learn from them?

The Initiation of the Bardic Grade.

THE CEREMONY THAT FOLLOWS will require you to be perfectly familiar with the opening and closing ceremony of the Bardic temple, the Pentagram Rituals of the four elements, the symbolism of the four inner groves, the methods of meditation taught in previous lectures, and the art of casting and interpreting a geomantic chart using the Druid wands. Like the Ovate Grade initiation you have already received, this ritual only has such power as you are capable of bringing to it by virtue of the work you have already done in your Bardic Grade studies. You are therefore most earnestly advised, if you have not performed the meditations and ritual work, studied the material presented in previous knowledge lectures, and completed the Bardic Grade examination to the best of your ability, to return to the studies and exercises already given and prepare yourself more fully for the initiation of the Bardic Grade.

On a more formal level, to perform the ceremony you will need all the items required for the altar of a Bardic temple, along with your set of Druid wands and the four spagyric tinctures representing the influences of the four inner groves, which you have prepared according to the instructions you have received. You will also need your white robe and green Ovate's sash, and another sash, blue in color, identical to the Ovate sash except that it is worn across the body from the right shoulder to the left hip. This will represent your rank as a Bard and will be put on at a certain point in the ceremony.

* * *

When you are ready to begin the initiation ceremony of the Bardic Grade, set up the temple as you have been taught to do, with the altar at the center draped in white, the three candles, the cauldrons of water and fire, and the cross and circle in their Bardic positions. Wear your white robe and green Ovate's sash. A chair should be placed in the west of the space where you will perform the ritual. Near the altar have your blue Bard's sash, your Druid wands, a sheet of paper and a pen, a small bowl, a larger bowl, a glass, a small pitcher or other vessel of water, an eyedropper, and the jars containing the spagyric tinctures of the four herbs you have selected by divination.

Begin the ceremony by performing the complete opening ceremony as you have been taught to do. When you have finished the opening and are standing at the west side of the altar facing east, say: "By all the powers here invoked, and in the presence of the Guardians of the Bardic temple, I present myself as one who has successfully completed the required examination and who therefore seeks to take the obligations and attain the blessings that the four elements bring to the Bardic initiate. I therefore enter the realm of earth."

Perform the complete Calling of Earth as you have learned and practiced it. When you have completed it, while you are still standing in the Sign of Earth and before returning to the altar, say: "I, (say your full name here), in the presence of all the holy powers of earth and the light of the Golden Dawn, do promise and bind myself anew to fulfill every part of my Ovate obligation in letter and in spirit; and I furthermore take upon myself the first of the four great obligations of the Mysteries, which is to Know."

Release the Sign of Earth, return to the altar, and stand at the south of the altar facing north. Pour a small amount of water into the small bowl and a similar amount into the glass; put seven drops of your tincture of earth into the bowl and the same amount into the glass. Say: "Having taken the obligation of earth, I ask that I may receive the blessing and empowerment of earth." Lift the glass containing the water and tincture, holding it high as though in offering, and then lower it and drink its entire contents. Then dip the index and middle fingers of your right hand into the bowl and trace the Sigil of the Winter Solstice on your forehead and the palm of your left hand. Empty the rest of the water from the small bowl into the large bowl. Say: "Having taken the obligation and received the blessing of earth, I now enter the realm of water."

Now perform the complete Calling of Water as you have learned and practiced it. When you have completed it, while you are still standing in the Sign of Water and before returning to the altar, say: "I, (say your full name here), in the presence of all the holy powers of water and the light of the Golden Dawn, do again promise and bind myself anew to fulfill every part of my Ovate obligation in letter and in spirit; and I furthermore take upon myself the second of the four great obligations of the Mysteries, which is to Dare."

Release the Sign of Water, return to the altar, and stand at the east of the altar facing west. Pour a small amount of water into the small bowl and a similar amount into the glass; put seven drops of your tincture of water into the bowl and the same amount into the glass. Say: "Having taken the obligation of water, I ask that I may receive the blessing and empowerment of water." Lift the glass containing the water and tincture, holding it high as though in offering, and then lower it and drink its entire contents. Then dip the index and middle fingers of your right hand into the bowl and trace the Sigil of the Autumn Equinox on your forehead and the palm of your left hand. Empty the rest of the water from the small bowl into the large bowl. Say: "Having taken the obligation and received the blessing of water, I now enter the realm of air."

Now perform the complete Calling of Air as you have learned and practiced it. When you have completed it, while you are still standing in the Sign of Air and before returning to the altar, say: "I, (say your full name here), in the presence of all the holy powers of air and the light of the Golden Dawn, do again promise and bind myself anew to fulfill every part of my Ovate obligation in letter and in spirit; and I furthermore take upon myself the third of the four great obligations of the Mysteries, which is to Will."

Release the Sign of Air, return to the altar, and stand at the west of the altar facing east. Pour a small amount of water into the small bowl and a similar amount into the glass; put seven drops of your tincture of air into the bowl and the same amount into the glass. Say: "Having taken the obligation of air, I ask that I may receive the blessing and empowerment of air." Lift the glass containing the water and tincture, holding it high as though in offering, and then lower it and drink its entire contents. Then dip the index and middle fingers of your left hand into the bowl and trace the Sigil of the Spring Equinox on your forehead and the palm of your right hand. Empty the rest of the water from the small bowl into the large bowl. Say: "Having taken the obligation and received the blessing of air, I now enter the realm of fire."

Now perform the complete Calling of Fire as you have learned and practiced it. When you have completed it, while you are still standing in the Sign of Fire and before returning to the altar, say: "I, (say your full name here), in the presence of all the holy powers of fire and the light of the Golden Dawn, do again promise and bind myself anew to fulfill every part of my Ovate obligation in letter and in spirit; and I furthermore take upon myself the last of the four great obligations of the Mysteries, which is to be Silent."

Release the Sign of Fire, return to the altar, and stand at the north of the altar facing south. Pour a small amount of water into the small bowl and a similar amount into the glass; put seven drops of your tincture of fire into the bowl and the same amount into the glass. Say: "Having taken the obligation of fire, I ask that I may receive the blessing and empowerment of fire." Lift the glass containing the water and tincture, holding it high as though in offering, and then lower it and drink its entire contents. Then dip the index and middle fingers of your left hand into the bowl and trace the Sigil of the Summer Solstice on your forehead and the palm of your right hand. Empty the rest of the water from the small bowl into the large bowl.

Circle the altar until you are at the west side of the altar and face east. Place your left hand on the circle and cross upon the altar, and raise your right hand, palm forward, facing the east, and repeat the following words:

"I thus pledge myself to Know, to Dare, to Will, and to be Silent: to Know the teachings of these Druidical Mysteries and the secret wisdom of the holy powers of nature; to Dare all the challenges that the way of the Mysteries and the blindness of unawakened humanity may place upon my path; to Will the healing, blessing, and unfolding of all beings whatsoever toward the better and the best; and to be Silent concerning every secret confided in me, now and in times to come.

"To all these things I pledge and bind myself, placing myself in the hands of the Guardians of the Bardic temple and the holy powers of the four elements, and should I ever violate this, my Bardic obligation, in any particular or under any pretense, I freely and willingly consent to the loss of whatever powers may be conferred upon me by this initiation, the course of study and practice that has prepared me for it, and the further studies and practices I shall pursue in the Druidical Mysteries hereafter, in the knowledge that I shall regain such powers only when by labor and suffering I shall again have proved myself worthy of them. May the holy powers of nature and the rays of the Golden Dawn uphold me in this, my Bardic obligation."

Be seated in the chair in the west of the temple; enter into meditation, and meditate on the obligation you have taken until your forehead and palms are dry. Pay close attention to any insights you may receive and any thoughts or images that come to you during this meditation. When you are finished, advance to the west side of the altar, facing east, and say, "Having taken the obligations and received the blessings and empowerments of the Bardic Grade, and being mindful of the responsibilities I do accept thereby, I do proclaim myself a Bard of the Druidical Order of the Golden Dawn, and I clothe myself in the garment of that grade." Put on the blue sash; it is worn over the green Ovate sash so that the two form a saltire, or diagonal cross, upon your body.

At this point, say: "I now ask the holy powers of nature for an omen to guide me in my work as a Bard." Take your Druid wands and cast a geomantic chart with them; draw up the chart and interpret it. The chart you cast at this time should be saved and reviewed repeatedly during your studies of the subsequent grade.

When you have finished casting and interpreting the divination, set it aside. Standing at the west of the altar, facing east, say: "In the presence of the holy powers of nature and the light of the Golden Dawn, I proclaim that this ceremony of initiation into the Bardic Grade has been duly performed, and I ask the Guardians of the Bardic temple to guide me until and unless the time may come that I pass to a grade beyond."

Now perform the License to Depart of the elements of fire, air, water, and earth, in that order. When you have finished this, perform the complete closing ritual of the Bardic temple. This completes the ceremony of initiation.

*   *   *

After the completion of this ceremony, once again, a choice of great importance faces you: to continue with your studies in the Druidical Mysteries as presented in these lessons or to take what you have learned in your Ovate and Bardic studies and depart. In either case, your rank and initiation as a Bard remain with you, and you may freely use the teachings you have already received in whatever way may correspond to the requirements of your Bardic obligation and your own personal decisions and needs.

The work of the Druid Grade surpasses that of the Bardic Grade to an even greater degree than the Bardic Grade surpasses that of the Ovate. So far, your studies and practices have focused, as the basic and intermediate training of every Mystery School must focus, on the training, purification, and transformation of the individual. That work continues in the Druid Grade at an even greater degree of intensity, but to it is added the more practically and spiritually challenging work of ceremonial magic, which is capable of transforming not only the practitioner but the wider world.

This work cannot be pursued halfheartedly with any chance of success. If you continue beyond this point, you will be committing yourself to a course of study and practice that will challenge you to your core, for only thus can the hidden powers of the self be awakened and brought under conscious control. If you are not prepared to enter on this more demanding course of study, it would be better for you to leave it for another time or another life than to enter into it and stop partway through.

It is therefore strongly recommended that, just as you did before beginning your Bardic studies, you take some time to glance over the lessons of the grade ahead and be sure that you are willing and able to undertake the course of work that is before you, before proceeding to the introductory lecture of the Druid Grade.

DRUIDICAL ORDER OF THE GOLDEN DAWN

— △ —

The Druid Grade

— ▽ —

*T*hrice welcome, Bard!

You have now successfully completed the studies and practices of the first two degrees of our order, and you stand at the portal of a wider world. All the teachings you have learned on your journey to this point will be necessary for your journey into that world. Thus you will find it helpful to review the knowledge lectures of the Ovate Grade and the rituals, lectures, and recommended readings of the Bardic Grade to remind yourself of the context that gives meaning to the more advanced teachings you will meet in this grade. You may expect to devote at least one year, and as much more beyond this as you find useful, to the work required for this grade.

The manner of instruction in the Druid Grade is the same as that in the Bardic Grade, but the nature of that instruction differs in an important respect. In the earlier grades of our order the theory of practical occultism is presented to the student along with a graded series of preparatory disciplines. This preparation is essential to success in magic; those who plunge directly into an attempt to shape the self and the world by magical means without first undergoing an appropriate training too often find themselves in a condition like a man who has done no exercise since his school days and then attempts to copy the weightlifting feat of some famous strongman. The failures and self-induced harm caused by such misguided attempts have had more than a little to do with the dubious reputation of magic in modern times.

At this point in your training, however, you have accomplished the work of basic and intermediate training we have required of you, and you are now prepared for the more demanding work of practical magic. That work is now before you. The papers that follow will instruct you in how to prepare and consecrate the magical working tools of the Druid, which are the wand, the sickle, and the serpent's egg. Then you will learn how to perform each of the three basic categories of Druidical ceremonial magic: the consecration of amulets and magical substances, the conjuration of elemental intelligences and spirits, and ceremonies of transformation for such purposes as invisibility and the projection of consciousness into animal forms, as well as ritual workings to draw down the power of the heavens on the solstices and equinoxes, the four great holy days of the Druidical calendar. In addition to these papers, a series of additional lectures cover more advanced topics in the theory and practice of Druidical magic, and these also await your careful attention.

All these ceremonies and teachings rest on a foundation that will already be familiar to you: the core daily practices of meditation, ritual, and divination. These should under no circumstances be neglected as you proceed to the teachings of the Druid Grade. Quite the contrary; you should plan on continuing your daily exercise of the Central Ray, meditation, and geomantic divination, just as you did while you studied the Bardic Grade teachings; the practical magic of the Druid Grade should be *added* to this rhythm of daily practice, not put in its place. You will find, as you make these daily disciplines a continuing part of your life, that they reveal more and still more depth and power the longer they are practiced.

In the work of preparing yourself for initiation into the Druid Grade, then, the fundamental practices you have already learned remain a necessary part of the work, and you will also be expected to perform at least one ritual of each of the three basic categories mentioned above—that is, one ritual of consecration, one of conjuration, and one of transformation—as well as an additional ritual of self-initiation. Beyond this, however, a great deal will be left to your own preferences.

It is part of the distinctive nature of the Druid Grade that its initiates tend to specialize; some devote more time to alchemy, others to geomancy; rituals of evocation appeal more to one, while ceremonies of consecration are more attractive to another; there are those who work with the already established rituals and teachings and those who add new material to the traditional lore of the Druidical path. All this is appropriate, and indeed necessary, for the talents and needs of one individual differ from those of another. While a common fund of teaching and practice is essential to a school of the Mysteries, the binary that inevitably exists between such a common fund, and everything that is not incorporated in it, is best resolved into a ternary by the third factor of individual choice.

For the same reason, while you will be expected to read and study at least nine books on occultism and the Druidical tradition during the time you spend preparing for your Druid Grade initiation, only one of these books is prescribed for you. This is *Dogme et Rituel de la Haute Magie* by Éliphas Lévi, usually known in its English translation as *Transcendental Magic*.

The fountainhead of modern magical theory and practice, Lévi's book is more often cited than read and more often read than understood. Lévi himself, in accordance with the occult traditions of his time, concealed much of what he had to teach beneath a sometimes evasive symbolism and a dry and distinctive sense of humor. He expected students to apply the tools of study, meditation, and magical experience to his work, and that expectation has too often proven unfounded. It is also unfortunate that the only English translation commonly available is that of A. E. Waite, who made comprehension of the work more difficult with his famously leaden prose style and a barrage of unhelpful footnotes that, evidently intended to show that Waite's own knowledge of occultism was superior to Lévi's, reveal the opposite with painful clarity.

Such difficulties are common in encountering the heritage of occult tradition, which has, after all, had to pass through the hands of generation after generation of all-too-human exponents. As you take your place in the golden chain of initiates of the Mystery Teachings, it is to be hoped that you remember your own limitations as you assess those of the teachers and writers whose work has guided you to this point. In this spirit, we welcome you again to this further stage of your path in the Druidical Mysteries.

The Guardians of the Order

The Supreme Ritual of the Pentagram.

IN THE INITIATION OF the Bardic Grade, the pentagram rituals assigned to the four elements are performed one at a time to summon and banish all four of the elements. That was appropriate in the context of that initiatory work, but a less cumbersome approach will be found more useful for most purposes. This is the Supreme Ritual of the Pentagram, which combines the pentagrams of the elements and the words of summoning and banishing. This ritual plays an important part in much of the ceremonial work before you, and it should be learned and committed to memory as soon as possible in your training in this grade.

The Supreme Ritual of the Pentagram is to be performed whenever the power of all four elements is to be summoned or banished together; when a single element is to be summoned or banished, the ritual forms you have already learned—the elemental rituals of the pentagram, the calling of the elements, and the License to Depart—are to be done in the same way as before.

Several of the ceremonial workings discussed in the lectures of this grade specify that the Supreme Ritual of the Pentagram or, alternatively, one of the elemental rituals, is to be used. In order to develop skill with the Supreme Ritual, you may find it useful when time permits to perform it in place of the Lesser Ritual of the Pentagram in your daily ritual working, before performing the exercise of the Central Ray.

The Supreme Ritual of the Pentagram is performed in two modes, one to summon and the other to banish.

I. *Summoning Supreme Ritual of the Pentagram*

1. Perform the Rite of the Rays in the usual form, standing at the west of the altar, facing east.

2. Go to the east and trace a summoning pentagram of air. Imagine that you are drawing it in the air in lines of glowing yellow light. Point to its center and say: "In the great name **BELISAMA**, the lady of air, Spirits of Air, behold the rays of the Golden Dawn! Come ye forth and assist me in this work of air."

   Next, in the center of the pentagram draw the Sigil of the Spring Equinox, and visualize it drawn in glowing yellow light. Point to its center and say: "By the hawk of May in the heights of heaven and the mystical gate of the eastern stars, Spirits of Air, behold the rays of the Golden Dawn! Come ye forth and assist me in this work of air."

   Now make the Sign of Air. Say: "By all the powers of the eastern quarter of the world, by the splendor of the dawn and the renewal of spring, by the strength of the rushing winds and the everlasting sky, Spirits of Air, behold the rays of the Golden Dawn! Come ye forth and assist me in this work of air."

3. Point again to the center of the air pentagram and draw a line a quarter of the way around the temple to the south, visualizing the line drawn in pure white light. There draw a summoning pentagram of fire. Imagine that you are drawing it in the air in lines of glowing red light. Point to its center and say: "In the great name **TOUTATIS**, the lord of fire, Spirits of Fire, behold the rays of the Golden Dawn! Come ye forth and assist me in this work of fire."

   Next, in the center of the pentagram, draw the Sigil of the Summer Solstice and visualize it drawn in glowing red light. Point to its center and say: "By the white stag who dwells in the summer greenwood and the mystical gate of the southern stars, Spirits of Fire, behold the rays of the Golden Dawn! Come ye forth and assist me in this work of fire."

   Now make the Sign of Fire. Say: "By all the powers of the southern quarter of the world, by the brilliant light of noon and the heat of summer, by the glory of the dancing flame and the verdant fire of life, Spirits of Fire, behold the rays of the Golden Dawn! Come ye forth and assist me in this work of fire."

4. Point again to the center of the fire pentagram and draw a line a quarter of the way around the temple to the west, visualizing the line drawn in pure white light. There draw a summoning pentagram of water like those you traced in the pentagram ritual you have just completed. Imagine that you are drawing it in the air in lines of glowing blue light. Point to its center and say: "In the great name **SIRONA**, the lady of water, Spirits of Water, behold the rays of the Golden Dawn! Come ye forth and assist me in this work of water."

Next, in the center of the pentagram draw the Sigil of the Autumn Equinox and visualize it drawn in glowing blue light. Point to its center and say: "By the salmon of wisdom who dwells in the sacred pool and the mystical gate of the western stars, Spirits of Water, behold the rays of the Golden Dawn! Come ye forth and assist me in this work of water."

Now make the Sign of Water. Say: "By all the powers of the western quarter of the world, by the peace of evening twilight and the bounty of autumn, by the power of the rolling waves and the river flowing toward the sea, Spirits of Water, behold the rays of the Golden Dawn! Come ye forth and assist me in this work of water."

5. Point again to the center of the water pentagram and draw a line a quarter of the way around the temple to the north, visualizing the line drawn in pure white light. There draw a summoning pentagram of earth; imagine that you are drawing it in the air in lines of glowing green light. Point to its center and say: "In the great name **CERNUNNOS**, the lord of earth, Spirits of Earth, behold the rays of the Golden Dawn! Come ye forth and assist me in this work of earth."

Next, in the center of the pentagram draw the Sigil of the Winter Solstice, visualizing it in glowing green light. Point to its center and say: "By the great bear who guards the turning heavens and the mystical gate of the northern stars, Spirits of Earth, behold the rays of the Golden Dawn! Come ye forth and assist me in this work of earth."

Now make the Sign of Earth. Say: "By all the powers of the northern quarter of the world, by the silence of midnight and the cold of winter, by the strength of the standing stone and the bare and leafless tree, Spirits of Earth, behold the rays of the Golden Dawn! Come ye forth and assist me in this work of earth."

6. Point again to the center of the earth pentagram and draw a line a quarter of the way around the temple to the east, completing the circle. Return to the altar. Stand at its western side, facing east, and extend your arms downward and to the sides, taking on the posture of the Three Rays of Light. Say: "Before me, the hawk of May and the powers of air. Behind me, the salmon of wisdom and the powers of water. To my right hand, the white stag and the powers of fire. To my left hand, the great bear and the powers of earth. For about me flame the pentagrams and upon me shine the Three Rays of Light."

7. Perform the Rite of the Rays as before. This completes the ritual.

II. Banishing Supreme Ritual of the Pentagram

1. Perform the Rite of the Rays in the usual form, standing at the west of the altar, facing east.

2. Go to the east and say: "With the blessings of **BELISAMA** and of the hawk of May in the heights of heaven, and with thanks for your assistance in this work of air, Spirits of Air, I license ye to depart. Go in peace, and peace be between ye and me." Then trace the banishing air pentagram toward the east, visualizing the pentagram drawn in yellow light. Point to the center and trace a line of white light a quarter of the way around the temple, ending in the south.

3. Say: "With the blessings of **TOUTATIS** and of the white stag who dwells in the summer greenwood, and with thanks for your assistance in this work of fire, Spirits of Fire, I license ye to depart. Go in peace, and peace be between ye and me." Then trace the banishing fire pentagram toward the south, visualizing the pentagram drawn in red light. Point to the center and trace a line of white light a quarter of the way around the temple, ending in the west.

4. Say: "With the blessings of **SIRONA** and of the salmon of wisdom in the sacred pool, and with thanks for your assistance in this work of water, Spirits of Water, I license ye to depart. Go in peace, and peace be between ye and me." Then trace the banishing water pentagram toward the west, visualizing the pentagram drawn in blue light. Point to the center and trace a line of white light a quarter of the way around the temple, ending in the north.

5. Say: "With the blessings of **CERNUNNOS** and of the great bear who guards the turning heavens, and with thanks for your assistance in this work of earth, Spirits of Earth, I license ye to depart. Go in peace, and peace be between ye and me." Then trace the banishing earth pentagram toward the north, visualizing the pentagram drawn in green light. Point to the center and trace a line of white light a quarter of the way around the temple, ending in the east and completing the circle.

6. Return to the altar, standing at its western side, facing east, and extend your arms downward and to the sides, taking on the posture of the Three Rays of Light. Say: "Before me, the hawk of May and the powers of air. Behind me, the salmon of wisdom and the powers of water. To my right hand, the white stag and the powers of fire. To my left hand, the great bear and the powers of earth. For about me flame the pentagrams, and upon me shine the Three Rays of Light."

7. Perform the Rite of the Rays as before. This completes the ritual.

The Ritual of the OIU.

The Ritual

FIRST, stand in the center of the ritual space, facing east. In silence make the following three signs:

1. The sign of the Bounty of Nature. Extend your left hand down and out to your side in a straight line, hand extended, palm facing forward. Place your right hand, palm up, at the level of your solar plexus, so that your forearm is parallel to the ground; your elbow is extended out to your side.

2. The sign of the Cauldron of Annwn. Raise both arms to the sides, curving them to form the outline of a cauldron; the hands are a little above head level, with the fingertips pointing straight up and the palms facing each other.

3. The sign of the Child of Light. Bring the fingertips of your right hand to the point of your left shoulder; allow your right forearm to rest across your chest in a diagonal line, so that your right elbow is at your right side; bring your left hand across so that the fingers cup the right elbow, the left forearm being parallel to the ground and the left elbow being at the left side.

SECOND, light a stick of incense. Go to the southeastern corner of the space, face southeast, and trace the Three Rays of Light / | \ with the burning end of the stick of incense: first the left-hand ray / , then the right-hand ray \ , then the central ray | . Visualize the rays drawn in pure white light. Point the stick to the middle of the central ray and vibrate the divine name HESUS.

THIRD, trace a line with the end of the incense stick a quarter of the way around the space to the southwest corner, draw the Three Rays in the same way, point the stick to the middle of the central ray, and vibrate the same name. Repeat this process twice more, drawing the rays and vibrating the name in the northwest and northeast corners of the space. Complete the circle by drawing the line back around to the southeast.

FOURTH, pause briefly at the southeast, again visualizing the three rays you have drawn there, and then draw a line of light with the incense up as far as you can reach, and then across the ceiling to a point above the center of the space. There draw the three rays again and vibrate the name. Draw a line across the ceiling to its northwest corner and then down, pausing briefly at the symbol you have drawn in the northwest, and then continue the line down to the floor and then across to the middle of the floor; there draw the three rays and vibrate the name again. Then complete the circle by tracing a line across the floor to its southeast corner and then back up to the starting point in the southeast.

FIFTH, pause, trace again the line of light around from southeast to southwest, pause there, and then draw a line of light up and across the ceiling to the symbol above the middle of the space. Pause, and then continue across the ceiling to the northeast corner and down to the symbol in the northeast. Pause, and then continue down and then across the floor to the symbol at the center of the floor. Pause, and then continue across to the southwest corner of the floor and then back up to the symbol in the southwest, completing the circle.

SIXTH, trace again the line of light further from the southwest around to the northwest, northeast, and southeast, returning to your starting point. There, again facing the southeast, trace the three rays again, larger and somewhat lower in the air; point to the middle of the central ray and again vibrate HESUS. Then, above the rays you have just traced, trace the rays again in their alternate form \ | / with the stick of incense, first the right-hand ray /, then the left-hand ray \, and finally the central ray | ; point to the middle of the central ray with the stick of incense and vibrate the name HU. The completed form is called the Tribann and is shown in the diagram below:

SEVENTH, set aside the incense and perform the Analysis of the Grand Word. Say:

"In the beginning of things Einigen Gawr, the first of all created beings, beheld three rays of light descending from the heavens, in which were all the knowledge that ever was and ever will be. These same were three voices and the three letters of one name, the Name of the Infinite One: Gwron, Plennydd, and Alawn; Knowledge, Power, and Peace:

"A, Knowledge, the sign of the Bounty of Nature." Make the first of the three signs described in the first step of the ritual, the sign of the Bounty of Nature.

"W, Power, the sign of the Cauldron of Annwn." Make the second sign, the sign of the Cauldron of Annwn.

"N, Peace, the sign of the Child of Light." Make the third sign, the sign of the Child of Light.

"A." Make the sign of the Bounty of Nature again. "W." Make the sign of the Cauldron of Annwn again. "N." Make the sign of the Child of Light again. "**AWEN.**" (Pronounce this ah-oo-en, drawing out the syllables.) "As in that hour, so in this; may the light that was before the worlds descend!"

Visualize a ray of light descending from infinite space above you to fill the space with pure brilliance. Maintain the image as long and as intensely as you can. When you are ready to release the visualization, say: "Gwron. Plennydd. Alawn. All are one in the infinite **CELI.**" This concludes the ritual.

The Uses of the Ritual

1. It veils the enaid, or body of aetherial energies, against outside influences and makes it difficult for any hostile being, incarnate or otherwise, to reach you. The pentagram rituals protect, but they also light up the aetherial realm and make entities on that plane aware of you. In practical magic the pentagram rituals are thus more useful; the OIW Ritual is for those times when you wish to withdraw from the aetherial realms for rest or healing, or when you seek to work with higher and more spiritual influences. When you are much distracted, use the Lesser Ritual of the Pentagram to banish and the Ritual of the OIW to establish peace with power.

2. It is a call to higher modes of consciousness and withdraws you from the physical and aetherial alike. It is thus a very good preparation for meditation

or for any situation in which you may need or desire to make contact with the highest levels of your own being and the divine influences of the cosmos.

3. It may be done to bless and heal others who are in pain or difficulty. To do this, build up with your imagination a clear image of the person to be helped, as though he were standing in the middle of the ritual space. Perform the ritual, weaving the pattern of rays and lines around the person you wish to help, and then call down the light with the intention that it descend on that person. When the ceremony is done, send the imagined form to the person you wish to help, with a strong intention that it will bring healing and peace with it. This will be found to be a very effective method for healing at a distance.

The Grand Word and Its Analysis

The letters OIW, as you learned in the first knowledge lecture of the Ovate Grade, were used among Welsh Bards to conceal the Grand Word they had inherited from the ancient Druids; the letters OIV (or, in modern spelling, OIU) were also used for this purpose. The secret hidden in these letters may be readily found by reviewing the history of the Welsh alphabet. There were anciently five vowels in Welsh, A E I O U, to which was added in early times W, and more recently Y. Take the six older vowels and remove O, I, and W, and the remaining letters are A, E, and U; if O, I, and U are removed instead, A, E, and W are left. O, I, and W (or U) are out of their proper order; this served as a reminder that the remaining letters also needed to be read in a different order. The proper order is AUE or AWE, the ancient spelling of the word now spelled and pronounced AWEN.

No word in the old Welsh tongue is of greater importance in religion, poetry, or philosophy than awen. In modern Welsh it means "muse" or "source of inspiration," and the word *awenydd*, "one who has awen," is a common word for "poet." In medieval times, according to the twelfth-century author Geraldus Cambrensis, awenyddion (this is the plural of awenydd) were seers who foretold the future while in trance. Old Welsh poetry, and texts such as *Barddas* that claim to descend from the old Bardic tradition, use the word constantly and with a variety of meanings, all related to concepts of spirit and inspiration. More generally, awen is the heart of the Druidical Mysteries, the personal inspiration of the initiate born of the flowing spirit that descends from the sun and rises from the earth.

The two versions of the Three Rays of Light used here are the evoking and the invoking forms. The first form / | \ evokes (literally, "calls forth") the vestiges of the three great creative forces already present in material things. The second form \ | / invokes (literally, "calls in") the creative forces themselves, which exist outside of manifestation. The evoking form prepares the space and those within the space to receive the descent of the light by evoking the light that is already in them; the invoking form brings down the pure light in response.

The three signs used in this ritual and elsewhere in the Druid Grade are based on an archaic symbolism that can be traced in the Welsh legend of Ceridwen and Taliesin, as well as elsewhere. The first sign imitates the gesture of one who scatters seeds upon the ground, as nature does with such abundance; the second imitates the shape of the great cauldron in which, according to Celtic legend, all things are transformed and renewed; the third imitates the gesture of a mother holding an infant in swaddling clothes. Each sign also imitates the form of a corresponding letter—A for the first, W for the second, and N (more precisely, EN) for the third.

The Druid Temple.

THE METHOD OF OPENING and closing the temple in the Druid Grade is the same as that used in the Bardic Grade, with three differences. The first is that the arrangement of the circle and cross upon the altar is not the same. In the Druid Grade the cross is placed beneath or to the west of the circle to form the emblem of the alchemical quintessence—the "perfect perfection" that transforms all things into their highest natures. This is done in the usual way before the temple is opened.

The second difference is that when the Druid Grade temple is opened, either the Supreme Ritual of the Pentagram in its summoning mode or the calling of one of the elements is done immediately after the opening, and either the Supreme Ritual of the Pentagram in its banishing mode or the relevant License to Depart is done immediately before the closing. The Druid Grade temple is always a place of power, and it should only be opened when you are prepared to call upon the great powers of the cosmos. It should be noted that the pentagram rituals performed at this stage of the work are separate from the Lesser Rituals of the Pentagram that open and close each working in your temple.

The third difference is simply that when you begin you will announce that you are about to open the temple in the Druid Grade, and when the temple is declared open you will declare it open in the Druid Grade rather than the Bardic Grade.

You will have ample opportunity to practice opening and closing your temple in the Druid Grade as you pursue the work before you. It may be worth noting that you may choose at any point, if you wish to do work other than the magical rituals before you, to open a temple in the Ovate or Bardic Grades. You will find that the former is an excellent preparation for meditation and for the simpler forms of ceremonial magic, particularly those working with a single elemental influence, and the latter is valuable as a preparation for pathworking and related experiences in the realm of the four elements, as well as for ceremonial magic working with all four of the elemental influences together. Be prepared to experiment with the rituals of the grades, and see what uses are best suited for them; you will find that they have capacities that proceed far beyond the obvious.

The Working Tools of Druidical Magic.

THE PRACTICE OF MAGIC relies primarily on the skills of will, imagination, and memory that you have already acquired during your training in the previous grades of our order. Several outward tools, however, will be found useful in the work of this grade and in magic more generally. Most of these are included in the furnishings of your altar, which you have had since your Ovate training, but three are reserved for Bards in training for the Druid Grade: the wand, the sickle, and the serpent's egg.

The Wand

This is for general use in magical working. The wand is a length of wood between one-half inch and one inch in diameter, and in length equal to the distance between the tip of your longest finger and the point of your elbow. (This is best measured when your arm is held up and bent at a right angle.) An inch back from one end is a ring or band of gold or copper, and an inch back from the other end is a ring or band of silver or another white metal. The body of the wand may be painted or treated with a finish such as linseed oil or left plain, as you prefer.

The two ends of the wand correspond to the two currents of force discussed in the lectures of the Bardic Grade—the solar ray and the earth spirit. The gold or copper ring corresponds to the former, the ring of white metal to the latter. When working with the solar ray you will use the end with the ring of red metal (hereafter called the sun end) to draw in influences from above, and the end with the ring of white metal (hereafter called the earth end) to project or banish those influences; when working with the earth spirit in any of its variegated manifestations, you will use the earth end to summon and attract influences, and the sun end to project or banish them. Thus, as will be demonstrated in the consecration ritual, the sun end is always used to trace the summoning pentagrams in the Lesser Ritual of the Pentagram and the banishing pentagrams in the elemental and supreme pentagram rituals; the earth end, correspondingly, is always used to trace the banishing pentagrams in the Lesser Ritual and the summoning pentagrams in the others.

The wand is always held toward the middle, where the insulating properties of the wood will prevent an excessive flow of either influence from entering your body. For the same reason, either end of the wand may be directed toward your or another's body, but neither should ever be brought into direct contact with a living body, or closer than a few inches at most.

The wand must be made and consecrated by you yourself, without any other person's assistance, and no one else should touch it at any time. It may be made as decorative or as plain as you desire and as your skills and resources permit. Even a very simple wand—a piece of ¾-inch dowel purchased from a hardware store, perhaps, with a strip of copper and one of zinc cut with snips from thin sheets purchased at the same store and wrapped around the wand to form the rings, then fastened in place with a good all-purpose glue—will do everything in your magical work that the most ornate and elegant piece of craftsmanship would do.

You will also need a bag or wrapper made of silk or linen to cover the wand when it is not in use. You may make this yourself or buy it ready-made; its purpose is to keep unwanted influences from affecting the wand rather than to impart any influence of its own. Silk or linen must be used because these fibers resist penetration by aetherial forces.

When you have the wand and bag or wrapper ready for use, you may proceed to the ceremony of consecration, which will awaken the powers that are latent in the wand and prepare it for the work of practical magic.

Ceremony of Consecration

1. Set up the temple for a ceremony in the Druid Grade, with the new wand lying across the altar, the sun end to the south, and the earth end to the north. Have the bag or wrapper for the wand nearby.

   When all is in readiness, light the candles and incense. Open the temple in the Druid Grade in the usual manner, following the opening ceremony with the Supreme Ritual of the Pentagram. The wand is not used in any part of this initial work since it has not yet been consecrated.

2. When you have finished the opening ceremony and have summoned the powers of the four elements by means of the Supreme Ritual of the Pentagram, take the wand in both hands and raise it high, as though in offering. Say: "In the presence of the holy powers of nature and the light of the Golden Dawn, let all spirits and powers behold this wand, which I have made for myself as a sign of light and a sacrament of will. Let it be purified by the waters of the sacred well." Lower the wand, dip the left hand into the cauldron of water, and sprinkle the wand nine times with water from your fingertips. Turn the wand between every three sprinklings so the whole surface of the wand receives some of the spray.

   Take the wand into the left hand. Say: "Let it be consecrated with the smoke of the sacred fire." Using the right hand, wave the smoke of the burning incense nine times over the wand, directing the smoke over every part of the wand.

3. Say: "Purified and consecrated, let this wand enter the realms of the four elements." Go to the northern quarter of the working space. Face north and hold the wand upright, sun end up and earth end down, in the middle of the space where you drew the earth pentagram earlier. Say: "Spirits and powers of earth, by the great name CERNUNNOS, Lord of Earth, behold this wand. With your aid, let it be charged and filled with the influences of earth."

   At this point you will use the pore breathing you learned in the Ovate Grade and practiced in the Bardic Grade for a new purpose. Draw in a breath and, as you do so, visualize yourself drawing in the green light of the element of earth. As you breathe out, however, direct the light of earth to flow down your right arm, through your hand and into your wand, so that all the energy that was in your body is now in the wand. Repeat this until you have done it a total of seven times and the wand blazes in your inner vision like a green thunderbolt.

   When this stage is reached, turn the wand in your hand, draw an invoking earth pentagram with the earth end of the wand, then point the earth end of the wand to the center of the pentagram and vibrate the name CERNUNNOS. Turn the wand in your hand so that it again stands upright, with the sun end upwards, and say: "So shall this wand ever be for me a sign of light and a sacrament of will. I thank the powers of earth for their blessing."

4. Go to the western quarter of the working space. Face west and hold the wand upright, sun end up and earth end down, in the middle of the space where you

drew the water pentagram earlier. Say: "Spirits and powers of water, by the great name **SIRONA**, lady of water, behold this wand. With your aid, let it be charged and filled with the influences of water."

Draw in a breath and, as you do so, visualize yourself drawing in the blue light of the element of water. As you breathe out, direct the light of water to flow down your right arm, through your hand and into your wand, so that all the energy that was in your body is now in the wand. Repeat this until you have done it a total of seven times and the wand blazes in your inner vision like a blue thunderbolt.

When this stage is reached, turn the wand in your hand, draw an invoking water pentagram with the earth end of the wand, then point the earth end of the wand to the center of the pentagram and vibrate the name **SIRONA**. Turn the wand in your hand so that it again stands upright, with the sun end upwards, and say: "So shall this wand ever be for me a sign of light and a sacrament of will. I thank the powers of water for their blessing."

5. Circle around to the eastern quarter of the working space. Face east and hold the wand upright, sun end up and earth end down, in the middle of the space where you drew the air pentagram earlier. Say: "Spirits and powers of air, by the great name **BELISAMA**, lady of air, behold this wand. With your aid, let it be charged and filled with the influences of air."

Draw in a breath and, as you do so, visualize yourself drawing in the yellow light of the element of air. As you breathe out, direct the light of air to flow down your right arm, through your hand and into your wand, so that all the energy that was in your body is now in the wand. Repeat this until you have done it a total of seven times and the wand blazes in your inner vision like a yellow thunderbolt.

When this stage is reached, turn the wand in your hand, draw an invoking air pentagram with the earth end of the wand, then point the earth end of the wand to the center of the pentagram and vibrate the name **BELISAMA**. Turn the wand in your hand so that it again stands upright, with the sun end upwards, and say: "So shall this wand ever be for me a sign of light and a sacrament of will. I thank the powers of air for their blessing."

6. Go to the southern quarter of the working space. Face south and hold the wand upright, sun end up and earth end down, in the middle of the space where you drew the fire pentagram earlier. Say: "Spirits and powers of fire, by the great name **TOUTATIS**, lord of fire, behold this wand. With your aid, let it be charged and filled with the influences of fire."

Draw in a breath and, as you do so, visualize yourself drawing in the red light of the element of fire. As you breathe out, direct the light of fire to flow down your right arm, through your hand and into your wand, so that all the energy that was in your body is now in the wand. Repeat this until you have done it a total of seven times and the wand blazes in your inner vision like a red thunderbolt.

When this stage is reached, turn the wand in your hand, draw an invoking fire pentagram with the earth end of the wand, then point the earth end of the wand to the center of the pentagram and vibrate the name **TOUTATIS**. Turn the wand in your hand so that it again stands upright, with the sun end upwards, and say: "So shall this wand ever be for me a sign of light and a sacrament of will. I thank the powers of fire for their blessing."

7. Return to the west of the altar, facing east. Place the wand upon the altar as it was in the beginning, with the sun end to the south and the earth end to the north. Say: "Let the power of the Solar Ray now descend into this wand." Continue with the Analysis of the Grand Word from the OIW Ritual, beginning with the words "In the beginning of things" and ending with "the infinite **CELI**" (see page 273). During the Analysis of the Grand Word, concentrate on the idea that the descending light is filling the wand with power and blessing.

When you have completed the Analysis of the Grand Word, take up the wand in your right hand and, with the sun end of the wand, trace a pentagram above the altar, beginning with the topmost point and proceeding clockwise, visualizing it drawn in white light exactly as in the summoning form of the Lesser Ritual of the Pentagram. *This form is the summoning pentagram of spirit.* When you have finished tracing the pentagram, hold the wand upright in the midst of the pentagram, sun end upwards, and vibrate the nine divine names assigned to the spheres of the Tree of Life below Celi: **HU, KED, BELI,**

TARAN, HESUS, ELEN, MABON, either COEL or SUL (depending on your gender), and OLWEN.

8. Say: "In the presence of the holy powers of nature and the light of the Golden Dawn, this wand is duly consecrated as a sign of light and a sacrament of will." Next, perform the banishing form of the Supreme Ritual of the Pentagram, using the sun end of the wand to trace the banishing pentagrams. Proceed to close the temple in the Druid Grade, and again use the wand to trace the banishing pentagrams in the Lesser Ritual of the Pentagram, using the earth end.

When the ceremony is completed, put the new wand into its bag or wrapping. It should never be removed from this except when it is to be used. Now that it is consecrated, you may use it in any magical working you perform to trace pentagrams and other signs and for other purposes that will be mentioned later or that may occur to you in the course of your studies.

The Sickle

A more specialized magical working tool than the wand, the sickle serves the Druid initiate primarily as an instrument of banishing and of defense against hostile and malevolent influences. The blade is to be made of iron or steel; the handle, of wood or any other insulating material. A small sickle purchased from a gardener's supply may be used, or the initiate may cut a blade from sheet iron or soft steel with a hacksaw, and fit this into a handle made from wooden dowel of one inch diameter. The entire sickle should be no more than twenty-four inches at most in a straight line from the point to the far end of the handle, and a size smaller than this is preferable. Like the wand, it may be made as plain or as richly ornamented as your desire, skills, and available resources permit.

The sickle's power in Druidical magic comes partly from its consecration and partly from the magical effects of iron, which has disruptive and dissolving effects on aetherial forms. A sharp pointed instrument of iron brought into contact with the aetherial body of a spirit can utterly destroy the aetherial form, resulting in a state akin to physical death in an incarnate being, and it has similar results on artificial forms of the kind created by malevolent magic. It is thus a potent protection against many of the magical dangers a Druid may expect to encounter and is especially needful when practicing rituals of evocation.

A wooden box should also be provided for the sickle, as a bag or wrapper will too easily be cut or pierced by the sickle's point. The box should be lined with silk or linen for best results; a single layer of fabric glued to all inside surfaces is sufficient.

Ceremony of Consecration

1. Set up the temple for a ceremony in the Druid Grade with the new sickle upon the altar. The box for the sickle should be nearby. When all is in readiness, light the candles and incense and open the temple in the Druid Grade in the usual way, and then perform the Supreme Ritual of the Pentagram in its summoning mode. You may use your wand in the opening and pentagram ritual.

2. After you have finished the opening ceremony and have summoned the powers of the four elements with the Supreme Ritual of the Pentagram, take the sickle in both hands and raise it high, as though in offering. Say: "In the presence of the holy powers of nature and the light of the Golden Dawn, let all spirits and powers behold this sickle, which I have made for myself as a sign of light and a sacrament of will. Let it be purified by the waters of the sacred well." Lower the wand, dip the left hand into the cauldron of water, and sprinkle the sickle nine times with water from your fingertips. Turn the sickle as you sprinkle it so its whole surface receives some of the spray.

    Take the sickle into the left hand and say: "Let it be consecrated with the smoke of the sacred fire." Using the right hand, wave the smoke of the burning incense nine times over the sickle, directing the smoke over every part of the sickle.

3. Place the sickle back upon the altar. Say: "Let the power of the Solar Ray now descend into this sickle." Continue with the Analysis of the Grand Word from the OIW Ritual, beginning with the words "In the beginning of things" and ending with "the infinite CELI" (see page 273). During the Analysis of the Grand Word, concentrate on the idea that the descending light is filling the sickle with power and blessing.

4. Say: "In the presence of the holy powers of nature and the light of the Golden Dawn, this sickle is duly consecrated as a sign of light and a sacrament of will."

Take it in your right hand, proceed to the eastern quarter of the temple, and face east. Hold the sickle high, with the point facing east. Say: "From this sign of light let all the phantoms of air flee to the uttermost realms of the east." Go to the south; raise the sickle high, with the point facing south, and say: "From this sign of light let all the phantoms of fire flee to the uttermost realms of the south." In the west, taking the same position, say: "From this sign of light let all the phantoms of water flee to the uttermost realms of the west." In the north, finally, taking the same position, say: "From this sign of light let all the phantoms of earth flee to the uttermost realms of the north."

5. Return to the altar, perform the Supreme Ritual of the Pentagram in its banishing mode, and then go on to close the temple in the Druid Grade. When you have finished, the sickle should be placed in its box. It should not be taken out except when it is to be used either in ritual or in less formal contexts when hostile influences or entities are to be dispelled.

The Serpent's Egg

A rich albeit contradictory body of lore surrounds this, the most famous working tool of the ancient Druids. A fanciful tale taken down solemnly by Greek and Roman authors held that it was formed from the congealed breath or spittle of many serpents and had to be stolen away from its makers by the intrepid Druid, who was required to leap on horseback with his prize and gallop away as fast as he could until crossing running water put an end to the reptiles' pursuit.

Those "serpent's eggs" that have been handed down through the ages in certain Celtic families, by contrast, are beads or spheres of glass. It has been suggested by certain scholars, notably Lady Flavia Anderson, that the original serpent's eggs were spheres of clear crystal that were used by the Druids of old to light the Beltane fires by means of focused sunlight.

Be this as it may, the serpent's egg as a working tool in this school of the Druidical Mysteries is different from either of these. It is instead a hollow spherical or egg-shaped container of glass or pottery, no bigger than a hen's egg, that is worn around the neck on a ribbon or cord. It has an opening that is carefully sealed once it is filled.

Strictly speaking, it may be of any convenient shape or material, for its power resides not in its form or color but in its contents; a properly made serpent's egg contains the prepared alchemical salts of vervain, which you used in your Ovate initiation, and of the four herbs you used in your Bardic initiation. It is therefore a unique emblem of your own initiations and serves as a focus and a fount for the magical influences of the whole Druidical tradition. Once made and consecrated, it should be worn whenever you perform magical workings, for it will increase in strength with each such use.

Making Your Serpent's Egg

A suitable container may be found or made. Like the other working tools, it may be made as plain or as ornate as you desire and as your skills and the available resources will permit.

Once it is prepared, you will need six ounces each of vervain and of each of the herbs you used to make spagyric tinctures for your Bardic Grade initiation. (If the divination that determined your Bardic tinctures assigned the same herb to more than one element, multiply the number of elements assigned to that herb by six; this gives you the number of ounces you need.)

All this must be reduced to ash in the usual way, one herb at a time. To do this, soak the herbs in enough pure alcohol to thoroughly wet the herbal material. Then put the herbal mass, or as much of it as you can safely do at once, into your iron pan, take it outside on a windless day, and burn it to dry black cinders. Place the pan in the hottest part of the gas or charcoal grill and reduce the cinders to white or gray ash, which is allowed to cool, ground to a fine powder in your mortar and pestle, and stored in a dry jar. This process is repeated until all the herbs have been turned to ash, and the ash of each herb is stored in its own jar.

At this point, the alchemical tinctures you prepared earlier and saved for future use are again needed. Again, one herb at a time, the white ash is placed in a shallow dish and moistened with the tincture; add the tincture of the same herb a few drops at a time until all the ash is moist, and then leave it to dry in a safe and windless place. (If the weather is humid, it should be placed upon a very low heat, such as the top of a water heater; otherwise it may simply be allowed to stand in a safe place.) Do this with each of your herbs. When all the alcohol has evaporated and the ash is dry, repeat the process, let it dry again, and then repeat a third time.

Once the ashes have dried after their third moistening, put them into the container you have chosen for your serpent's egg, and seal the container permanently with a good all-purpose glue. Fasten the serpent's egg to the cord or ribbon that will support it around your neck at a level that causes it to hang directly in front of your solar plexus. Once this is done, the serpent's egg is ready for its consecration.

You will also need a bag of silk or linen in which to keep the serpent's egg when it is not in use. A padded bag is best to minimize the risk of breakage.

Ceremony of Consecration

1. Set up the temple for a ceremony in the Druid Grade with the serpent's egg on the altar, resting on the place where the circle and cross touch. Have the bag for the egg nearby. When all is in readiness, light the candles and incense, and open the temple in the Druid Grade in the usual way, following the opening ceremony with the Supreme Ritual of the Pentagram. Use your wand in the opening ceremony and pentagram ritual; you will need it later in the ceremony.

2. When you have finished the opening ceremony and the Supreme Ritual of the Pentagram, take the serpent's egg in both hands and raise it high, as though in offering. Say: "In the presence of the holy powers of nature and the light of the Golden Dawn, let all spirits and powers behold this serpent's egg, the emblem of the initiated Druid, which I have made for myself as a sign of light and a sacrament of will. Let it be purified by the waters of the sacred well." Lower the egg, dip the left hand into the cauldron of water, and sprinkle the egg nine times with water from your fingertips. Turn the egg as you do this so the whole surface of the egg receives some of the spray.

    Take the serpent's egg into the left hand and say: "Let it be consecrated with the smoke of the sacred fire." Using the right hand, wave the smoke of the burning incense nine times over the egg, directing the smoke over every part of the egg.

3. Say: "Purified and consecrated, let this serpent's egg go forth to receive the blessings of the four elements." Go to the northern quarter of the working space. Face north and hold the egg in the middle of the space where you drew the earth pentagram earlier. Say: "Spirits and powers of earth, by the great name **CERNUNNOS**, behold this serpent's egg, the emblem of the initiated Druid. With your aid, let it be charged and filled with the influences of earth." Pause and allow the influences of earth to flow into the egg. Do not use pore breathing, as you did with the wand; the wand is an active tool, and so you

took an active role in charging it, but the serpent's egg is a receptive tool, and your role in this part of the consecration is therefore receptive. Simply wait attentively; you will know when it is time to go on. When you feel that the egg has been charged, say: "So shall this serpent's egg ever be for me a sign of light and a sacrament of will. I thank the powers of earth for their blessing."

4. Go to the western quarter of the working space. Face west and hold the egg in the middle of the space where you drew the water pentagram earlier. Say: "Spirits and powers of water, by the great name **SIRONA**, behold this serpent's egg, the emblem of the initiated Druid. With your aid, let it be charged and filled with the influences of water." Again, pause and wait for a sense that the charging has been accomplished. When you feel this, say: "So shall this serpent's egg ever be for me a sign of light and a sacrament of will. I thank the powers of water for their blessing."

5. Circle around to the eastern quarter of the working space. Face east and hold the serpent's egg in the middle of the space where you drew the air pentagram earlier. Say: "Spirits and powers of air, by the great name **BELISAMA**, behold this serpent's egg, the emblem of the initiated Druid. With your aid, let it be charged and filled with the influences of air." Pause as before until you feel that it is time to go on, and then say: "So shall this serpent's egg ever be for me a sign of light and a sacrament of will. I thank the powers of air for their blessing."

6. Go to the southern quarter of the working space. Face south and hold the egg in the middle of the space where you drew the fire pentagram earlier. Say: "Spirits and powers of fire, by the great name **TOUTATIS**, behold this serpent's egg. With your aid, let it be charged and filled with the energies of fire." Pause as before, and then say: "So shall this serpent's egg ever be for me a sign of light and a sacrament of will. I thank the powers of fire for their blessing."

7. Return to the west of the altar, facing east. Place the serpent's egg upon the altar as it was in the beginning, resting on the circle and cross. Say: "Let the power of the Solar Ray now descend into this serpent's egg." Continue with the Analysis of the Grand Word from the OIW Ritual, beginning with the words "In the beginning of things" and ending with "the infinite **CELI**" (see page

273). During the Analysis of the Grand Word, concentrate on the idea that the descending light is filling the serpent's egg with power and blessing.

When you have completed the Analysis of the Grand Word, take your wand and, with its sun end, trace a summoning pentagram of spirit above the altar, beginning with the topmost point and proceeding clockwise, visualizing it drawn in white light. When you have finished tracing the pentagram, hold the wand upright in the midst of the pentagram, sun end upwards, earth end pointing directly toward the serpent's egg, and vibrate the nine divine names assigned to the spheres of the Tree of Life below Celi: **HU, KED, BELI, TARAN, HESUS, ELEN, MABON**, either **COEL** or **SUL** (depending on your gender), and **OLWEN**. As you vibrate each of these names, visualize a current of force descending from infinite space above you, through the wand and into the serpent's egg.

8. Say: "In the presence of the holy powers of nature and the light of the Golden Dawn, this serpent's egg is duly consecrated as a sign of light and a sacrament of will. Let it empower and protect me now and always." Put the ribbon or cord around your neck and settle the serpent's egg above your solar plexus. Wearing it, perform the banishing form of the Supreme Ritual of the Pentagram and close the temple in the Druid Grade.

When the ceremony is completed, put the serpent's egg into its bag. It should never be removed from this except when it is to be used. You should wear it whenever you perform magic, and you may find it valuable also to wear it during meditation, divination, and other Druidical practices.

The Formulae of Ceremonial Magic.

"THE GREAT WORK," WRITES Éliphas Lévi, "before anything else, is the creation of man by himself, that is to say the full and entire conquest that he makes of his faculties and his future; it is above all the perfect emancipation of his will, which assures him the universal empire of Azoth and the domain of Magnesia, or in other words a complete mastery of the universal magical agent."

The first magical operation that must be performed by any student of the Mysteries, therefore, is that which transforms an ordinary human being, stumbling blindly and without self-knowledge through a world of shadows and illusions, into an initiate who has learned to know, to dare, to will, and to be silent, and who can apply these four powers of the soul to the tasks and riddles of life and the mastery of the subtle forces and influences of the cosmos. This is nothing less than the creation of a self out of the raw materials flung together at random by heredity and environment. It is the work in which you have been engaged, knowingly or not, since the day that you first began to study the teachings and practice the magical disciplines of this order; and it will remain central to your work as long as you remain upon the path of the Druidical Mysteries. This first and highest of all magical operations is named initiation.

The act of initiation has a secondary importance alongside its central role in magical training. Initiation may be understood, magically speaking, as a process in which something common, belonging entirely to the realm of the everyday and transitory, is drawn apart from other things of the same kind, translated to a new plane of action and perception, and given a purpose and a direction it did not previously possess. Apply this process to a human soul and you have initiation. Apply it to any other subject, in turn, and you have one of the other formulae of practical magic.

This is among the great secrets of every Mystery tradition: time spent following the path of initiation is time spent learning the arts of practical magic.

In those orders and traditions that rely on ceremonial initiation in a lodge or temple and conferred by a group of experienced practitioners, many difficulties can interfere with this learning process. If the initiate does not pay close attention during the initiation ceremony or fails to study and meditate upon the experience afterwards; if mistakes are made in the ritual or if it is performed by rote in that dry, plodding manner that can make the most potent ceremony have no more effect on its participants than the reading of a laundry list—in any of these cases the initiation will not have its usual effects, and a variety of problems may follow.

The great advantage of the process of self-initiation through which each initiate of our order has passed is that these risks are all but eliminated. So long as the student does the work assigned to the grades, the steady repetition of rituals, meditations, pathworkings, and other practices will build up precisely those patterns in consciousness that a ceremonial initiation in a lodge or temple is meant to establish; the awkward performance of a ritual here or a meditation there will be of far less importance than the rhythm of steady practice and improvement; forms unfolded in daily practice over a period of months and years will be far more thoroughly understood and internalized than those experienced in a rush of unfamiliar images and words on one's first admission to a temple. If, on the other hand, a student of these Mysteries neglects to do the work, the formulae of practical magic given in these papers will remain useless to him because he will not have built up the patterns in consciousness upon which those formulae are based.

The attentive student will have noticed that he has already applied two formulae derived from the ceremonies of initiation in the three rituals of consecration already presented: those of the wand, the sickle, and the serpent's egg, the three working tools of the Druid initiate. Examine them closely and you will find that the first and the third take their structure from the Bardic Grade initiation, while the second takes its structure from that of the Ovate Grade. These are examples of the first of the three great classes of magical ceremonies—the ceremonies of consecration—and the same formulae may be applied equally to the other two classes, the ceremonies of conjuration and transformation.

These terms require further definition. Consecration is the act of taking a material object or substance and charging it with a specific magical influence, which thereafter radiates from the object and influences its surroundings. It is by way of consecration that amulets and working tools are made effective and magical potions, oils, and other substances are prepared for the work assigned to them.

Conjuration is the act of entering into contact with a disembodied being—an intelligence, a spirit, or some other entity dwelling in the aethereal realms. It is by way of conjuration that intelligences are consulted and spirits called forth to accomplish magical works.

Transformation is the act of bringing about changes within the threefold being of the magician by directing magical influences upon the magician's own material, aethereal, or intellectual bodies. It is by way of transformation that works of invisibility and projection are accomplished and more lasting changes pursued.

Each of these classes of ceremonial magic may be understood with reference to the structure of the Ovate and Bardic Grade initiations, as mentioned already. The following index will be helpful in understanding that structure. It is specific to the Ovate Grade initiation; the Bardic Grade extends steps I and J into a fourfold elemental structure and adds an invocation and banishing of the elemental powers to the structure. The way in which this works in practice will be understood by example.

General Index of the Ovate Initiation

1. A—The purpose of the ceremony
2. B—The candidate for initiation
3. C—The magical influences invoked in the ceremony
4. D—The temple
5. E—The proclamation of the working and preliminary pentagram ritual
6. F—The purification, consecration, and circumambulation of the temple
7. G—The invocation of the Golden Dawn
8. H—The candidate calls upon the powers governing the obligation
9. I—The candidate takes the obligation or obligations of the grade
10. J—The candidate receives the blessing and empowerment of the grade
11. K—The period of meditation

12. L—The candidate proclaims that he has received the initiation of the grade

13. M—The candidate casts and interprets a geomantic chart concerning the initiation

14. N—The candidate proclaims the ritual complete

15. O—The purification, consecration, and reverse circumambulation of the temple

16. P—The final banishing and closing

To expand this outline for use with the Bardic Grade formula, which invokes all four elements and spirit, steps H, I, and J are repeated; it may be useful in practice to denote the invocation of earth as H1, the obligation of earth as I1, and the empowerment of earth as J1; those of water as H2, I2, and J2; those of air as H3, I3, and J3; those of fire as H4, I4, and J4; and the final obligation taken at the altar as I5. Step N is also expanded to include the banishing of the elemental powers, which is done at this point in the ceremony.

Consecration

CEREMONIES OF CONSECRATION, AS already explained, are used to draw down magical influences into material things and establish them there in a lasting manner. The items to be consecrated range from working tools such as the wand, sickle, and serpent's egg, through amulets and other items meant to radiate a particular influence for an extended period, to potions, baths, washes, oils, and other substances used to communicate a magical influence to a person, place, or thing for a short time only.

All forms of ceremonial magic depend on the use of an effective ritual structure and on the concentrated will and imagination of the magician working through that structure. Unlike the other two classes of ceremonial magic, however, ceremonies of consecration also depend on a material basis that is in harmony with the goal of the working. It is for this reason that the student of Druidical magic is earnestly counseled to study the occult lore of herbs and determine which of the herbs and other vegetable substances that are readily available to them have traditionally been used for the various purposes of practical magic. It is useless to attempt to consecrate an amulet of protection if it contains herbs that have the effect of stirring passion; the knowledge of the proper material basis is essential to consecration.

The material basis for a work of consecration in Druidical magic may usefully consist of one, three, five, seven, or nine herbs, which have the same elemental character—for example, all hot and dry, belonging to fire—and which have either the same magical properties or complementary ones. An amulet made in this way consists of a small cloth bag in the color appropriate to the element; other preparations of herbal magic are made simply by processing the herbs themselves in whatever manner is appropriate. The student should consult books on herbalism for instructions in the processes involved in making oils, ointments, and the like.

Thus, for example, an amulet for protection against hostile magic might be made with equal parts of angelica root, St. John's wort leaf and flower, and dill weed placed in a small red bag. This is then consecrated and placed in a room where protection is needed or worn around the neck by a person who desires protection. A floor wash for the same purpose may be made of the same three herbs steeped in boiling water and then strained out; the infusion is cooled, consecrated with the appropriate ritual, and then added to water, and this is used to clean the floor in a usual way but with a new mop; the room or house that is cleansed in this way will be barred to hostile magic and noxious spirits for some weeks or months, depending on the strength of the consecration.

The Ovate initiation formula is sufficient for the consecration of amulets and herbal preparations, as it lends itself well to workings that call upon the influences of a single element. Only for working tools that are meant to be used with all four of the elemental powers may the Bardic formula be needed; the consecration ceremony for the wand is an example of the type. The following index, based on the general index above, may be used as a guide to creating consecration ceremonies for amulets and herbal preparations:

A—Specify the purpose of the amulet or preparation; this should be simple and clear enough to be written out in a single sentence in plain English, and a geomantic divination should be done in advance of the ritual to make sure that the working is appropriate.

B—Prepare the material basis for the working; this consists, for the present, of one, three, five, seven, or nine herbs or other plant materials either placed inside a bag of colored cloth or prepared in some other way for magical use. This is placed upon the altar.

C—The spirits and powers governing the element that rules the herbal materials included in the material basis, invoked by means of the name of the god or goddess ruling the element.

D—Any room or other space set up as a temple of the Ovate Grade, when possible; when circumstances do not permit this, any place whatsoever, provided that the appropriate rituals can be performed there. The wand and serpent's egg should be present for the working: the wand upon the altar and the serpent's egg worn about the neck. A chair should be set up on the side opposite the quarter of the element to be invoked.

E—The standard words of the opening, followed by the Lesser Ritual of the Pentagram in its summoning mode.

F—The standard purification, consecration, and circumambulation of the temple.

G—Say the following words: "I invoke the rising of the eternal spiritual sun! May this amulet"—or potion, or whatever you happen to be consecrating—"be illumined by a ray of that Golden Dawn." Visualize the rising sun in the usual manner, imagining the rays of the sun falling upon the amulet or preparation. When the sun has risen, say: "In the light of the Golden Dawn and the presence of the holy powers of nature, I proclaim this temple open in the Ovate Grade for a ceremony of consecration."

H—Perform the calling of the element governing the work. Return to the altar, facing the direction of the element across it, and say: "By all the powers here invoked, and in the presence of"—here vibrate the divine name governing the element—"I present this amulet (or other preparation) as a proper material basis for the influences of (element)."

I—Take the wand in your right hand and raise it high, with the sun end up and the earth end down. Extend your left hand to place your palm just above the amulet or other preparation. Visualize a current of force descending from infinite space above you and into the wand, from the wand through your right arm, shoulders, and left arm, and emanating from your palm into the amulet. Say: "Creature of (element), by all the powers of (element), I instruct you in your purpose. It is"—here state the purpose you have determined under heading A.

J—Now, with the earth end of the wand, trace a summoning pentagram of the element over the amulet or other preparation, as though the amulet stood upright above the amulet or preparation. Trace the appropriate sigil—for example, the Sigil of the Winter Solstice, should the working be of the element of earth—in the pentagram, again with the earth end of the wand. The wand is then held upright, with the earth end in the midst of the pentagram and the sun end just above the amulet or preparation, and with an effort of focused will and imagination, the influences of the element are projected into the amulet or preparation. This effort should be maintained as long as it may be done without slackening.

K—Lower the wand and set it upon the altar. Sit in the chair, enter into meditation in the usual way with breathing in the color of the element, and concentrate for a time on the purpose of the amulet or preparation you have just charged. Think of it as though its work is already accomplished and is about to manifest in your life. Feel that as a reality. When you are ready, rise from the chair and return to the altar.

L—Say: "In the name and the presence of (divine name ruling element) and all the powers of (name of element), I proclaim that this amulet (or other preparation) has been duly consecrated for the purpose of (state the purpose)."

M—At this point, if appropriate, cast a geomantic chart to determine how best to use the amulet or preparation you have consecrated.

N—Standing at the west of the altar, facing east, say: "In the presence of the holy powers of nature and the light of the Golden Dawn, I proclaim that this ceremony of consecration is complete, and I ask the powers of (name of element) to guide its results in accordance with the great harmony of nature." Then perform the License to Depart of the element you have previously summoned.

O—Perform the standard purification, consecration, and reverse circumambulation of the temple.

P—Perform the Lesser Ritual of the Pentagram in its banishing mode, followed by the standard words of the closing. As soon as possible after the ceremony, the amulet is put in the place or worn on the person for which it was made or the preparation is used for its intended purpose.

Conjuration

THE ART OF CONJURATION, or the summoning and commanding of spirits, has been an important part of magical practice since the oldest times from which records come down to us, and there is every reason to think that the ancient Druids practiced it. It is worth noting in this regard that records of magical practice in the English-speaking countries include many ceremonies of conjuration that claim Celtic origins; one example is the conjuration of the spirit Luridan, a spirit of the Orkneys previously conjured by Welsh Bards, which is among the workings recorded in the enlarged third edition of Reginald Scot's *Discoverie of Witchcraft*.

An abundance of lore concerning spirits and the means of conjuring them survives from the later years of the Middle Ages, the Renaissance, and the early modern period, and some magicians of the present time make use of these. Many of these same texts teach, however, that each practitioner of conjuration must obtain his own grimoire or register of spirits, whom he alone may summon. Says the eighteenth aphorism of the *Arbatel of Magick*, a guide to magical practice first published in the seventeenth century, in speaking of the names of spirits:

> They only are effectual, which are delivered to any one, by the Spirit the revealer, visible or invisible; and they are delivered to every one as they are predestinated; therefore they are called Constellations; and they seldom have any efficacy above 40 years. Therefore it is most safe for the young practicers of Art, that they work by the offices of the Spirits alone, without their names; and if they are preordained to attain the art of magic, the other parts of the art will offer themselves unto them of their own accord.

That is to say, a list of spirits more than forty years old is like a city directory of the same age. One who attempts to send a letter to an address found therein may or may not have that letter delivered anywhere at all, and only sheer chance will allow the letter to reach the person to whom it was intended. It is for this reason that the student is instructed to call upon spirits by their offices rather than their names, until such time as he may learn names of spirits from the spirits themselves or, more usefully still, from his own Guardian Genius or Higher Self.

This is how the aspiring initiate of the Druidical Mysteries should proceed. The intelligences and spirits of the elements may be summoned using their titles alone and the divine names and ceremonial forms already learned; a ceremony for this purpose is given in outline form below. Each intelligence and spirit should be requested by the conjurer to give its name and seal—this latter being a geometrical pattern or simple drawing of lines and curves that serves to identify the spirit—and these names and seals should be recorded and used in future conjurations. (The lore of intelligences and spirits is discussed in the lecture "On the Macrocosm and Microcosm," which is included in the papers assigned to this grade.)

Aspirants to the Druid Grade who wish to specialize in conjuration or merely seek to proceed further in that art than the minimum required for the examination will do well to acquire a blank notebook or journal to serve as a Book of Spirits. This may be purchased or, better still, made by the hands of the aspirant; instructions for making a suitable book may be found in many books on handicrafts. Once made or purchased, the Book of Spirits should be consecrated using a ceremony like the one given previously for the serpent's egg; thereafter, the names, seals, and other identifying information received from the intelligences of each element should be copied into it, and it should be kept close at hand during any ceremony of conjuration. The names and seals of spirits above the elemental realm are best learned from the Guardian Genius or Higher Self of the aspirant. The ritual forms used to enter into communion with this great being are discussed later.

It should be noted that among the things that can be done by means of ceremonies of conjuration is the consecration of amulets and other preparations. In workings of this sort, an amulet or herbal preparation is readied in advance using herbs of a nature appropriate to the effects desired. The amulet or preparation is then placed not on the altar but in the quarter of the temple assigned to the element to be invoked. An intelligence is summoned and asked to call a spirit; the spirit is then instructed to charge the amulet or preparation so that it will accomplish the purpose for which it is made. Those students who find conjuration more congenial and effective than consecration will find that this is an effective method for creating amulets and other magical substances.

One additional matter needing reference at this time is the mode in which intelligences and spirits summoned in ceremonies of conjuration are to be made visible and audible. Here three methods have been in common use. One, more common in those magical traditions that come from continental Europe, is conjuration to visible appearance—that is, to a degree of solidity in which the physical eyes of the magician are capable of perceiving the spirit. This requires the burning of large quantities of certain herbs that facilitate such materializations; it also requires the use of a protective circle, since a spirit brought this close to the material plane is quite able, if it should be so minded, to assault the magician.

The second, more common in magical traditions native to Britain, is conjuration to appearance in the crystal. Here a crystal ball, magic mirror, or similar tool is used to assist the magician—or, more often, a scryer or seer with the gift of vision in the crystal—to see the spirits. This form of conjuration is considerably less dangerous and no magical circle need be used, but it depends on either having (or having an assistant who has) the peculiar mental arrangement necessary to see visions in a crystal or other reflective surface.

The third, found primarily in those schools of the Mysteries that share in the heritage of the Golden Dawn, is conjuration to appearance in the spirit vision. The pathworkings and similar practices you have already done are training for this method, in which the human imagination—or, as it is sometimes called in old books of magic, the diaphane—is used to perceive spirits and intelligences. This form of conjuration is both relatively safe and accessible to all, and it is the method of perceiving spirits used in the ritual outline that follows.

The Ovate initiation formula may be used for conjuring any intelligence or spirit of the elemental realms. The following index, based on the general index previously given, may be used as a guide to creating conjuration ceremonies for elemental intelligences and spirits:

A—Identify the purpose of the ritual of conjuration; such rites should not be done for the purpose of idle curiosity, but only in order to request that a specific service, appropriate to the element being invoked, be done by the intelligence or spirit. An intelligence should be conjured to gain knowledge; a spirit should be conjured to bring about effects in the world. The purpose should be simple and clear enough to be written out in a single sentence in plain English, and a geomantic divination should be done in advance of the ritual to make sure that the working is appropriate.

B—Identify the spirit or intelligence that is to be conjured, together with its name and seal if these are known. These should be written on paper of the elemental color and placed upon the altar.

C—Identify the spirits and powers governing the element that rules the spirit, invoked by means of the name of the god or goddess ruling the element and the name of the elemental intelligence.

D—Create a temple of the Ovate Grade that can be closed off against any interruption during the duration of the ceremony. The wand, sickle, and serpent's egg should be present for the working: the wand and sickle upon the altar and the serpent's egg worn about the neck. A chair should be set up on the side opposite the quarter of the element to be invoked.

E—Recite the standard words of the opening, followed by the Lesser Ritual of the Pentagram in its summoning mode.

F—Perform the standard purification, consecration, and circumambulation of the temple.

G—Say: "I invoke the rising of the eternal spiritual sun! May I be illumined and strengthened for this working by a ray of that Golden Dawn." Visualize the rising sun in the usual manner. When the sun has risen, say: "In the light of the Golden Dawn and the presence of the holy powers of nature, I proclaim this temple open in the Ovate Grade for a ceremony of conjuration."

H—Perform the calling of the element governing the work. Return to the altar, facing the direction of the element across it, and say: "By all the powers here invoked, and in the presence of"—here vibrate the divine name governing the element—"I call forth an intelligence of (element) appropriate to the following purpose." State your purpose as you have determined it under heading A. Say: "Come forth, creature of (element)!"

At this point, look beyond the temple in the direction assigned by the element, and imagine a vast space of a kind appropriate to the element reaching off into the distance. (For example, in a working of the element of air, imagine a cloudscape; in one of fire, imagine a vast realm of flame, and so forth.) Wait for an intelligence to appear. If none does, repeat the words just given, and again wait; repeat a third time if necessary, and then the intelligence will infallibly appear.

I—Take the wand in your right hand and raise it high, with the sun end up and the earth end down. Extend your left hand toward the intelligence as though in greeting. Visualize a current of force descending from infinite space above you into the wand, from the wand through your right arm, shoulders, and left arm, and radiating from your palm like a beacon. Say: "Creature of (element), by all the powers of (element), I have conjured you for the following purpose. It is—" Here state the purpose you have determined under heading A. If the conjuration is done for the purpose of knowledge, finish: "In the name of (divine name ruling the element), I ask you to fulfill it." You may converse with the intelligence at this point, or proceed directly to heading K.

   If the working is done for the purpose of bringing about effects in the world, finish: "In the name of (divine name ruling element), I ask you to call forth a spirit of (element) whose work it is to fulfill such purposes." You may converse further with the intelligence at this point, or proceed to heading J.

J—Wait for the spirit to appear; it will do so, becoming visible in the imagined space. When it has appeared, take the wand and, with the earth end, trace a summoning pentagram of the element over the altar, as though the amulet stood upright above the altar. Trace the appropriate sigil (for example, the Sigil of the Winter Solstice, should the working be of the element of earth) in the pentagram, again with the earth end of the wand. Then, holding the wand in the right hand, take the sickle in the left, hold both high, and say, "Spirit of (element), I have bid you be summoned for the following purpose. It is—" Here state the purpose you have determined under heading A. "In the name of (divine name ruling element), I instruct you to accomplish it."

K—Remain at the altar, and continue to hold the wand (when conjuring an intelligence) or the wand and sickle (when conjuring a spirit). The intelligence will then provide you with the knowledge you have requested, or the spirit will depart and busy itself with the work you have instructed it to perform.

L—Say: "In the name and the presence of (divine name ruling element) and all the powers of (name of element), I thank you, creature (or creatures) of (name of element). Receive my blessing and that of all the holy powers of nature."

M—At this point, you may address the intelligence and ask it to provide you with its name, its seal, and the work that it accomplishes in the realm of its element You may also ask it for the name, seal, and work of the spirit it has summoned, if this has happened, or with the names, seals, and work of one or more spirits assigned to it who accomplish work relevant to your needs and desires. Inquire also about how the intelligence prefers to be conjured, and about how the spirit or spirits should properly be conjured. All this should be done with the utmost courtesy; intelligences are not subject to human beings, but to their own elemental hierarchies; the aid they provide initiates of the Mysteries is a gracious favor of their realm to ours, and should be recognized and treated as such.

N—Still facing the direction of the element across the altar, say: "In the presence of the holy powers of nature and the light of the Golden Dawn, and in the name of (divine name ruling element), I thank you, (name of elemental and, if appropriate, name of spirit), for your aid and assistance in this work, and I bid you depart with my blessing to your own realm." Trace the banishing pentagram of the element above the altar, and then perform the License to Depart of the element you have previously summoned.

O—Perform the standard purification, consecration, and reverse circumambulation of the temple.

P—Perform the Lesser Ritual of the Pentagram in its banishing mode, followed by the standard words of the closing.

Once the name and seal of a spirit has been obtained, it may be conjured without previously conjuring its governing intelligence; the words under heading H should be revised in this case to summon the spirit directly, and the ritual should then pass directly to heading J.

Transformation

CEREMONIES OF TRANSFORMATION ARE among the most remarkable of all magical workings and include two classes of magic commonly dismissed as mere folklore, that is, workings of invisibility, on the one hand, and workings of transformation into an animal form on the other. It may seem surprising to the student that such things can be done or that such things should be done in the world of today, so seemingly different from those ages of romance when a *Tarnkappe* (a magical cap of invisibility and shapeshifting in the old German legend of Siegfried) might make its wearer invisible or tranform him into salmon or hawk. Still, invisibility has its practical value in time of danger, and the power to take on an animal form, with its very different senses and power of movement, also has its uses; furthermore, both teach in no uncertain terms the extraordinary power magic has over human perception.

It is true and should be remembered by the student that no magical operation will prevent light from falling upon a human body, reflecting from it, and reaching the eyes of any observers who may be present, just as no magical operation will enable human flesh to be molded into the form of another living creature. Still, such overly material expressions are far from the only options available for magical working.

The practice of invisibility is among the most common attainments of advanced occultists all over the world. It is accomplished by building up, from the substance of the aetherial realm, a species of veil or shroud that surrounds the physical body. Those who look upon the shroud, unless they themselves have achieved some level of initiation or are possessed of uncommon powers of concentration and perception, are swayed by the intention formulated in it; their eyes receive the image of the person thus veiled, but their minds are distracted and never quite notice what is before them.

The practice of shapeshifting, as it is called in folklore, is subject to similar laws. Here the shape of aetherial substance does not surround the material body; instead, what is called an animal body of transformation is created. The magician projects his consciousness into it and goes forth in an animal form that is not quite material in nature. While any living thing may in theory be used as the basis for an animal body of transformation, it is difficult in the extreme to create a working form outside the vertebrate animals—

mammals, birds, reptiles, amphibians, and fish—and mammals and birds are easiest, especially for the novice in this work.

A variety of means have been used in folk magic to make the formulation of the body of transformation easier and more complete; it is for this reason, for example, that the werewolf cult of the Middle Ages practiced its rites on nights of the full moon, when the aetherial tides are at their strongest, and often used ointments containing various herbs to assist the separation of consciousness from the physical body and its implantation in the body of transformation. Such aids are not necessary when effective magical formulae and adequate training are combined.

It is possible to use either of the previously discussed classes of ceremonial magic, consecration and conjuration, to assist workings of this third class. For example, an amulet or ointment of invisibility may be prepared using herbs traditionally considered to foster invisibility, consecrated with an appropriate ceremony, and worn or applied when performing an invisibility working and thereafter while going about invisible. A spirit of the element of air, to which invisibility is assigned, may also be conjured to place influences conducive to invisibility into a properly prepared amulet or the like. Any of these things can be done equally to assist the work of taking on a body of transformation.

Workings intended to take on an animal body of transformation, in addition, must include a material basis drawn from the body of the animal whose form is to be taken: a piece of fur, a feather, or some other physical link with the animal form needs to be present to provide a template upon which the aetherial form can be built. This serves as a natural amulet. To take on an animal form, it is also necessary beforehand to study the animal's form, life, and ways of moving and acting so that the building up of the body of transformation may not suffer interference from wrong ideas held in the mind.

Both these forms of magic have a curious effect not found in the other classes of ceremonial magic: regular practice of either one enables the magician to dispense with ceremony at need and formulate either the shroud of invisibility or the animal body of transformation by an act of will and imagination. The shroud or body formed by ceremony, however, will be found to be stronger and more effective than that done without ceremony, and the simpler approach in practice is usually reserved for emergencies.

The Ovate initiation formula is *not* usually sufficient for works of transformation, at least until experience is gained with such ceremonies, and the Bardic formula should be used instead. The following index, based on the previous general index, may be used as a guide to creating transformation ceremonies for invisibility and animal bodies of transformation:

A—Define the purpose of the working, either invisibility or the creation of an animal body of transformation, and any more specific purpose for which one or the other may be sought.

B—Gather the aetherial substance that will be formed into the shroud of invisibility or the animal body of transformation, as well as any amulets or consecrated substances that may be used in the working, and the piece of animal material that will be used as the template for the animal body of transformation. This latter must be worn or carried on the body throughout the ceremony.

C—Define the deities, spirits, and powers of the four elements, who are invoked to assist in creating the shroud of invisibility or the animal body of transformation.

D—Create a temple of the Bardic Grade that can be closed off against any interruption for the duration of the ceremony but from which the magician has access to the outside world to accomplish whatever invisibility or an animal form will make possible. The wand and serpent's egg should be present for the working: the wand upon the altar and the serpent's egg worn about the neck. A chair should be set up in the western quarter of the temple.

E—Recite the standard words of the opening, followed by the Lesser Ritual of the Pentagram in its summoning mode.

F—Perform the standard purification, consecration, and circumambulation of the temple.

G—Say: "I invoke the rising of the eternal spiritual sun! May I be illumined by a ray of that Golden Dawn." Visualize the rising sun in the usual manner. When the sun has risen, say: "In the presence of the holy powers of nature and the light of the Golden Dawn, I proclaim this temple open in the Ovate Grade for a ceremony of transformation."

H1—Return to the west of the altar, face east and say: "By all the powers here invoked, I now begin taking on the shroud of invisibility/a body of transformation of a (name of animal). I therefore enter the realm of earth."

I1—Perform the complete Calling of Earth, tracing the pentagram with the earth end of the wand. While you are in the northern quarter, standing in the Sign of Earth, say: "In the presence of the holy powers of earth and the light of the Golden Dawn, and in the great name (divine name ruling earth), I call on all the magical influences of earth to formulate about me a shroud of invisibility/a body of transformation of a (name of animal)."

J1—At this point, imagine the shroud of invisibility or the animal body of transformation taking shape. The shroud is like an egg-shaped mass of dark mist surrounding your physical body and obscuring it from all eyes, including your own; as it takes shape, imagine your body becoming dim and transparent so that, looking down, the floor becomes visible through you. The animal body of transformation looks exactly like the animal it is meant to duplicate and stands just before your own body, facing north. Maintain your concentration on this as long and intensely as possible. When your concentration begins to weaken, say: "I thank the earth and the powers of earth for their aid in this work."

H2—Return to the west of the altar, keeping your awareness of the shroud of invisibility about you or the animal form moving ahead of you; in the latter case, it should move in whatever way is typical of the animal. When you have reached the altar, face east and say: "By all the powers here invoked, I now continue taking on the shroud of invisibility/a body of transformation of a (name of animal). I therefore enter the realm of water."

I2—Perform the complete Calling of Water, tracing the pentagram with the earth end of the wand and continuing to maintain the visualization. While you are in the western quarter, standing in the Sign of Water, say: "In the presence of the holy powers of water and the light of the Golden Dawn, and in the great name (divine name ruling water), I call on all the magical influences of water to formulate about me a shroud of invisibility/a body of transformation of a (name of animal)."

J2—At this point, imagine the shroud of invisibility or the animal body of transformation becoming even more definitely present. Maintain your concentration on this as long and intensely as possible. When your concentration begins to weaken, say: "I thank the water and the powers of water for their aid in this work."

H3—Return to the west of the altar, face east, and say: "By all the powers here invoked, I further continue taking on the shroud of invisibility/a body of transformation of a (name of animal). I therefore enter the realm of air."

I3—Perform the complete Calling of Air, tracing the pentagram with the earth end of the wand. Continue to maintain your visualization. While you are in the eastern quarter, standing in the Sign of Air, say: "In the presence of the holy powers of air and the light of the Golden Dawn, and in the great name (divine name ruling air), I call on all the magical influences of air to formulate about me a shroud of invisibility/a body of transformation of a (name of animal)."

J3—At this point, imagine the shroud of invisibility or the animal body of transformation becoming ever more distinctly present, so that your body is completely obscured or the animal form is as clearly visible as though it was physically present. Maintain your concentration on this as long and intensely as possible. When your concentration begins to weaken, say: "I thank the air and the powers of air for their aid in this work."

H4—Return to the west of the altar, face east, and say: "By all the powers here invoked, I complete taking on the shroud of invisibility/a body of transformation of a (name of animal). I therefore enter the realm of fire."

I4—Perform the complete Calling of Fire, tracing the pentagram with the earth end of the wand. Continue to maintain your visualization. While you are in the southern quarter, standing in the Sign of Fire, say: "In the presence of the holy powers of fire and the light of the Golden Dawn, and in the great name (divine name ruling fire), I call on all the magical influences of fire to formulate about me a shroud of invisibility/a body of transformation of a (name of animal)."

J4—At this point, imagine the shroud of invisibility or the animal body of transformation wholly present. In your imagination, make their effect more than natural—thus the shroud of invisibility becomes so intense that your body is not merely hidden but seems completely nonexistent, or the animal body of transformation seems more solid, real, and alive than a real animal. Maintain your concentration on this as long and intensely as possible. When your concentration begins to weaken, say: "I thank the fire and the powers of fire for its aid in this work."

I5—Return to the west of the altar and face east. Raise your wand on high, with the sun end upwards and the earth end directed toward yourself if the working is to create a shroud of invisibility, or toward the animal form if the working is to create an animal form of transformation. Say: "Let the holy powers of nature and the light of the Golden Dawn bless and perfect this working, so that all who behold me see me not/so that all who behold me see the form I have created." Visualize light descending from the heavens into the wand, and from the wand into the shroud of invisibility or the animal form of transformation, completing and perfecting it in every way.

K—Lower the wand and set it upon the altar. If you have created a shroud of invisibility, leave the temple, leaving everything in place and locking the room behind you so that no one but yourself may enter it until you return. As you go about whatever work you have it in mind to do in a state of invisibility, maintain your concentration on the shroud of invisibility and keep perfect silence. Maintaining this twofold focus requires practice, and it is normally wise not to attempt it for long periods at first; with experience, it will become easy. Return to the temple when you are done.

If you have created an animal body of transformation, sit in the chair and see the animal form standing in front of you. Relax your physical body and then, with an effort of will, imagine yourself seeing through the animal form's eyes, hearing through its ears, moving with its muscles, and residing in its body. Depending on your degree of concentration, you may or may not lose track completely of your physical body, but this is the goal to be sought; with practice, the shift is total and nearly instantaneous. When you are in the animal body of transformation, go out into the world—being an aetherial body, the body of transformation will pass readily through walls—and do whatever work you have it in mind to do, maintaining your concentration on the animal form. Return to the temple when you are done.

L—When you have finished and returned to the temple, in the case of a shroud of invisibility, go to the west of the altar and face east. Say: "In the presence of the holy powers of nature and the light of the Golden Dawn, I thank the powers of the elements for their aid in this work and dissolve the shroud of invisibility I have created." Now, concentrating as forcefully as possible, imagine the shroud of concealment dissolving from around your body and your body coming back into full visibility. You may find it helpful to imagine that the aetherial substance composing the shroud streams away in four streams, one to each of the elemental quarters. Maintain this visualization until the shroud is entirely dispersed and your body is entirely visible.

In the case of an animal body of transformation, return in the body of transformation to the chair where your physical body is placed, have your animal body stand in front of your physical body facing toward the altar, and then with an effort of will see again through your physical eyes, hear through your ears, and indwell your physical body, leaving the animal body of transformation empty. Rise in your physical body and go to the west of the altar. Say: "In the presence of the holy powers of nature and the light of the Golden Dawn, I thank the powers of the elements for their aid in this work and dissolve the body of transformation of a (name of animal) that I have created." Imagine the animal body of transformation going first to the south, then to the east, then to the west, and then to the north; in each quarter it becomes less solid and definite, until in the north it dissolves completely and can no longer be seen. Concentrate as forcefully as possible on this process of dissolution.

M—Say: "I now ask the holy powers of nature for their help in learning from my experience and using the abilities I have gained in accordance with the great harmony of nature."

N—Now perform the License to Depart of fire, air, water, and earth in order. When you have done this, return to the west of the altar, face east, and say: "In the presence of the holy powers of nature and the light of the Golden Dawn, I proclaim that this ceremony of transformation is complete."

O—Perform the standard purification, consecration, and reverse circumambulation of the temple.

P—Perform the Lesser Ritual of the Pentagram in its banishing mode, followed by the standard words of the closing.

On Rituals of Self-Initiation

THE FORMULAE OF CEREMONIAL magic imparted in this paper have an open and a concealed use. The first is that of practical magic, in which the magician causes changes in the world he experiences and in the experiences of others. This is an essential part of magical training and practice, for it is by success in practical magic that the initiate may measure the growth of his skill and also judge accurately of the truth of magical teachings and the ignorance of those who dismiss magic as evil or useless. When the influences of an amulet bring an improbable event to pass or an intelligence communicates information no incarnate mind could have known or an invisibility working allows the magician to pass unseen through an angry crowd, the resulting gain in confidence is a great advantage in further workings, and for this reason among others practical magic should be explored and used by the student.

Yet there is another higher and more concealed application of these magical formulae, and this is the work of self-initiation or, as it is also called, spiritual development. Of this there are three forms, which correspond to the three classes of ceremonial magic described above.

The first form is that of consecration. It calls down magical influences, not into an amulet or herbal preparation but into the physical, aetherial, and intellectual bodies of the magician, so as to perfect them and bring about the full awakening of the potentials within these bodies.

The second form is that of conjuration. It summons not an elemental intelligence or spirit but the Guardian Genius or Higher Self of the magician, opening up channels of communication and power between the magician's own lower and higher selves.

The third form is that of transformation. It transforms not the outward appearance of the magician but his inward nature, raising this up from its present imperfect and incomplete status to the more perfect and complete expression of its capacities.

Consecration calls down an influence, conjuration summons forth an entity, and transformation raises up a personality. In each case the goal is the establishment of a connection between the self and what is above it. The relation between the individual magician and the higher reaches of human possibility can be understood in any or all of these ways.

No outline is provided here for any of these ceremonies, though a close study of the ceremonies and outlines already provided will readily show the attentive student how such ceremonies may be written and performed. Your task as an aspirant to the Druid Grade is to make such a close study, create a ritual based on one of these three forms, and perform it. It must use the Bardic initiation formula—that is, it must invoke all four elements—and must include at its culmination, at heading 15 of the formula, the OIW signs and their analysis, which are the distinctive signs of the Druid Grade. Beyond this, the details are left up to the individual student.

It will be found helpful to perform at least one working of each of the forms listed earlier—consecration, conjuration, and transformation—for the purposes of practical magic. This is also required in order to qualify for the Druid Grade initiation, but it will also have the effect of teaching the student which of these ways of performing magic is most congenial. That form, in most cases, will also be the best form to use for the ritual of self-initiation you must write and perform. Heretofore you have followed teachings and practices provided for you; now you must create and perform a working of your own, unique to yourself.

Equinox and Solstice Ceremonies.

IN THE FORTHCOMING LECTURE on the macrocosm and microcosm, one of the two additional lectures assigned to the Druid Grade, it will be explained that the relationship between sun and earth is the source of all magic in this world, just as it is the source of all life and of the great cycles of nature that maintain the world in balance. The solar ray—manifesting in its seven sub-rays, which are the colors of the solar spectrum—descends from the heavens to the earth; the telluric ray or earth spirit, differentiated into an infinite number of expressions by the subtle variations of stone, soil, and plant growth, rises up from the earth to the heavens and returns eventually to the sun. It is from the dance of these interpenetrating influences that Druidical magic receives its power.

At four times in the cycle of each year, the spring and fall equinoxes and the summer and winter solstices, the relationship between sun and earth has its turning points. To make use of a traditional metaphor, they are the four gates of the year through which powerful currents of magical influence flow, and ceremonial workings done at these times can draw upon these currents and direct them to bring fertility to the land, harmony and healing to the people of the land, and wisdom and power to the initiated Druid. The regular practice of these ceremonies is an important dimension of the work of the Druid Grade and should not be neglected by any initiate of that grade.

It is of some importance that all four gates of the year should be worked. At one point in the history of our tradition, it was common to perform ceremonial workings only at the equinoxes. The reasoning behind this custom derived from the recognition that it is at the two equinoctial points that the sun and earth are, magically speaking, in closest contact with one another. It is at the equinoxes that the sun, as it proceeds along the ecliptic—its apparent track through the heavens relative to earth—crosses the celestial equator, the projection of the earth's center into space, and thus the solar ray descends to earth most directly on the day of the equinox and for forty-eight hours to either side. The initiates of the period just mentioned concluded that the direct ray from sun to earth was sufficient to their needs.

The results of this choice, however, were not good. By defining the furthest separation of sun and earth, the solstices also have their role in the cycle of the year's energies, and that role especially is one of providing balance to the whole; the stability of the cycle depends on the relation of its extremes, just as a tightrope-walker in a circus extends his arms to either side in order to maintain balance. Those orders that neglected the solstice observances thus suffered from a lack of stability that expressed itself in various ways, none of them helpful. An order that neglected the equinoxes and celebrated only the solstices would tend to fall correspondingly into stagnation. It is the mutual relation between mobility and stability—between the full flow of the solar influence at the equinoxes and the points of interchange and reversal at the solstices, where the ecliptic and the celestial equator are at their furthest separation in space—that makes for best results.

The energies of the solstices and the equinoxes, then, differ; the rituals that work with these energies, however, are in essence the same. These rituals should always be performed within forty-eight hours of the moment of equinox or solstice, so as to make best use of the change of energies at the gates of the year. The opening and closing rituals are those of the Druid Grade; the wand and serpent's egg should be present, along with the ordinary furnishings of the altar and the materials for casting a geomantic divination. A chair should be placed in the west of the temple, facing the altar.

One additional detail should be provided before the ceremony begins. This is a watchword, a single word or phrase that is used to represent a concept or theme the aspirant wishes to make part of his life during the three months that follow the ceremony. For example, "harmony" might be a watchword suitable for a time when this quality appears to be lacking in the world, and "unity of will" might be suited to a student who wishes to develop this quality in himself. The watchword should be chosen after careful meditation, and a divination cast to ensure that it is appropriate.

Ceremony of the Equinox or Solstice

1. Set up the temple for a ceremony in the Druid Grade. The wand should be upon the altar and the serpent's egg about the neck of the celebrant, who should wear his white robe and the regalia of his grade of initiation. The watchword for the next three months should also be present, written on paper and placed somewhere convenient to the altar.

   When all is in readiness, light the candles and incense, and open the temple in the Druid Grade by the usual ceremony, following the opening ceremony with the Supreme Ritual of the Pentagram in its summoning mode. The wand should be used to trace all pentagrams.

2. When these preparatory ceremonies are complete, go to the west of the altar and face east. Raise the wand on high, with the sun end upwards, and say: "In the presence of the holy powers of nature and the light of the Golden Dawn, I proclaim that the"—here state the day the ritual is meant to celebrate: spring or fall equinox, or summer or winter solstice—"has arrived and that the watchword of the previous term is abrogated." (If this is the first time you have performed this ceremony, the reference to the watchword may be omitted.) "Let us celebrate according to ancient custom the return of the equinox/solstice."

3. Return the wand to the altar, and turn your attention to the elements of air and water, the powers of which you have summoned in the east and west respectively. Visualize again the yellow pentagram of air before you and the blue pentagram of water behind you, and feel the presence of the winds of heaven in the east and the mighty waters in the west. When this imagery is well established, say: "Light; darkness. East; west. Air; water. I am the reconciler between them."

4. Turn your attention now to the elements of fire and earth, the powers of which you have summoned in the south and north respectively. Visualize again the red pentagram of fire to your right and the green pentagram of earth to your left, and feel the presence of the solar fire in the south and that of soil and stone in the north. When this imagery is well established, say: "Heat; cold. South; north. Fire; earth. I am the reconciler between them."

5. Now become aware of all four elements and all four pentagrams. When the appropriate imagery is well established, say: "Powers that create; powers that preserve; powers that destroy; powers that redeem. One is the reconciler between them." At this point, in silence, make the three signs of the OIW.

6. Take up the wand and go to the eastern quarter of the temple. Hold the wand high in the right hand, sun end up, and extend the left hand toward the east, palm forward. Say: "May the light of the Golden Dawn extend through all the realms of air! Let the east receive its blessing." Visualize a tremendous stream of golden light rushing forth from the altar behind you, past you, and out into infinite space to the east.

7. Go to the southern quarter of the temple, raise the wand, and extend the left hand in the same manner. Say: "May the light of the Golden Dawn extend through all the realms of fire! Let the south receive its blessing." Visualize another tremendous stream of golden light rushing forth from the altar behind you, past you, and out into infinite space to the south.

8. Go to the western quarter of the temple, raise the wand, and extend the left hand in the same manner. Say: "May the light of the Golden Dawn extend through all the realms of water! Let the west receive its blessing." Visualize another tremendous stream of golden light rushing forth from the altar behind you, past you, and out into infinite space to the west.

9. Go to the northern quarter of the temple, raise the wand, and extend the left hand in the same manner. Say: "May the light of the Golden Dawn extend through all the realms of earth! Let the north receive its blessing." Visualize another tremendous stream of golden light rushing forth from the altar behind you, past you, and out into infinite space to the north. The altar now stands at the center of a vast equal-armed cross of light, and your movement around the temple has traced the circle: the two emblems upon the altar are now projected onto the scale of the cosmos.

10. Return to the west of the altar, face east, lay down the wand, and perform the complete Analysis of the Grand Word from the OIW Ritual, calling down the light. Visualize the light descending with utmost intensity upon the altar, where it divides into five currents; one descends to the center of the earth and the

other four radiate outwards along the four streams of light you have established. Extend your arms out to your sides, mirroring the cross of the elements, and say: "In this time of equinox/solstice, may the light of the Golden Dawn extend through all the realms of being. May it bring fertility to the land, healing and harmony to the people, and to me such wisdom and power as I am prepared to receive." Maintain the visualization of the descending light as long and as intensely as possible.

11. Say: "In the presence of the holy powers of nature, I proclaim the watchword for the term now beginning. It is (say it aloud)." Then go to the west, be seated in the chair, and enter into meditation. Meditate on the season that is beginning at the equinox or solstice you are celebrating and on the watchword you have chosen.

12. When you have finished your meditation, you may cast a geomantic divination as an oracle for the following three months. Its interpretation is slightly different from usual in that the figures in the First Triplicity provide an omen for the first month; those in the Second Triplicity, for the second; those in the Third, for the third; and those in the Fourth, for the three months as a whole. The Witnesses and Judge are interpreted in the normal way.

13. When you have finished your divination and put away your divinatory tools, raise the wand high, with the sun end upwards, and say: "In the presence of the holy powers of nature and the light of the Golden Dawn, I proclaim that the (spring or fall equinox/summer or winter solstice) has been duly celebrated and its blessings extended to the land and the people."

14. Perform the Supreme Ritual of the Pentagram in its banishing mode, tracing all pentagrams with the wand, and follow it with the complete ceremony of closing the temple in the Druid Grade.

Additional Lectures of the Druid Grade.

On the Macrocosm and Microcosm

"THAT WHICH IS ABOVE," states Hermes Trismegistus in *The Emerald Tablet*, "is as that which is below, and that which is below is as that which is above, to perform the miracles of the One Thing." This is the law of macrocosm and microcosm, among the most ancient and essential of the teachings of all Mystery Schools. The word *macrocosm* means "great universe," and the word *microcosm* means "little universe." From the human perspective, one could as well speak of the *macranthropos* and the *micranthropos*, the "great human" and the "little human"; the older terminology, however, has the advantage that every other thing and being in the macrocosm is also a microcosm. Humanity expresses only one set of possible reflections of the macrocosm; other living things, and those things we call nonliving as well, are equally microcosms.

To put the same law in another and perhaps a more useful form, everything in the cosmos is made of the substance of the cosmos; it is formed according to the basic structure of the cosmos, and whatever its capacities of perception, thought, and knowledge may be, these are capable of experiencing the cosmos and the cosmos alone. The sum total of the substance, form, and capacities of perception, thought, and knowledge of the things that compose the cosmos provide the cosmos in turn with its own substance, form, and capacities.

Thus each being in the cosmos has a twofold existence. It is at once a life unto itself and a part of the One Life—a microcosm and a part of the macrocosm. Between the poles of this twofold existence a range of intermediate possibilities unfold, each providing the third factor that resolves the binary of macrocosm and microcosm into a ternary.

I. Three Planes in the Microcosm

The Mystery Teachings divide the existences perceived by human beings in a variety of ways, depending partly on the requirements of training and partly on the symbolism of sacred numbers. Divisions into two, three, four, five, seven, and ten levels or planes are common. In our work we divide the planes of being into three—material, aetherial, intellectual—and hint at a fourth: divine. In the same way, we speak of the material, aetherial, and intellectual bodies of the individual human being and hint at a fourth level, the divine spark.

This division into three is of great use both on the microcosmic and on the macrocosmic level. In the realm of the microcosm—meaning here the individual human being—a very little meditation or simple introspection will reveal the existence of three kinds of experience: those that come to us through the material senses; those that come to us through the forms of inner experience such as thought, imagination, and memory; and those that come to us through the higher, formless capacities of the mind.

Open a drawer and take out a memento of some past time—a card, let us suppose, from some once beloved person whom death or estrangement has taken from your life. You see the card—its shape and colors, the forms of the ink tracing out letters and words—and you feel its weight and other properties as it rests in your hand. As you consider it, there comes to mind some scene from your memories of the person who sent the card—for a moment you are back in some once familiar room, in a conversation that ended long since, and perhaps your mind leaps from there to imagine how the future might have unfolded had you said or done something different.

Beyond these images of memory and imagination, finally, there comes a series of formless and wordless intuitions—first, perhaps, a feeling of regret; then a sense of the quality or flavor, so to speak, of that time in your life or in the world; then, as your awareness opens out, a realization of the transience of all things, or of the way in which two lives like threads in a tapestry drew together and then moved apart. The first set of perceptions, those of the senses, belong to the material plane; the second, those of memory and imagination, belong to the aetherial plane; the third, beyond these latter, belong to the intellectual plane.

The degree to which each of these planes is present to conscious awareness varies from person to person and also, for each person, over the course of the lifespan. In general, attention to the material plane emerges in infancy, is at its height in childhood, and wanes as adulthood comes. Attention to the aetherial plane emerges in adolescence, is at its height in young adulthood, and continues throughout life unless consciousness of the third plane displaces it. This does not always happen. Indeed, attention to the intellectual plane may never emerge at all—many people go through their lives without noticing the existence of anything beyond the planes of form—and if it does emerge, that emergence may come at any point between young adulthood and old age.

Unlike consciousness of the two lower and more basic planes, which occurs naturally in the ordinary process of maturation, the awareness of the intellectual plane requires a stimulus from outside as well as a state of readiness within. The ancient Mystery Schools with their ceremonies of initiation had in their care, as an important part of their work, the task of identifying those who had reached the state of readiness and providing them with the stimulus. Few of the descendants of the old Mystery Schools in the modern world still recall this mission in any but the most cursory sense. Yet it is still far from uncommon, for example, that a man's first awakening on the intellectual plane, and thus his first efforts to think thoughts that someone else has not first thought out for him, follows his initiation into Freemasonry or some similar order.

It is important to realize, however, that even those who have no conscious awareness of a given plane may still exist and function upon it. A child of six who has not the least insight into the workings of his mind among the forms and images of the aetherial plane is not hindered in the least from having keen memories, a lively imagination, and a mind full of images and words. The absence of consciousness of the aetherial plane shows itself in the way that the child habitually treats mental experiences as though they were material—for example, converting the inner experience of night terrors into a conviction that a monster lurks under his bed.

Similarly, a young person of sixteen may—indeed almost certainly will—have a lively inner life full of intellectual perceptions but will confuse them with the forms and images of the aetherial plane with which they happen to be associated in his mind. The passions of youth have their source in this confusion; what makes a singer or a style of garment or a potential lover the center of a young person's world is nearly always a cluster of intellectual realizations that have become attached to the apparent object of attention for some reason more or less accidental or absurd. Many people, as already noted, continue in this state through their lives; the church they attend, the political party they support, the ethnic or religious group they hate and despise—all have fixed roles in the furnishings of their mind having little, if anything, to do with the realities of these things and everything to do with the unrecognized intellectual dimension of their lives.

It is rare for a person to be attracted to a school of the Mysteries unless he has achieved at least some readiness to pass beyond this stage, but that readiness typically requires much stimulation and development. One of the many benefits of the regular practice of meditation is that it aids the ripening of the mind's ability to discriminate between aetherial and intellectual contents, and thus dissolves rigid thinking of the kind that causes so many human troubles.

II. Three Planes in the Macrocosm

It is among the superstitions of contemporary Western culture that only one of the three planes of human existence—the material plane—is considered to be real, while the other two, if they are granted any existence at all, must exercise it strictly within the confines of any one human skull. The teaching of the Mystery traditions on this point has always been that what we have here called the aetherial and intellectual planes are realities in their own right, with as definite and interpersonal an existence as any material object, but on their own appropriate levels.

It is an important law of magic that the planes of being are discrete and not continuous. This means that realities existing on one plane need not follow the same laws as those existing on another; it also means that the capacity of changes on one plane to affect changes on another is sharply limited by the availability and nature of specific channels or connections that allow influences to pass from plane to plane.

The material presence of ink upon the page you are now reading is capable of creating aetherial forms in your awareness because a complex set of relationships between written letters and words in the mind has been established over the centuries, making use of the sense of vision, which connects the material and aetherial planes. The intention, ultimately intellectual, that the page of the book should be turned when you are finished reading it is expressed in turn by the muscles of your hand. If you doubt the importance of these connections between the planes, attempting to absorb the information in this book without opening its covers or turning its pages without touching the book may prove instructive.

Human beings are entities of three planes, and they therefore possess the capacity not only to perceive and act on all three planes but to transfer influences from one plane to another through channels interior to them. There are other beings in the cosmos—other microcosms of the macrocosm—that also exist on three planes. Other beings exist on two planes or one plane only. Beings of two or one planes are in no sense lower or lesser than those of three; each has its place in the cosmos, and a three-plane existence imposes limits as well as capacities.

Of beings existing on two planes only, those most familiar to us are plants and animals, which exist on the material and aetherial planes but not the intellectual plane. It will be noticed that beings of this kind vary remarkably on both of the planes upon which they exist; on the material plane their bodies are of countless shapes, sizes, and capacities; on the aetherial plane their capacities for perception, memory, and imagination vary widely, from the simple consciousness of the single-celled algae to the nearly human capacities of the larger mammals. It is thought that a very few animals, such as whales and dolphins, are in fact three-plane beings with an intellectual body of very different nature from ours, but the truth of this matter is not known to dwellers in Abred.

Another class of beings existing on two planes only are those that exist on the aetherial and intellectual levels but not the physical. Of these, the most common on earth at present are human beings who are between physical incarnations or for one reason or another have stepped outside the normal cycles of rebirth. Certain other beings also exist on these two planes, among them the fays, archfays, and kindred beings who are described in legends of elves and faeries as well as in some magical traditions. It is rarely wise to attempt to summon the human dead, and it is neither wise nor, in most cases, possible to summon other beings of two planes; the greatest of these latter are of far more intelligence and power than any human being, and the methods of conjuration have no effect upon them.

Beings of one plane exist in great abundance in the cosmos. Those existing only on the material plane are those entities we are pleased to call inanimate substances, such as stone, wind, water, and the like. The material aspects of the four elements belong to this class. They are, in fact, not inanimate—nothing in the cosmos is without some degree of life and consciousness—but theirs is undifferentiated, having not yet separated out into individual beings.

Beings of one plane existing only on the aetherial plane include those that have traditionally been called elemental spirits or elementals. These beings are differentiated according to the four elements, and they are very numerous, dwelling wherever there is fire, air, water, or earth. Those who come into contact with human beings have for the most part a well-developed aetherial consciousness, and thus their thoughts and actions bear some resemblance to those of children. They are lively and nimble beings, playful and irresponsible, but they have great powers over the aetherial plane and also have the capacity to shape the material elements that are their homes.

Beings of one plane existing on the intellectual plane only are called intelligences. Some are differentiated by the elements, while others have other correspondences. Some part of their nature may be grasped by imagining them as thoughts that think themselves, contemplate themselves, and understand themselves. They have a curious relationship to the elementals, one which some works on magic represent awkwardly by saying that the elemental intelligences rule over the elemental spirits.

The reality is subtler than this phrasing would suggest. Elementals are receptive to influence from the intellectual plane, and it is therefore easy for an elemental intelligence to call an elemental spirit of the same element and direct its actions. For elementals, this is a game; for intelligences, it is something more, for they are, by and large, fascinated by the three-plane consciousness of human beings, so similar to theirs in its manifestation on the intellectual plane, so different in its capacity to direct itself to the other planes of being, and so often less completely developed on the intellectual plane than theirs. Intelligences and spirits, those of the elements and those of other kinds, may therefore be conjured with good effect by the skilled magician, and so long as they are treated with appropriate courtesy and not put to base or destructive purposes, the magician will find it relatively easy to establish cordial relations with them. The Druidical Mysteries have a special relationship with the intelligences and spirits of the four elements, and the student of conjuration who approaches these beings as he would approach visitors from another country or another world will find that he can learn much from the intelligences and accomplish much with the help of the spirits of all four elements.

III. *The Solar Ray and the Earth Spirit*

In a lecture of the Ovate Grade, you learned about niter $\oplus$ and salt $\ominus$, the two great principles of Druidical alchemy: niter, the active principle, which descends from heaven to earth, and salt, the passive principle, which ascends from earth to heaven. In a lecture of the Bardic Grade, in turn, you learned of the solar ray, which descends from the sun through human beings and other animals, and of the earth spirit, which ascends from the earth through every variety of plant. These are simply different ways of speaking of the same phenomenon, the cycle of ascending and descending energies that brings about the birth, life, death, and rebirth of all living things and the creation, preservation, destruction, and redemption of the entire cosmos.

This endless twofold flow by which spirit descends into matter and matter arises into spirit is not only the central secret of alchemy and of plant magic but of the entire work of the Druidical Mysteries. Everything we do as Druids may be understood either as bringing down a spiritual influence into material manifestation or lifting up a material manifestation into spirit or creating a dialogue between these two processes. (These three options may be used, for instance, to describe ceremonies of consecration, transformation, and conjuration, respectively.)

The three planes that we have been discussing so far in this paper may be understood in turn as the three stages in the descending or ascending process. This may be understood in a wholly personal and even prosaic sense. What are the three stages, for example, by which anything is created? First the desire for that thing makes itself felt in the mind of at least one being as a formless intuition that it might be necessary or desirable. That formless sense crystallizes into a recognition of what is desired, and this takes form in the imagination, moving from a general pattern to an exact realization of what the thing will be. In the final stage, it leaps from mind to matter at the hands, perhaps, of a craftsperson. The descending current thus moves from the intellectual plane to the aetherial plane, and then to the material plane.

What are the three stages, in turn, by which anything, however ordinary, is learned? First, the thing that will be learned is encountered with the physical senses: it is seen or heard, or its traces become apparent to the senses. Second, the thing seen or heard becomes an image in mind and memory; it is combined with other images, made more general, until the essentials become clear. Third, it is understood, and form gives way to principle. The ascending current thus moves from the physical plane to the aetherial plane, and then to the intellectual plane.

These same currents also work on a grander scale. The process by which the earth was created follows the same threefold descending rhythm as the process by which a child makes a paper hat: first the abstract potentiality, then the concrete form, then the material manifestation. The process by which the soul achieves its ultimate freedom follows the same threefold ascending rhythm as the process by which the same child learns to add two and two: first, the material fact repeatedly experienced; second, the aetherial model of that fact in the mind, memory, and imagination, repeatedly contemplated; third, the realization of meaning within the form, or experience transmuted to thinking, and thinking to understanding. All this should be explored in meditation.

These general considerations, though, also apply to something much more specific. The solar ray is one distinctive influence that descends from heaven to earth, from the intellectual realm of abstract principle to the material realm of concrete fact. The earth spirit is another distinctive influence that travels the same path in the other direction. All metaphor aside, the solar and animal niter descend from sun to earth, and the telluric and vegetable salts ascend from earth to sun. These powers can be grasped and harnessed by the initiated Druid, and indeed you have already begun to grasp and harness them.

The core ritual practices of this tradition—the Rituals of the Pentagram, the Exercise of the Central Ray, and the OIW Ritual—all use the imagination, the most important expression of the aetherial body in the human individual, to provide a channel for the descent of the solar ray from heaven to earth. This descending flow is naturally present in human beings and all other animals, as you have already learned; the point of the ritual work is to participate in it consciously and to begin to direct it in ways that will further the work of initiation.

Several other aspects of the tradition—notably the lore of elemental herbalism introduced in the Ovate Grade and the practices of plant alchemy—all use material substances to balance the descending solar ray or animal niter with the vegetable salts that are the material expression of the earth spirit. This also is natural in human beings, who, like all other animals, consume vegetable substances to balance the influx of the solar ray. Here, too, the point of this study and practice is to participate in that process consciously and to begin to direct it in ways that will further the work of initiation.

IV. Standing Stone and Oak Tree

It remains to comment on the older and, it may be, original form that Druidical work with the descending and ascending currents formerly took.

In ancient times these same processes were pursued under different conditions and with different tools. Standing stones have much the same affinity for the solar ray as do animals, and the ancients raised them in places carefully selected for the purpose: to draw down the solar and animal niter in greater quantity so that it might be transmuted into the earth spirit and bring fertility to the fields and flocks. Great trees received the upwelling vegetable salt and returned it to the atmosphere, where it shed its material envelope and returned to the sun. In past centuries, it must be remembered, subsistence farming required most of the available labor and resources of a society, and a single bad harvest could mean hunger and death for many. The efforts of Druids to improve the harvests through their skillful knowledge of natural magic were thus among the most important factors that, in ancient times, won them the loyalty and love of the populace and the protection of kings.

The coming of Christianity, though it replaced the old Druid teachings with the theology of a newer faith, imposed few changes on this ancient pattern. Stone churches proved to be as efficient an instrument for attracting the solar ray and earthing it in the ground as the old menhirs and standing stones. A great deal of Druidical teaching on this subject passed into common use within the medieval church in Ireland, Britain, and France, where it lingered for centuries, especially in the older monastic orders. The guilds of Masons whose responsibility it was to site, align, build, and maintain parish churches and monasteries across the countryside also acquired a great deal of this lore.

Over time, however, the art of attracting the solar ray became encrusted with superstitions of various kinds; the purpose behind many of the old observances was forgotten; and farmers and landowners struggling to maintain faltering harvests turned to other methods to make up for the waning influence of the solar ray. At the time of the Reformation, the very real abuses practiced by institutionalized religion made it easy for men greedy for wealth and power to seize much of the property of the church, and in the process most of what remained of the old traditional lore was lost. Only the standing stones themselves, a scattering of folk custom, some few of the writings of the medieval church, and the rituals and customs of the Freemasons bear witness to the old lore of the solar ray. Even within today's Druid orders it is little known. Observances at stone circles, a few teachings on sacred geometry, and the basic theory of the solar and terrestrial rays remain, but the science of which these were once parts has been lost even to the heirs of those who once created it.

Druids at the present time have other tasks, focusing more on the microcosm and less on the macrocosm. Still, there is good reason to think that the old lore may again someday be necessary for the survival and welfare of communities; what remains of it should be preserved and, if possible, enlarged with new discoveries when these can be made.

On the Paths Above the Veil

THE TEACHINGS ASSIGNED TO the Ovate Grade include a set of attributions assigning the sixteen figures of geomancy to sixteen spheres and paths of the Tree of Life, specifically those below the Veil or crossing it and the sphere Muner, which lies immediately above. Many students have found this attribution puzzling, not for itself—for, indeed, the relation between each sphere or path and the corresponding geomantic figure may readily be understood through meditation—but insofar as it provides no corresponding symbolism for the paths and spheres that lie further up the Tree of Life, in the portions assigned to the circles of Gwynfydd and Ceugant.

There is, in fact, such a symbolism, and it is among the studies assigned to aspirants to the Druid Grade. Similarly reserved to this stage of your studies are the methods of pathworking on the paths that lead upwards from Abred to the threshold of Gwynfydd. The present lecture treats of both these themes.

1. *The Genesis of the Geomantic Figures*

The sixteen geomantic figures, as you have learned, are each composed of four lines, and each line is composed of either one or two points. The practical papers on geomancy you have studied heretofore do not touch on figures composed of fewer lines, since these are irrelevant to the work of geomantic divination. To understand the full attribution of the geomantic figures to the Tree of Life, however, it is necessary to follow the genesis of the sixteen figures from their source.

Here the teachings of the Pythagoreans, which ancient authors state were closely akin to those of the Druids of old, offer a helpful guide. The division between single and double points in a geomantic figure is understood as a difference between odd and even, as you will have learned from the method of adding up figures that produce the Nieces, Witnesses, and Judge. In the Pythagorean writings, though, 3 is considered to be the first odd number and 4 the first even number; 1 and 2 are not numbers but principles: the monad and the indefinite dyad, the creative or procreative pair from which all numbers are born. In sacred geometry these are the point and the line: the first defining a position from which all else may unfold, the second producing a division that may be extended to the ends of space. Behind the monad and dyad, in turn, lies the unmanifest reality that a later mathematics calls zero, from which monad and dyad have not yet emerged; behind the point and the line lie the unmarked page upon which no geometrical form has yet been traced.

The lesson here is that behind the pattern made manifest even in a single or double point there lie three realities that may not be expressed in form: the primordial wholeness from which monad and dyad, odd and even, have not yet begun to separate out, and the paired principles by which that separation takes place, the one giving birth to odd numbers, the other giving birth to even.

To these three we may add a single point and a double point, the two most basic figures; the four figures made from two lines, single or double; the eight made from three lines; and the sixteen made from four. The total number of figures thus generated is thirty-three.

You will observe that in each stage of the progression shown, a new line consisting of a single or double point is added to the bottom of the existing figure. Thus the fire line is generated first and may be either active and present or passive and latent. The air line is generated next, and the presence or latency of air is combined with the two conditions of fire. The water line follows, added to each of the four previously combined conditions of fire and air, and the earth line is added last to create the sixteen geomantic figures used in divination and magic.

Thus the generation of the geomantic figures follows the pattern of the generation of the cosmos itself and echoes another pattern shown in the knowledge lectures of the Ovate Grade, the genesis of the Tree of Life itself from point to line, line to surface, and surface to solid. It is along the lines of the same structure that the application of the one-, two- and three-line figures to the Tree of Life may be properly understood.

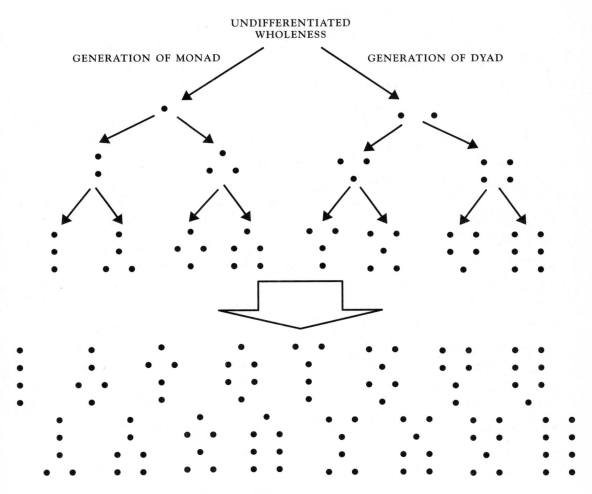

UNDIFFERENTIATED
WHOLENESS

GENERATION OF MONAD

GENERATION OF DYAD

Genesis of the Geomantic Figures

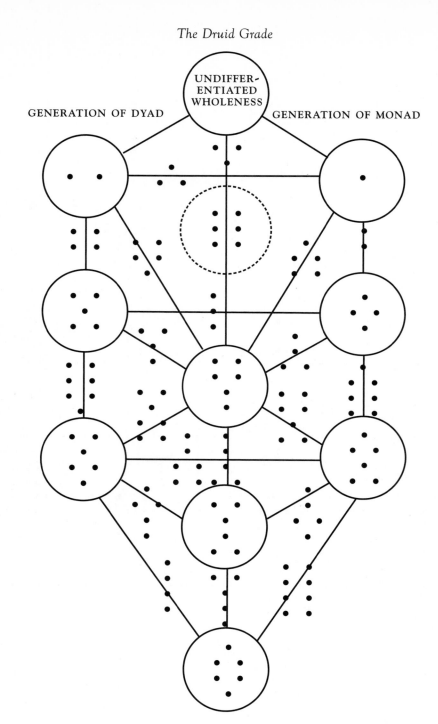

The Geomantic Tree of Life

Undifferentiated wholeness: Celi, the first sphere			
•	Perydd, the second sphere	• • • • • •	Muner, the sixth sphere
• •	Dofydd, the third sphere	• • • • • •	Byw, the seventh sphere
• • • • • •	Iau, the Place of Meeting	• • • • • •	Byth, the eighth sphere
• • • •	Ener, the fourth sphere	• • • • • •	Ner, the ninth sphere
• • • • •	Modur, the fifth sphere	• • • • • •	Naf, the tenth sphere

Spheres of the Tree of Life

	First Path— Ner to Naf		Eleventh Path— Muner to Modur
	Second Path— Ner to Byth		Twelfth Path— Byw to Ener
	Third Path— Naf to Byth		Thirteenth Path— Muner to Ener
	Fourth Path— Ner to Byw		Fourteenth Path— Modur to Ener
	Fifth Path— Naf to Byw		Fifteenth Path— Muner to Dofydd
	Sixth Path— Byth to Byw		Sixteenth Path— Modur to Dofydd
	Seventh Path— Ner to Muner		Seventeenth Path— Muner to Perydd
	Eighth Path— Byth to Muner		Eighteenth Path— Ener to Perydd
	Ninth Path— Byw to Muner		Nineteenth Path— Perydd to Dofydd
	Tenth Path— Byth to Modur		Twentieth Path— Muner to Celi
Generation of Dyad: Twenty-first Path—Dofydd to Celi			
Generation of Monad: Twenty-second Path—Perydd to Celi			

Paths of the Tree of Life

2. Patterns on the Tree of Life

The entire Tree of Life may be understood as a diagram of the process by which primordial and undifferentiated wholeness unfolds its potential through the interplay of active and passive potencies. In this context several points may be worth making.

1. The sixteen geomantic figures of four lines each correspond to the circle of Abred, the world as experienced by incarnate human beings; to the five paths that descend into the circle of Abred from above; and Muner, the sixth sphere, which does not itself belong to Abred but gathers into itself all the influences of the higher reaches of the Tree and transmits them through the Veil to the spheres and paths of Abred. These are therefore the spiritual influences with which the initiate incarnate in a physical body has to do; it is for this reason that these figures and no others play an active role in divination, magic, and pathworking.

2. The figures of three, two, and one lines each represent realities above the circle of Abred and do not manifest directly in the world as experienced by incarnate beings. Their indirect influence, however, is great and may be understood through meditation. Each figure of three lines consists of fire, air, and water, and its influence may be traced in both four-line geomantic figures that share the same fire, air, and water lines; thus the influence of the fourteenth path, which extends from Modur to Ener, will be found reflected in the figure Llosgwrn y Ddraig, which governs the seventh path from Ner to Muner, and the figure Ffordd, which governs the second path from Naf to Byth. Each figure of two lines, being fire and air, may be traced in each of the four figures that share the same fire and air lines; each figure of one line, being fire, may be traced in each of the eight figures that share the same fire line; and the influence of the single sphere and two paths in which active and passive have not yet differentiated themselves may be traced in all the figures without exception.

3. Of the figures of three lines, one is placed in a special position not previously discussed in the knowledge lectures. This is the figure formed by three double points in the dotted circle midway between Celi and Muner, along the central ray of the Tree. The dotted circle located here is not a sphere, though in some ways it functions as one; it is called Iau, the Place of Meeting, in our teachings,

and Daath in the terminology of the Kabbalah. It is the point of contact between Ceugant and Gwynfydd: from the one side, the act of union by which the seven lower spheres come into existence out of the conjugal joining of Perydd and Dofydd, the masculine and feminine powers of Ceugant; from the other side, the nearest approach of created being to the uncreated realities of Ceugant. It is from this latter symbolism that it receives its geomantic symbol, that is, all three elements in Gwynfydd rendered passive and latent. Here the nearest approach to knowledge about the realities beyond the Abyss may be gained.

3. The Paths Above the Veil

In the course of your preparation for initiation into the Bardic Grade, you worked the six paths uniting the four spheres of the elements with one another. In preparing for your Druid Grade initiation, five more paths await you; in our numeration, these are the seventh, eighth, ninth, tenth, and twelfth paths, extending respectively from Ner to Muner, from Byth to Muner and Modur, and from Byw to Muner and Ener. The methods of pathworking you learned in the previous grade are to be used here as well, with certain alterations made necessary by the task that stands before you.

Your goal in preparing for the Druid Grade is to establish, as far as possible, a link between your own ordinary consciousness and the state of consciousness represented by Muner, the lowest of the spheres of Gwynfydd. This work may be accomplished in several different modes, and these modes may assist one another rather than entering into conflict. It is for this reason that you have been requested to continue with your regular practice of meditation, ritual, and divination, for this is one mode of establishing the link that must be formed; it is for this reason that you are expected to prepare and perform a ceremony of self-initiation using one of the three formulae of ceremonial magic explicated in a previous paper of this grade; and it is for this reason that you are now instructed to work the paths connecting the spheres of the four elements with the sphere that, within the realm of Abred, represents the fifth element of spirit.

To accomplish this you will perform a series of pathworkings beginning from the inner grove of earth. Open a temple in the Druid Grade in the usual way, perform the Calling of Earth, and establish yourself in the inner grove of earth, which is also the grove of Naf. You will discover here, however, that the ghostly portals have changed their position;

the portal leading to the inner grove of water, formerly to the right, is now directly ahead of you, while that of air is to the left and that of fire is to the right.

You are now on the threshold of the Druid Grade, and the inner groves and paths now reflect the Tree of Life more than the square of the elements. You will therefore go to the middlemost of the ghostly portals, which is covered with a blue cloth and marked with the geomantic character of Pen y Ddraig. Here you will call and test a guide in the name of **SIRONA** and traverse the first path to the inner grove of water, which is also the grove of Ner.

When you arrive in the inner grove of water, however, you will not close the working in the usual way. Instead, you will examine the grove carefully, and find that there is a fourth ghostly portal, not previously observed by you, that leads away from that inner grove in another direction. A white cloth veils this fourth portal, and upon it is the geomantic character of Llosgwrn y Ddraig.

Llosgwrn y Ddraig

You will approach this portal in the usual way and seek and test a guide by the divine name HESUS, which is the divine name ruling over Muner. When you have found an appropriate guide, follow his guidance and proceed up the seventh path. We do not provide you with a description of that path; your previous work with the paths of the elemental realm of Abred will have prepared you sufficiently to make that journey without such assistance.

The first time you venture on the seventh path, your guide will not take you all the way to the inner grove of spirit, the destination of this pathworking. You will be taken there the second, third, or some subsequent time. Whatever the highest point you reach on this journey, when you are finished, you must retrace your steps all the way back through the inner grove of water to the inner grove of earth, and from that latter point perform the License to Depart and the closing ritual. This is necessary because the ascent to Muner often causes a certain disorientation; returning to the level of earth is literally grounding and also helps bring whatever has been gained by the exercise down to earth in the sphere of Naf, where it most needs to manifest.

Continue working the first and seventh paths in this way until you have entered into the inner grove of spirit, which is also the grove of Muner. This is not described to you in advance; it differs—sometimes slightly, sometimes greatly—for every person who arrives there, and you will need to use your own abilities to perceive the form it takes for you. Once you have done this, begin working up to Muner along a second route, by way of the second and eighth paths. This is done in exactly the same way as the ascent via the first and seventh paths, except that you will take the right-hand portal, call and test a guide in the name **BELISAMA**, and travel the second path from there to the inner grove of air.

There, as you did in the inner grove of water, you will find a fourth ghostly portal, not previously observed by you, which leads away from the grove in another direction. A white cloth veils this portal, and on it is the geomantic character of Coch, as shown here. Approach this portal in the usual way, seek and test a guide in the name of **HESUS**, and follow your guide's lead as far along the path as he leads you.

Coch

As happened with the seventh path, your first journey along the eighth path will not end in the inner grove of spirit; not until the second, third, or some subsequent path-working will you arrive there. Whether or not you reach that goal in any given path-working, you must again retrace your steps all the way back via the inner grove of air to the inner grove of earth in order to close.

Once you have reached the inner grove of spirit by this route several times, a valuable side trip awaits you. This is the tenth path, which rises straight up the left-hand ray of the Tree from Byth toward Modur. This working should follow the same pattern as the ones you have already performed, rising up from the inner grove of earth to that of air and proceeding from there. You will find a fifth ghostly portal in the inner grove of air, leading in yet a new direction; it is veiled with a white cloth, and on this is the geomantic character of Tristwch, as shown below.

Tristwch

Here you will call and test a guide in the name of **TARANIS**, the god that rules over the sphere Modur, and follow that guide's lead as far as he takes you. Do not seek to ascend yet all the way to the inner grove that lies at the end of this path; you may do so later, when you have completed your work with the paths to Muner, and the method for doing so will be explained shortly. Your task here is to learn what you can of the direct influence of the left-hand ray of the Tree, so that you understand more fully what it is that is brought together in synthesis in the unifying sphere of Muner. Several pathworkings should be done along this path before you proceed; each of them, as with the pathworkings you have already performed in this sequence, must begin and end in the inner grove of earth.

The final sequence of pathworkings assigned to you in preparation for the Druid Grade initiation are those that ascend to Muner by a third route, proceeding from the inner grove of earth to that of fire by the fourth path, and then to the inner grove of spirit by the ninth. All the points made concerning the first two routes to Muner apply equally to this journey. You will again begin and end each of these workings in the inner grove of earth.

In the inner grove of fire, the ghostly portal you did not previously observe is draped in white and bears the geomantic character of Gwyn, as shown here. You will seek and test a guide in the name of **HESUS**, and follow his guidance upon the path; you will again not reach the inner grove of spirit on the first attempt, but the second, third, or some subsequent attempt will bring you to that point, completing the threefold ascent.

Gwyn

Once you have done this as many times as seems appropriate, exploring the twelfth path upwards from Byw toward Ener is a worthwhile side trip. The fifth ghostly portal in the inner grove of fire, which is again veiled in white, bears the geomantic character of Llawenydd, as shown here, and the guide to the path should be called and tested in the name of **BELINUS**, who is the god ruling over the sphere Ener. Here again you should not yet seek to ascend all the way to Ener at this time. Several pathworkings should be done along this path, following the same principles as the parallel journey toward Modur.

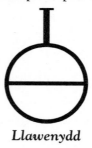

Llawenydd

4. The Paths Beyond Muner

These are optional for the student of the Druidical Mysteries. Among incarnate human beings, the whole work of Druidical initiation in Abred is that of ascent to Muner, and this may not be fully completed in incarnation; even the greatest of initiates embodies only a very small part of the immense power and wisdom of the sixth sphere, and Muner itself is but the lowest of the three spheres that belong to the circle of Gwynfydd. The higher reaches of Gwynfydd are unimaginable and incomprehensible to the incarnate human mind, as are the potencies and attainments of those who have risen to dwell in those realms.

Still, there is a point to working the paths of the Tree of Life above Muner. What is experienced on these paths can at most be a faint foreshadowing of the realities to be encountered when the corresponding planes of existence are reached in reality; still, that foreshadowing can be of value in its own right. There is, however, no established structure for attempting these pathworkings, nor can there be; the ways that proceed beyond Muner are unique to each individual who attempts them and must be learned by experience. Two methods of doing so may be described here.

The first is to make use of the material already imparted to you concerning the tenth and twelfth paths. When you have completed the pathworkings already described and received the initiation of the Druid Grade, you may proceed from the inner grove of earth to that of air, call and test a guide upon the tenth path, and ask that guide not only to lead you to the inner grove corresponding to Modur but to instruct you on how to make the equivalent ascent from Muner to Modur. Write down the instructions you receive and follow them precisely.

When you have completed your journeys on the tenth and eleventh paths and are ready to proceed, repeat the same process on the twelfth path, ascending from Naf to Byw and calling and testing a guide at the portal of the twelfth path. Once you have contacted a guide, ask him not only to lead you to the inner grove corresponding to Ener but also to instruct you in how to make the equivalent pathworkings from Muner and Modur. Write down these instructions as well, and follow them precisely.

The second way to gain the knowledge you will need to ascend above Muner is to make use of the art of ceremonial magic and conjure an intelligence capable of providing you with that information. This should be attempted only by those who have already gained some experience in conjuration and are familiar with intelligences and their varying capacities and concerns. No further details, therefore, will be provided here; if you wish to use this approach, your own experiences must guide you.

This same point is equally true of pathworkings across the Abyss or above it. If you desire to attempt these and are meant to accomplish this very challenging work, enough has already been said to enable you to find the way there for yourself.

Preparation for the Druid Grade Initiation.

BEFORE YOU PROCEED TO the initiation of the Druid Grade, one year should have passed since your Bardic Grade initiation. During that year you are required to complete the following tasks:

1. Continue the daily practice of meditation, the Lesser Ritual of the Pentagram and Central Ray exercises, and geomantic divination.

2. Study at least nine books on magic and Druidical lore, one of them being Éliphas Lévi's *Transcendental Magic*, the others being chosen yourself.

3. Learn, commit to memory, and regularly practice the Supreme Ritual of the Pentagram and the OIW Ritual, and make and consecrate your wand, sickle, and serpent's egg.

4. Prepare and successfully perform at least one ceremony of consecration (in addition to those for the working tools just named), at least one ceremony of conjuration, and at least one ceremony of transformation, using the ritual forms provided in the paper on ceremonial magic assigned to this grade.

5. Perform the complete set of pathworkings on the paths crossing the Veil, as described in the paper on pathworking assigned to this grade.

6. Celebrate, over the course of one year, the rituals of both solstices and both equinoxes.

7. Design a ceremony of self-initiation using either the formula of consecration, that of conjuration, or that of transformation, as described in the paper on ceremonial magic. Do not perform it until you have taken the examination.

When you have completed this work, you may proceed to the Examination of the Druid Grade.

The Examination of the Druid Grade.

WRITE OUT A DETAILED account of the work you have done to complete the previously described requirements, including the texts of your ceremonies of consecration, conjuration, and transformation, and of your self-initiation ceremony. This account is your examination for the Druid Grade.

The Initiation of the Druid Grade.

AFTER COMPLETING THE EXAMINATION of the Druid Grade, perform your ceremony of self-initiation at least nine times. The ninth performance of the ceremony is your initiation into the Druid Grade.

Thrice welcome, Druid!

It is with the greatest pleasure that we congratulate you on your successful completion of all the work assigned to you and on your initiation as a Druid. Over the two years or more that you have spent studying and practicing the Druidical Mysteries, you have learned many things and ventured into what almost certainly were branches of knowledge and methods of practice unfamiliar to you.

It may thus come as some surprise to hear now that your education as a Druid has only just begun. Still, this is quite true. You have finished your assigned studies and practices, and learned the things that we can teach you. Now you must pursue your own studies and practices, and learn the things that only you yourself and the holy powers of nature can teach you.

The fundamental practices of meditation, ritual, and divination that were introduced to you during your studies in the Ovate Grade and became your daily companions in your studies in the Bardic and Druid Grades do not lose their value at this point. Quite the contrary—the longer you pursue daily practice with them, the more you will gain from them. In the same way, it will be to your advantage to take the time to review the instructional materials you have studied, beginning with the Ovate knowledge lectures, and to repeat this review at intervals. The wise initiate is never too proud to revisit even the most basic elements of study and practice, and soon learns that every review of the basics brings a new level of understanding.

From this point the roads that lie open before you diverge to cover many realms. You may choose to revisit the herbal lore of the Ovate Grade and study herbal medicine in more detail. You may choose to explore the rich lore of plant alchemy or even venture into the alchemy of minerals and metals. You may choose to expand your knowledge and practice of geomancy or of sacred geometry or of the lore of colors and sounds. You may choose to build on the foundations provided you in the art of ceremonial magic. You may choose to do several of these things or all of them or something else entirely. You may pursue this work together with others or you may travel the path alone. All this is left to your own free choice.

Whatever you choose, in the presence of the holy powers of nature and the light of the Golden Dawn, we wish you good fortune in your further travels upon the path of the Druidical Mysteries.

The Guardians of the Order

THOSE READERS WHO ARE interested in working with the
system outlined in this book together with others are invited to
contact the Druidical Order of the Golden Dawn at:

HTTP://WWW.DRUIDICAL-GD.ORG

Sources and Additional Reading.

LIKE THE TEACHINGS OF the original Hermetic Order of the Golden Dawn, the material in this book is partly original and partly derived from older traditions. Much of it is modeled, of course, on the original Golden Dawn teachings, and a good deal more is based on the teachings of the old Druid Revival orders, which have come down to me by a variety of channels. A third set of sources, though, include a variety of published works on Druidry, magic, alchemy, divination, and related subjects.

I have given below an outline of the sources of this third kind that I have used in creating the Druidical Order of the Golden Dawn. Partly this is so that readers interested in following up on the teachings in this book will know where to look; partly, though, it is meant to give those readers interested in adapting the Golden Dawn system to other symbolic and spiritual traditions some idea of how this can be done.

I have also included modern reading lists for the Bardic Grade supplementary lectures, which can be used in place of the early twentieth-century resources listed in those lectures.

The Ovate Grade

First Knowledge Lecture

The symbolism in this lecture and the Welsh Druid symbolism that appears throughout the knowledge lectures is taken from J. Williams ab Ithel's *Barddas*, a collection of Iolo Morganwg's notes and teachings originally published in 1862 (see bibliography for details). The quotations on p. 35 are from pp. 47, 49, and 21 respectively of the 1862 edition. The quote from the Chaldean Oracles on p. 36 is from Westcott's translation, p. 38.

The meditations given in the knowledge lectures are original but based on standard Druid Revival techniques and teachings.

Second Knowledge Lecture

The material on alchemy in this lesson, including the use of niter and salt as basic elements of existence, is largely taken from Kirchweger's 1723 alchemical text *Aurea Catena Homeri (The Golden Chain of Homer)*. The eighteenth-century English translation by Sigismund Bacstrom was circulated in a manuscript in the original Hermetic Order of the Golden Dawn, and this is the version I have quoted here.

The names of the geomantic figures are translations into modern Welsh of the standard Latin names of the figures. Most European languages translate such names as a matter of course—thus a French geomancer, for example, thinks of the first two figures as Garçon and Perte rather than Puer and Amissio (or Mab and Colled). English is quite unusual in insisting on Latin names for geomantic figures, zodiacal signs, and the like.

The healing system given in these lectures is standard medieval elemental medicine as found in hundreds of medieval Latin sources; Chishti 1991 is a good modern introduction. The teachings of the physicians of Myddfai, which are based on the classic medieval system, may be found in Pughe 1861. J. M. *Nickell's Botanical Ready Reference* was originally published in 1880 and was a standard herbal manual all through the early twentieth century; it may be replaced with any other herbal the reader prefers.

Third Knowledge Lecture

Most of the material in this lecture is standard Western magical lore—the attributions of the four elements, the basic concepts of alchemy and sacred geometry, and the meanings and elemental analysis of the geomantic figures may be found in dozens of books in and out of print.

Calling the simple geomantic tools introduced in this lecture "Druid wands" is a habit that seems to have sprung up in the American Pagan scene sometime in the 1980s—I have not been able to identify who invented the label—and their inclusion here under that name may be considered a scholarly joke; still, they make excellent tools for casting geomantic charts and may as well live up to the name they have been given.

Fourth Knowledge Lecture

The difference between the two aspects of nature was a commonplace of medieval and Renaissance philosophy, the sort of thing every literate sixteen-year-old knew in Shakespeare's time; I have long since forgotten the source in which I first encountered it. The quote from the *Aurea Catena Homeri* is the whole of chapter 1 in Sigismund Bacstrom's translation; see Kirchweger 1983, p. 1. The geometrical analysis of the Tree of Life is common in modern Cabalistic instruction—see, for example, Greer 1996, pp. 28–29. The Ovate Tree Working is a Druid exercise found, in one form or another, in most of the older Druid Revival traditions.

Fifth Knowledge Lecture

The genesis of the elements described in this lecture is derived from the *Aurea Catena Homeri*, chapters 6 through 9, though I have rephrased it in my own words. The outline of spagyric alchemy is based on the standard modern methods of spagyrics and can be studied in more detail in Albertus 1974, Junius 1985, Stavish 2006, and other books on the subject. The quote from Trismosin's *Splendor Solis* on p. 115 is the first sentence of the First Treatise, p. 17 of the Kohn translation; see Trismosin 1920 in the bibliography.

Sixth Knowledge Lecture

The selections from the *Aurea Catena Homeri* are from the prologue to the work, again in Bacstrom's eighteenth-century manuscript translation; see Kirchweger 1983, pp. ii–iv.

Seventh Knowledge Lecture

The geomantic characters are taken from standard Renaissance sources such as Cornelius Agrippa. The material on sacred geometry cited here is also part of the standard tradition; see, for example, Lawlor 1982. The passage quoted from the *Aurea Catena Homeri* is from the prologue; see p. ii in Kirchweger 1983.

The Bardic Grade

The Introductory Letter and the Work of the Elements

Everything in these papers is either lightly modeled Golden Dawn material or the sort of utterly standard elemental visualizations and pathworkings nearly all late twentieth-century ceremonial magic traditions practiced in one form or another.

On the Tree of Life

The relationship between the T'ai Chi T'u and the Tree of Life has fascinated me for decades, but I have yet to see a discussion of it in modern Cabalistic literature; this may be considered a first step in that direction. The information on the T'ai Chi T'u presented here has been collected over many years from dozens of references in English-language sources on Taoism. The attribution of the original Tree of Life to the school of Rabbi Isaac the Blind is found in Scholem 1987. The categories of Aristotle are fundamental to his logical theory; see Aristotle 1952.

Modern books on the Tree of Life worth including in a list for students include DuQuette 2001, Fortune 1984, Gray 1997, Greer 1996, and Knight 1978.

The Sacred Geometry of the Druids

The material in this lecture is the standard sacred geometry found in serious books on the subject. The writings of Jay Hambidge mentioned in the final section may be found conveniently summarized in Hambidge 1967. Among the modern works I have consulted, and which are recommended to the student, are Critchlow 1982, Doczy 1981, Ghyka 1977, Huntley 1970, Lawlor 1982, Lundy 2002, Michell 1988, and Sutton 2009.

Plants in Magic and Alchemy

This lecture is more or less a summary of my book *The Encyclopedia of Natural Magic*, which may be consulted for more detailed information. Other modern books worth studying on herbal magic include Smith 1989 and Zalewski 1990; worthwhile books on herbal alchemy include Albertus 1974, Junius 1985, and Stavish 2006.

Principles of Color and Sound

The material in this lecture is entirely original but drew some of its inspiration from Joscelyn Godwin's excellent books on the esoteric dimensions of music; see especially Godwin 1987.

Practical Geomancy

The material here is derived from three Renaissance handbooks of geomancy, none of which as far as I know is currently in print: Christopher Cattan's *The Geomancie of Master Christopher Cattan* (London, 1591); John Heydon's *Theomagia, or the Temple of Wisdome* (London, 1664); and Robert Fludd's *De Geomantia* (Verona, 1704).

The situation regarding classic geomantic texts, in other words, is not much better now than it was a century ago. My books (Greer 2006 and Greer 2009), Pennick 1995, and Skinner 2011 are worth recommending, however.

The Druid Grade

The Introductory Lecture (Letter)

The Supreme Ritual of the Pentagram and the OIW Ritual are based on Golden Dawn models; the latter uses Iolo Morganwg's creation myth of the Three Rays of Light, previously cited in the first knowledge lecture of the Ovate Grade, in place of the hybrid Christian-Egyptian symbolism of the Golden Dawn's Rose Cross ritual.

The Working Tools of Druidical Magic

The three working tools are derived from Druid Revival tradition, while the rituals of consecration combine Golden Dawn methods with ideas and words drawn from the writings of Éliphas Lévi.

The reference to Lady Flavia Anderson in the discussion of the serpent's egg is one of the few obvious anachronisms in the material, as her book *The Ancient Secret* was not published until 1953. For the egg itself, those plastic clays that can be baked to hardness in an ordinary oven are one entirely suitable choice for making the container.

The Formulae of Ceremonial Magic

The quotation from Éliphas Lévi is the opening sentence of book I, chapter XII, of *Dogme et Rituel de la Haute Magie*, translated by the present author; Lévi deserves better than Waite's leaden and pompous translation. The outline of the Ovate initiation, of course, is modeled on the outline of the Neophyte Grade in the original Golden Dawn manuscripts; see also Greer 1997, where a similar outline of the equinox ceremony is used as a basis for magical ceremonies.

Any convenient magical herbal may be used for the relevant lore needed to create amulets and other herbal preparations for consecration; for obvious reasons, I have relied on Greer 2000.

The quotation from the *Arbatel of Magick* is from page 193 of the original 1665 edition.

Equinox and Solstice Ceremonies

This is based mostly on the Golden Dawn equinox ceremony, with some original material.

Macrocosm and Microcosm

The division of macrocosm and microcosm into three planes here (and elsewhere in this book) is ultimately derived from Renaissance magical teachings but saw a great deal of development in French magical circles—see, for instance, Péladan 1892. The theory of the solar and telluric currents is found all through the lore of the Druid Revival; the discussion of standing stones and stone churches as tools for channeling the solar ray into the earth in order to bring fertility to the soil is also from this source and is discussed from another perspective in Greer 2007.

On the Paths Above the Veil

This is standard Golden Dawn pathworking technique adapted to the different version of the Tree of Life introduced in this book. The attribution of the geomantic figures to the Tree of Life given here is original.

Bibliography

Albertus, Frater (Albert Reidel). *Alchemist's Handbook*. New York: Weiser, 1974.

Anderson, Flavia. *The Ancient Secret*. Wellingborough, UK: Thorsons, 1987.

Anonymous. *Arbatel of Magic* in Henry Cornelius Agrippa's *Fourth Book of Occult Philosophy*. London, 1665; repr. Woodbury, MN: Llewellyn, 2009.

Aristotle. *Categories*, tr. E. M. Edghill, in *The Works of Aristotle*, vol. 1, ed. W. D. Ross. Chicago: William Benton, 1952.

Chishti, Hakim G. M. *The Traditional Healer's Handbook*. Rochester, VT: Healing Arts Press, 1991.

Colquhoun, Ithell. *Sword of Wisdom: MacGregor Mathers and the Golden Dawn*. New York: G. P. Putnam's Sons, 1975.

Critchlow, Keith. *Time Stands Still*. New York: St. Martin's Press, 1982.

Doczy, György. *The Power of Limits: Proportional Harmonies in Nature, Art, and Architecture*. Boston: Shambhala, 1981.

DuQuette, Lon Milo. *The Chicken Qabalah of Rabbi Clifford Ben Lamed*. York Beach, ME: Weiser, 2001.

Fortune, Dion. *The Mystical Qabalah*. York Beach, ME: Weiser, 1984.

Franck, Adolphe. *The Kabbalah*. New York: Kabbalah Publishing Co., 1926.

Ghyka, Matila. *The Geometry of Art and Life*. New York: Dover, 1977.

Ginsburg, Christian D. *The Kabbalah*. London: Longmans, Green and Co., 1865.

Godwin, Joscelyn. *Harmonies of Heaven and Earth: The Spiritual Dimensions of Music*. Rochester, VT: Inner Traditions, 1987.

Gray, William. *Qabalistic Concepts*. York Beach, ME: Weiser, 1997.

Greer, John Michael. *The Art and Practice of Geomancy.* San Francisco: Weiser, 2009.

———. *Circles of Power.* St. Paul: Llewellyn, 1997; repr. Chiang Mai, Thailand: Salamander & Sons, 2012.

———. *The Druid Grove Handbook.* Everett, WA: Starseed Press, 2011.

———. *The Druid Magic Handbook.* San Francisco: Weiser, 2007.

———. *The Druidry Handbook.* San Francisco: Weiser, 2006.

———. *The Encyclopedia of Natural Magic.* St. Paul: Llewellyn, 2000.

———. *The Geomancer's Handbook.* Iowa City, IA: Renaissance Astrology, 2006.

———. *Inside a Magical Lodge.* St. Paul: Llewellyn, 1998.

———. *Paths of Wisdom.* St. Paul: Llewellyn, 1996; repr. Loughborough, UK: Thoth, 2008.

Hambidge, Jay. *Elements of Dynamic Symmetry.* New York: Dover, 1967.

Huntley, H. E. *The Divine Proportion.* New York: Dover, 1970.

Junius, Manfred M. *Spagyrics.* Rochester, VT: Inner Traditions, 1985.

Kalogera, Lucy Shepard. *Yeats' Celtic Mysteries.* Ph.D. dissertation, Florida State University, 1977.

Kirchweger, Anton Joseph. *Aurea Catena Homeri.* San Francisco: Sapere Aude, 1983.

Knight, Gareth. *A Practical Guide to Qabalistic Symbolism.* York Beach, ME: Weiser, 1978.

———. *The Secret Tradition in Arthurian Legend.* Wellingborough, UK: Aquarian, 1983.

Lawlor, Robert. *Sacred Geometry: Philosophy and Practice.* New York: Thames and Hudson, 1982.

Lévi, Éliphas. *Transcendental Magic,* tr. A. E. Waite. York Beach, ME: Weiser, 1972.

Leyel, Hilda (as "Mrs. C. F. Leyel"). *The Magic of Herbs: A Modern Book of Secrets.* London: Jonathan Cape, 1926.

Lund, Fredrik Macody. *Ad Quadratum: A Study of the Geometrical Bases of Classical and Medieval Religious Architecture.* London: Batsford, 1921.

Lundy, Miranda. *Sacred Geometry.* Presteigne, Wales: Wooden Books, 2002.

Michell, John. *The Dimensions of Paradise.* San Francisco: Harper and Row, 1988.

Nickell, J. M. *J. M. Nickell's Botanical Ready Reference.* Chicago: Ottaway & Co., 1880; repr. Banning, CA: Enos Press, 1976.

Péladan, Sar Mérodack J. *Amphithéatre des Sciences Mortes: Comment on Devient Mage* Paris: Chamuel, 1892.

Pennick, Nigel. *The Oracle of Geomancy.* Chively, UK: Capall Bann, 1995.

Pughe, John, and John Williams ab Ithel. *The Physicians of Myddfai.* London: Longmans & Co., 1861.

Richardson, Alan, and Geoff Hughes. *Ancient Magicks for a New Age.* St. Paul: Llewellyn, 1989.

Scholem, Gershom. *Origins of the Kabbalah.* Princeton, NJ: Princeton University Press, 1987.

Skinner, Stephen. *Geomancy in Theory and Practice.* Singapore: Golden Hoard, 2011.

Smith, Stephen R. *Wylundt's Book of Incense: A Magical Primer.* York Beach, ME: Weiser, 1989.

Stavish, Mark. *The Path of Alchemy.* Woodbury, MN: Llewellyn, 2006.

Stewart, R. J. *The Miracle Tree: Demystifying the Qabalah.* Franklin Lakes, NJ: New Page, 2003.

Sutton, Andrew. *Ruler and Compass: Practical Geometric Constructions.* New York: Walker and Company, 2009.

Trismosin, Salomon. *Splendor Solis,* tr. Julius Kohn. London: Kegan Paul, 1920.

Westcott, William Wynn. *An Introduction to the Study of the Kabalah*. London: Watkins, 1910.

———, ed. *The Chaldean Oracles of Zoroaster*. Wellingborough, UK: Aquarian Press, 1983.

Williams ab Ithel, J. *Barddas*. London: Longman & Co., 1862; reprinted as *The Barddas of Iolo Morganwg*, York Beach, ME: Weiser, 2004.

Zalewski, C. L. *Herbs in Magic and Alchemy*. Bridport, UK: Prism, 1990.

Index.